SEEING THE CHURCH

WHEN YOUR PURPOSE COLLIDES WITH GOD'S PASSION

BY ANDREW MURRAY

Seeing The Church

Copyright 2017 Andrew Murray
All rights reserved

Published by Generation Builders

Book designed and formatted by Laura Murray at Peanut Designs www.pnutd.co.uk

CONTENTS

Acknowledgements

Laura - my biggest encourager and inspiration

Judah and Asher – my boys

Mum and Dad – for taking me to church

Matthew, Becky and Josiah – three of my heroes

Dave Jones – The principles in this book were either taught or modelled by you. Such a debt can never be repaid. Many blessings to you, Carolyn and the family.

Jarrod, Vicky and the Revive family for providing us with a place in which to flourish

John and Ann, Cleddie and Gaynell, Peter and Pam, Ken and Lois

The Generation Builders trustees – Kevin and Janet, Nigel and Angie, Steven and Sharon. Thank you for all you do.

Julie Turner, Annalieza Landa, Margaret Carr for proof reading and correcting!

Dedication

To all at Bethel Community Church Royston. The church that released me, as it has done so many others into their calling. Never forget that the true greatness of a church is never in how many are gathered but in how many are sent.

Preface

Several years ago I was preaching in a Church a few miles from where I live in South Yorkshire. It was a midweek meeting and Christians from across the region had been invited to gather. I was preaching on the subject of 'Revival' and for the need for God to pour out His Spirit on our nation. My attention began to focus on a man who was seated at the back of the hall. He was enthusiastically responding to everything I was saying, edging closer and closer to the edge of his seat, his excitement growing with every point I made.

Suddenly, mid-preach and without any warning, the man jumped up and ran to the front of the church. He stood before me, eyes closed, hands outstretched and facing upwards, which told me he desired to receive the gifts of the Spirit.

"I want your anointing!" he said, "And I want a double portion!"

I have to admit to being a little thrown by this interruption of my message, but at the same time I had to admire the man's obvious hunger for God. I politely asked him to sit down so I could continue, but promised him he would be the first to receive prayer during ministry time. He complied, seating himself on the front row, and stared at me throughout the remainder of the sermon with excitement in his eyes.

As soon as the message was over, people began to line-up for prayer. The first person I approached was my new best friend … "Double portion man"! Before I laid hands on him, I asked him a simple question: "Which church do you attend?" The man thought for a moment and responded by saying, "I go to *all* the churches!"

He went on to explain that, rather than belonging to one particular church family, he visited a different church each week, going "wherever the Spirit led him".

My follow up question was "Who is your Pastor?" He replied, "I don't need a Pastor. I have my own ministry, evangelising on the streets. That's why I need the anointing."

Sadly, I knew that I could lay hands on this man all evening and he would never receive the anointing he desired. This book will seek to explain why.

Over my time in ministry, I have met many Christians like this man - people with a sincere passion for God and His presence and a real longing to be used by God for His glory. Sadly, like this man, there are many who fail to see their need for the local church and its importance in the plan and heart of God. A failure to correctly see the Church can have a disastrous impact on our walk with God and can cut us off from the anointing and blessing that He desires to pour into our lives.

This book is written for the man in that meeting and the countless others like him all over the planet. It is not written to judge or condemn, but to allow the Holy Spirit to use God's Word to enable us to see the Church and our part in it.

Introduction

"Behold, how good and how pleasant it is for brothers to dwell together in unity. It is like the precious oil [of consecration] poured on the head, coming down on the beard, even the beard of Aaron, coming down upon the edge of his [priestly] robes [consecrating the whole body]. It is like the dew of [Mount] Hermon coming down on the hills of Zion; for there the Lord has commanded the blessing: life forevermore."

Psalm 133 (Amplified Bible)

The anointing oil was incredibly important to the nation of Israel. Oil was used to set apart and anoint prophets, priests and kings. It was a key component of the Jewish system of worship, in both the Tabernacle and, later, the Temple. The Hebrew word for anoint means "to pour or rub oil on a person or thing". For the New Testament Christian, the oil represents the anointing of the Holy Spirit.

When Jesus was born, He came as "The Anointed One", and it was His anointing that enabled Him to "do good and heal all who were under the power of the devil" (Acts 10v38).

Most scholars believe that the Holy Spirit anointed Jesus at His baptism. It was this anointing that enabled Him to heal the sick, raise the dead, cast out demons and preach with power and authority.

Many Christians today desire this same anointing - and rightly so. Jesus has called every believer to do the works that He did, and even greater works (John 14v12), whilst Paul encouraged the Church to "eagerly desire spiritual gifts" (1 Corinthians 14v1). It is clear from Scripture that moving in the power of God is only possible when we receive the anointing of God's Spirit.

Members of the early Church were called "Christians" because they were "anointed ones", little Christs who carried the same anointing that Jesus Himself carried. Today, there is a new hunger rising up in believers to experience and encounter the anointing of God. It could be argued that the anointing is the most important thing we can receive, as the anointing is God Himself – the Holy Spirit, abiding and dwelling in us and flowing out of us in power and glory.

Divine Principle

As we study Psalm 133 we see a very important lesson. It is a principle that unless understood can lead to great disappointment and frustration. There are many Christians praying for an increased awareness of the anointing and a greater manifestation of the Holy Spirit in their lives. These Christians will pray and fast with great desire and zeal. In their enthusiasm they will travel to conferences and events hoping to receive an impartation from the preacher. This can lead to great frustration and heartbreak, because once the meeting is over, the goose-bumps have left and the encounter has passed, their life is still as powerless as it was before. It is not that there was anything wrong with attending the conference or receiving prayer or going on a fast – these are all important, highly recommended and indeed Biblical – but unless they are combined with the Psalm 133 principle, they are utterly meaningless.

The principle is quite simply this – the oil always flows downwards.

When I am teaching on this scripture in front of an audience, I will usually ask for a volunteer to come and stand at the front. I will then hold a bottle of water over their head and begin to tip it slightly. This is usually followed by some nervous laughter from my now unwilling volunteer! I explain to the congregation that if I were to fully tip the bottle, the person underneath would get a good soaking. This usually results in the congregation urging me to do just that (I have so far resisted the temptation!) I then ask the (by now bemused) volunteer to take a step either to the right or to the left. I explain that if I were to pour the water now I could keep pouring all day and the volunteer would remain dry, because they were no longer in alignment with the flow of water. The key to the volunteer getting wet is only partly down to me pouring - they must also be willing to align themselves with the flow.

In the same way, receiving the anointing of God's Holy Spirit is only partly down to God pouring out. In fact, that is the easy bit!

2000 years ago on the day of Pentecost, Jesus poured out His Holy Spirit (Acts 2v33) and He has not stopped being poured out. God is not stingy with the person of the Holy Spirit. He gives Himself, His anointing and gifts to all those who would ask for them (Luke 11v13).

However, unless we come under God's flow and into alignment with His purposes, we can ask and God can pour out all day long, yet we remain outside of the blessing.

God's Flow

In Psalm 133, David - using the High Priest as an example - explains that the anointing flows down upon three places: the head, the beard and the robes. We must be connected to those three places if we are to receive the anointing, the life and the blessing of God.

The head in the Bible is a clear picture of Jesus Christ. Paul says in Ephesians 5 (and elsewhere) "Christ is the head of the Church". Unless we recognise the Headship of Jesus, we are never going to experience the power and presence of the Holy Spirit. God is not going to give His anointing to those who do not submit to His Anointed

One. Recognising the Headship of Jesus is simply to recognise His Lordship over our lives. We are called to serve Him, follow Him, obey Him, trust Him and worship Him. Failure to do this means we are coming out of alignment with the Head and, therefore, the flow of God's oil.

Most Christians are aware of the need to make Jesus their Lord and not just their Saviour so we won't discuss this point in any further detail. What many miss though is that from the head, the oil flows down upon the beard and the robes.

The beard speaks of those who are mature, specifically leaders who have been put in place by God. This can be leadership in the home, the workplace and society, but most significantly for Christians, leadership in the local church. As the oil flows down upon the Head, it then flows down upon the beard.

God's anointing never bypasses His ministers. Rather, the anointing flows from His ministers to the rest of the congregation. If we fail to recognise God's delegated authorities and fail to honour, submit and serve those who God, in His wisdom, has placed in leadership, we cut ourselves off from the flow of the anointing. Sadly, there are many today who, like the man I mentioned earlier, don't see their need for a Pastor or any kind of spiritual covering. This will ultimately lead to a powerless life, as they are coming out of alignment with God's flow. A correct understanding of submission and accountability positions you to receive the anointing and blessing that God longs to release into your life.

Finally the oil flows down upon the robes. The robes cover the body, and speak of Jesus' body (Christ being our High Priest). The body of Christ is the Church (Ephesians 5v23, Colossians 1v18, Colossians 1v24). The anointing flows down upon the body, the Church. And that is it. There is no follow up, no Plan B. If we want to encounter the Holy Spirit, yes pray and fast, yes attend the latest impartation meeting – but understand you must also connect to the body of Christ, the local church. To separate from the body, is to cut ourselves off from the flow of oil.

Old Testament anointing vs. New Testament anointing

As I read the Bible I see a major difference between the anointing in the Old Testament and the anointing in the New Testament. Although there are occasions in the Old Testament when the anointing came on groups of people, generally the anointing came on individuals – Samson, Gideon, David and the prophets are all examples of this. However, when we get into the New Testament, we see something very interesting – on every occasion in the book of Acts when we read of people being baptised in the Holy Spirit, it was always on groups of people. Of course, these groups of people were made up of individuals, but the emphasis is on the fact that they had come together as part of the body of Christ. When we do read of individuals being used by God in the New Testament, it is never the Old Testament lone ranger ministry. We never read of a lone prophet crying out in the wilderness after John the Baptist. All of God's servants in the new dispensation were all connected to each other as part of the Church.

In Exodus 30, God said that the anointing oil was only for the High Priest and his sons. In verse 32 He clearly states "do not pour it on anyone else's body". The anointing oil can only be poured on one body – the body of the High Priest – Jesus. That body is His Church. Unless we are a part of that body, we come out of alignment with God's purposes.

It is common these days for Christians to think that they can be part of Jesus but not part of the Church – this is simply not Biblical. To receive the anointing, the blessing and the life of God, we must be connected to the Body of our High Priest, Jesus. We must see His Church. This is what will we look at in this book.

SEEING THE CHURCH

"His intent was that now, through the Church, the manifold wisdom of God should be made known to the rulers and authorities in the heavenly realms, according to his eternal purpose that he accomplished in Christ Jesus our Lord."

(Ephesians 3v10-11)

In these two verses, the apostle Paul gives some of the greatest revelation on the Church that man has ever received. It is clear to see, as we read the New Testament, that the Church is central to the plans and purpose of God. It is our understanding of this and our response to it that will determine our own individual fruitfulness.

God's Plan

Ephesians 3v10-11 tells us that God has a plan, a purpose. This purpose is not an afterthought, not a Plan B, not a panic response to the Fall of Man. Instead this plan was conceived in the heart of God way back in eternity past. This plan is quite simply The Church. It is through the Church Paul tells us that God reveals His "manifold wisdom". The word manifold means "many sided", "many coloured", "multifaceted". We serve an awesome God, a God far bigger than our concept or understanding of Him. He is the unfathomable God, the unknowable God, the unapproachable God and the unseen God. Yet God's plan and purpose from eternity past was to make

Himself understood, knowable, approachable and visible. He does this by first giving us His Son Jesus, then His Church, which is the fullness of Him who fills everything in every way (Ephesians 1v23).

The scope of God's remit to unveil Himself goes far beyond our towns, villages and cities. He wants to reach the "rulers and authorities in the heavenly realms". This is the ultimate destiny of the Church – to show heaven, in its entirety, who God is and what He is like.

God is many sided, multifaceted - yet each expression of His Church is an expression of who He is. As a diamond, when held up to light, reflects many different colours yet remains one piece, the Church when shining with the light of God's presence, is one body, yet effulgently radiates different aspects of His glory and reality.

This verse shows us that the Church is not primarily here to educate people or reform society or meet people's social needs or to be a fellowship gathering, but it is a Spiritual organism, testifying of a Spiritual Being to other spiritual beings.
When we consider the magnitude of God's purpose for the Church, it is so humbling to think that He allows us to be a part of this wonderful plan.

When the Church is mentioned in the Bible, it is important to realise that it is always referred to as **His** Church. It is never mentioned as belonging to a Pastor or a group of leaders or a tithe-paying group of members, but always as belonging to God. In Matthew 16, Jesus famously said, "**I** will build **my** Church" – twice emphasising His ownership. In Acts 20v28, the Church is simply called "the Church of God", a title used elsewhere in 1 Corinthians 1v2 and 1 Corinthians 11v16. In Hebrews 12v23, the Church is called "the Church of the firstborn". God not only takes ownership of His Church, but chooses to identify Himself with His Church. He is not embarrassed or ashamed of His Church, but proudly and boastfully (if I can use those terms of

God) declares, "This group of people are mine! They belong to me!"

In scripture, God always chooses to identify Himself with His Church. When Saul of Tarsus persecuted the Church, Jesus accused him of "persecuting me" (Acts 9v4). Likewise Jesus said in Matthew 10v40 "Anyone who welcomes you welcomes me, and anyone who welcomes me welcomes the one who sent him." Our attitude to the Church is our attitude towards Jesus. How we treat the Church is how we treat Jesus. "Whatsoever you do to the least of these, you do unto me." (Matt 25)

In Acts 5, Ananias and Sapphira are judged by God and struck down dead. Peter declares that they "lied to the Holy Spirit" (v3). Interestingly, as we read the passage, it is clear that Ananias and Sapphira lied to the Church. But again, God so identifies Himself with His Church that lying to the Holy Spirit and lying to the Church are in effect the same thing. God never separates Himself from His Church. Jesus and His Church are one. The Holy Spirit and the Church are one.

When we understand that the Church *is* God's plan, it will perhaps help clear up some faulty thinking that many Christians have today. You often hear of Christians talking about the fact that "God has a plan for their life". This is true, as scriptures like Jeremiah 29v11 show. However as we have already seen, the plan of God *is* the Church. And that is it. He has no other plan. The plan that God has for your life as an individual can only be discovered and outworked as we connect to His Church. Many Christians are helplessly searching, trying to discover "what is the plan of God for my life?" – there is only one plan of God – the Church. In being part of God's plan, you discover your plan.

Again, Christians speak of "their destiny" and will buy books and attend seminars trying to discover what their destiny is. This risks narrowing down "our destiny" to a function: my destiny is to lead worship, to be a successful businessperson etc.

No, your destiny is far bigger and more exciting than that! Your destiny is to "make known to the rulers and authorities in the heavenly realms, the manifold wisdom of God" as you become part of this amazing organism called His Church!

In the book of Acts, we not only see the plans of God outworked but also the plans of Satan. Satan's plan is always to attack the Church. He tried attacking God directly and was defeated by Him on the cross; so today he attacks the Church. Acts 8v1 tells us that a persecution broke out "against the church". The New Testament and Church history show us that Satan always seeks to destroy the Church. Why? Satan has figured out what most Christians miss: the Church is God's plan. If he can stop the Church, he can stop God. The Church is the outworking of God's power, God's will and God's purpose. This is why Satan hates it so much and seeks to destroy it. Thankfully he never will. Jesus said the gates of Hades would never overcome His Church.

If only Christians would acquire the understanding that Satan has! "What is God's will for my life?" "What is the plan that God has for my life?" "What is my purpose?" God's will, God's plan and God's purpose is always – the Church. As we become part of the Church, we discover our own individual functions and roles, but never apart from the ultimate plan – the Church. In disconnecting us from the Church, Satan seeks to disconnect us from our own purpose and destiny.

The Devotion of the Devoted

"They devoted themselves to the apostles' teaching and to fellowship, to the breaking of bread and to prayer. Everyone was filled with awe at the many wonders and signs performed by the apostles. All the believers were together and had everything in common. They sold property and possessions to give to anyone who had need. Every day they continued to meet together in the temple courts. They broke bread in their

homes and ate together with glad and sincere hearts, praising God and enjoying the favour of all the people. And the Lord added to their number daily those who were being saved." (Acts 2v42-47)

Here we can see the extraordinary devotion of the devoted. The word devoted means "to be steadfast, enduring, faithful." This was the attitude of the disciples towards the Church. Notice that they devoted themselves. This wasn't about the leaders forcing or coercing or persuading people to come to meetings or to get involved in the vision. The Holy Spirit had so moved upon their hearts, that spontaneously and willingly these believers gave themselves, their lives, their time, their energy, their finances, their all into the local church.

The success of the ministry of the early Church was based upon the truth that every believer saw: life is about more than self. They chose to live for something and be part of something that was much bigger than they were. When we take our eyes off ourselves and see what God is doing through His Church and through community, we position ourselves to receive all that God has for us as individuals.

Paradoxically, when we live our lives "others-conscious", we discover our own identity, ministry and purpose. No one wanted for anything in the early Church because people had committed to pouring their lives into others. How different would Church be today, if instead of focusing on our needs, wants and desires we poured ourselves into meeting others' desires and focused on other people's needs and wants. I would meet your need, you would meet my need, and consequently, neither of us would have any need!

We require a bigger focus, a bigger vision and a bigger picture for our individual lives and ourselves. We need to see the Church, see each other and see how we individually fit into God's plan. We need to commit to devoting our lives to a cause that is bigger than we are.

This is what John meant when he said that "we ought to lay down our lives for our brothers" (1 John 3v16). Love always gives itself away, pours out, is never self-seeking, looks outwards and focuses on something other than itself. Imagine if we were so gripped by a vision of the Church that we poured out our lives and gave all that we were towards its success, growth and health!

John Cassian said, "the bond between friends cannot be broken by chance; no interval of time or space can destroy it. Not even death itself can part true friends."

I am reminded of the account of the four friends in Mark 2 who brought their paralysed friend to Jesus. These four men saw a need that was bigger than their own. Instead of focusing on their own miracle or encounter, they committed to transporting someone else into God's presence. They literally carried their friend to Jesus, doing what Paul told us all to do when he said, "carry each other's burdens" (Galatians 6v2). They used all of their strength and energy to ensure that someone else received a miracle. They risked their own reputation and, despite the embarrassment and even potential legal repercussions, tore open someone's roof so that their friend could have his encounter. Their passion, commitment and zeal were focused on someone other than themselves.

Consequently, before Jesus focused on the paralysed man, He focused on them: "When Jesus saw their faith …" (Mark 2v5). The act of perceiving, acknowledging and responding to a need that was bigger than their own received the attention, approval and commendation of heaven.

In 1 Samuel 14 we read the story of Jonathan and his armour-bearer attacking a Philistine outpost. An armour-bearer was an incredibly important, but dangerous, role in the army. An armour-bearer would help carry his commanding officers shield and other weapons so that these heavy tools didn't weigh down the officer. An armour-bearer literally carried someone else's burden. An armour-bearer also had the awesome responsibility of ensuring the success and safety of his commanding officer.

A sense of self-preservation prevails in battle: "How do I get out of this alive?" An armour-bearer doesn't think like this. An armour-bearer focuses on someone else: "How can I make sure that they get out of this alive?"

Imagine if we committed to being armour-bearers for each other in the Church? Imagine if we habitually focused on each other rather than self? Imagine if our automatic response to crises was "How can I help you get through this?" Imagine if our goal in life is not to fulfil our own destiny, but to help others to fulfil theirs?

When Jonathan proposed the risky strategy of attacking the enemy without backup, he was effectively going on a suicide mission. The response of his armour-bearer is a wonderful statement of courage and loyalty: "Go ahead, I am with you heart and soul" (1 Samuel 14v7).

This armour-bearer would stick with Jonathan no matter how great the danger. He would remain devoted to his friend no matter the cost to his own safety. Jonathan's success would be his armour-bearer's success. They would both share the victory that day (1 Samuel 14v14).

Oh, that God would raise up armour-bearers in the Church today … that he would raise up friends, like the friends of the paralysed man … that He would raise up a Church devoted not to self, but to each other … that He would give us all the eyes to see that we are a part of something so much bigger than ourselves!

God's Presence

In Ephesians 2v22 Paul declares that "**together** [i.e. The Church] is becoming a dwelling in which God lives by His Spirit". The New Testament makes it clear that God dwells, abides, moves and lives in His Church … not in buildings, conferences, events or organisations, but in His people who come together as one to worship Him. Jesus Himself declared, "For where two or three gather in my name, there am I with them" (Matthew 18v20). This is an incredible promise. Of course, Jesus is with you as an individual wherever you go, but there is a special manifestation of His Spirit and a special promise of His personal presence given to the corporate Church that meets in His Name. Jesus doesn't stipulate that we need to organise a conference with a "special guest" preacher before He will appear in our midst – it is simply that believers are gathered together in His Name.

In Revelation 2, Jesus is described as being amongst the lamp stands (the lamp stands being the Church). Jesus moves in the midst of His Church. When we meet together as the Church, Jesus is there. The power, glory, authority and presence of heaven are in our midst. Surely we are standing on Holy ground! Notice, Jesus never says part of Him will be present (as if somehow He can be divided up and portioned out). No, all of Him is with us. This is so important to grasp. There is as much of Jesus present in your local church on a Sunday morning as there is in the special "revival" service taking place in another part of the world. There is as much of the anointing and resurrection power of Jesus available whilst your Pastor is preaching, as there is when your favourite television evangelist is preaching. He gives Himself to His Church. He is present in His Church.

Paul writes in 1 Corinthians 3v16 "Don't you know that you yourselves are God's temple and that God's Spirit lives in you?" Who is He writing to? The Church! In fact, all of the epistles (except the Pastoral Epistles) are written to churches. God speaks to

His Church. "He who has an ear, let him hear what the Spirit *says to the churches*" (Revelation 2v11). If we want to hear God speaking, perhaps the best place to be is not always in the prayer line of a prophet, but in the pew of our local church, hungry and expectant for God to speak to us.

Ephesians 3v21 tells us that God's glory is in the Church. This is very important to grasp. I am a revivalist, passionate about God moving in the nations and desperately longing for a greater manifestation of the glory of God in our day. It is God's glory that changes lives, situations and communities. But it is vital to understand that God only gives His glory to His Church. The Church is the only habitation for His glory. When we talk about God's glory moving in our cities and nations, God will not click His fingers and cause His presence to somehow hover in the skies and transform our societies. No, God's glory fills His Church. National revival will never bypass the Church. That doesn't mean that God won't bypass certain groups of people or certain denominations (history sadly shows us that this often happens), but God will never bypass His corporate Church. I have even heard people preach that if the Church doesn't want revival, God will move amongst another group of people. This is wrong and un-Biblical. God only moves through His Church. His glory is only ever given to His Church. The Holy Spirit abides in the Church. Let me clarify, I am not saying that God only moves in church meetings. A quick overview of the New Testament actually shows that very few miracles took place "in church". Nearly every healing and miracle took place outside the four walls of the church. But the miracles were still done as the Holy Spirit worked through individuals or groups of people who were part of His Church. We desperately need the glory of God to move in our streets and communities. But God only works through His Church as it obeys the Great Commission.

When we understand that the Holy Spirit dwells in the Church, this may lead us to reconsider the meaning of questions such as "Have you heard about the move of God in such and such a place?" What we usually mean by this is that in some particular part of the world, Christians are gathering and there seems to be an unusual manifestation of God's presence. Often in these gatherings there seems to be an ease in which people are healed and a significant amount of people receiving salvation or being restored back to God. Church history shows us time and time again that in certain places there can be "spiritual hotspots", "revivals" or special "outpourings of God's Spirit". I believe and fully embrace all of that. I certainly desire that in my country. However, when we talk about "the move of God in such and such a place", there is a danger that we downplay what God is doing in our local church. Whilst there may be more of an awareness of God in certain places, the reality is that God is there whenever and wherever His people meet. The reality is that your local Church is just as much a move of God as whatever else God is doing around the globe. Your local church is just as important and as vital to the plans and purposes of God as the extended meetings that are on Christian television. Your community, town or village may be totally unaffected by the move of God that is taking place elsewhere. The answer to your community is not the move of God in such and such a place. The answer to your community is your church. The Church is God's plan, God's move, God's outpouring. Moves of God come and go, but your local church, God willing, will have a place in your community for generations to come.

Excitement or Abundance?

In John 10v10, Jesus famously said "I have come that you may have life and life in all its fullness". Many times Christians mistake Jesus' understanding of an abundant life and think that Jesus meant an exciting life. There is no doubt that being a Christian is exciting but it is immature to think that just because something is not exciting it's not God. Let's be honest, the chances are that the huge conference that's taking place next month is probably more exciting than your local church on a Sunday morning. Of course it's far more exciting to be amongst thousands of other Christians than the handful that meet in your local church. Of course it's far more exciting to sing along with the professional worship leader and their band, than sing along with brother so-and-so with his out of tune guitar. Of course it's far more exciting to listen to the dynamic preacher who you've seen on TV expounding his best message, rather than your local pastor who you've heard countless times before. Just because something is less exciting, doesn't mean it's any less God.

It's sad when Christians get excited about the next conference, but not about the next communion service or prayer meeting in their local church. I am all for conferences, but don't fall into the trap of thinking that somehow God is more passionate about the conference than He is your local church, or that He is somehow more God in those places than He is in your church.

Again, in our lust for excitement, we can buy tickets and fly half way around the world to visit the move of God in such and such a place. It's exciting to do that, but I am convinced that what Jesus meant when He talked about "an abundant life" was not excitement, but fruitfulness. The best way for a plant to remain fruitful is not to be constantly dug up and moved, but to remain where it is has been planted.

I have had the joy of experiencing moves of God around the world and attend several conferences throughout the year. Whilst recommended, we can receive a touch, an impartation or a Word as much from our local church as we can from places where revival seems to be breaking out. Less exciting doesn't equate to less powerful.

It disturbs me when Christians frequently leave their local church to experience what God is doing elsewhere. The local church needs our loyalty – and we need our local church. Give to it, tithe to it, serve in it, honour it and celebrate it! It may not always seem as exciting, but it is the only way to bear fruit and fruit that remains.

Conclusion

Some Christians today have totally failed to see the importance and value of the Church. Others may only see one particular aspect of many that makes up the Church.

The aim of this book is to look at each aspect of what the Church is according to the New Testament. These are:

The Assembly – this speaks of our physical meeting together
The Building – this speaks of our connection and unity
The House – this speaks of our commitment and relationship to the organism
The Family – this speaks of our commitment and relationship to each other
The Body – this speak of our ministry and service
The Bride – this speaks of our worship, love and passion
The Sheepfold – this speaks of our submission and obedience
The Army – this speaks of our mission and warfare

It is vital that we see and embrace all of these aspects of the Church. To only see one aspect leaves us unbalanced, our lives out of focus.

We will begin by seeing the Church as the Assembly and the physical aspect of us meeting together.

THE ASSEMBLING OF THE SAINTS

"The whole assembly became quiet as they listened to Barnabas and Paul..."

(Acts 15v12)

The word assembly speaks of a group of people coming together or meeting together. In the Bible it is used throughout the Old Testament. God's people would often assemble together for feasts and for fasts, for times of worship and for times of warfare. In the New Testament, the word is used only once in reference to the Church, in the above passage in Acts. However, the phrase "coming together" or "meeting together" is used time and again. Perhaps the most significant is found in Hebrews 10v25:

"Do not give up meeting together, as some are in the habit of doing, but encourage one another – and all the more as you see the Day approaching."

It seems to have become apparent that some believers had got into the habit of not attending church. They had stopped physically meeting together with other Christians. Notice this had not necessarily been a deliberate one-off decision to cut themselves off from the body of Christ. It had become a "habit". A habit is something that forms over time, perhaps something unknown to the person doing it. Apparently, some believers had started missing church meetings - perhaps they had become bored or busy - but now this had become a habit. Church attendance was becoming much less frequent for them.

The writer to the Hebrews simply says, "Do not be like this!" There are some habits that are good and then there are some that are bad. Missing Church is a bad habit! Notice the urgency of this warning. It is not given as a sound piece of advice, but as a command – do not give up meeting together. There are no specific reasons given in this passage for why meeting together is so good and why not meeting is so bad, but the writer clearly expects that those who belong to Christ will regularly meet together for fellowship and worship.

In seeing the Church, we must understand that Church is a literal meeting, an assembly of saints. Of course, Church is much more than a meeting, but nevertheless it is still an important aspect. Our connection to the Church has to be physical as well as spiritual. This is obvious as we look throughout the New Testament.

The Importance of Meeting

The importance of meeting together is clear throughout the book of Acts. Today many Christians claim that they can belong to a Church without regularly attending meetings. They may justify their lack of attendance by saying "I'm with you in spirit" or "I can't make it, but I'm praying for you". Of course, some believers may have genuine reasons why they can't get to church - people may be sick or elderly, for example. God sees the hearts of those who genuinely would love to attend a church meeting but physically can't. He can meet them right where they are. There are others, however, who due to boredom, business or other priorities and commitments have simply "got into the habit" of not meeting together with other Christians. When we do this we are in grave danger of cutting ourselves off from the purposes of God. Count Zindenzorf said, "there can be no Christianity without community". In his book 'First Day', Dr John Andrews says, "Ironically, although no book champions the cause of the individual more than the Bible, the individual is almost always seen in the frame of community".

Most theologians would agree that it was the outpouring of the Holy Spirit on the Day of Pentecost that brought about the birth of the Church. Acts 1 and 2 tells us that there were around 120 believers meeting together in one place for constant prayer. It is most likely this group that initially received the baptism in the Holy Spirit and became the first church. What is interesting is that we know from Paul's writings that after Jesus was raised from the dead He appeared to hundreds of His disciples not just those 120. We know of one instance, for example, when He appeared to 500 at one time (1 Corinthians 15). So it seems that hundreds of Jesus' disciples were not there in Acts 1 and 2. It doesn't say that they necessarily stopped believing in Jesus, just that they decided to miss the prayer meeting! When Jesus, ten days later, poured out the Holy Spirit, those disciples were not in a position to receive simply because they weren't there! Perhaps they were having "family time", perhaps they were at work, but we know that they didn't become the Acts 2 Church - not necessarily because they were bad, sinful people, but because they didn't come to the meeting. There is no indication that the 120 were more spiritual, more holy or more faith-filled than the others, but they were the ones who encountered the fire, received the gift of tongues, the infilling of the Spirit, heard the mighty rushing wind and saw the great harvest of souls in Acts 2. Why? They were the ones who met together! Never underestimate the power of just turning up. Acts 2 was a bad morning to have a lie-in!

It is true that "going to Church doesn't make you a Christian"; however it could be argued that it is equally true that being a Christian means that you will go to

Church! The concept of believing in Jesus and not attending Church is absent from scripture. Many accepted Peter's message of faith in Jesus after his preaching on the Day of Pentecost (Acts 2v41); however, the Bible only records those who were in the company of believers as those "who were added to their number". This same truth is repeated again in Acts 4. The book of Acts only counts and records those who became a part of the Church as being the number who gave their lives to Jesus. Salvation is not just about saying a prayer, filling in a decision card or raising our hand at the altar call. As Saint Augustine said, "He cannot have God for his Father who refuses to have the Church for his Mother".

The early Christians placed a clear importance on church attendance. Acts 2v46 tells us that they "continued to meet together" and Acts 5v12 tells us "*all* the believers used to meet together". Church attendance was something that they were obviously committed to and something they enjoyed. Acts 2v42 tells us they devoted "themselves" to fellowshipping together. The Pastor didn't need to ring around asking why they hadn't been to church for a month. Neither did they miss church for several weeks just to "test" the Pastor's concern for them! Instead, each individual believer made a conscious decision that fellowship together was going to be something that they devoted themselves to. Acts 2v1 tells us that they were "in one place" – it was a literal, physical, coming together to meet.

The Purpose of Meeting

One of the primary reasons why we meet together is to fellowship with other Christians.

I heard recently of a Christian who stated that, although he sincerely loved Jesus, he had decided he would no longer attend church on a regular basis. He said that instead he would do things he considered more fun and enjoyable like spending time with his family or taking the dog for a walk in the park. After all, Sunday was his day off so he was going to use it for recreation, not sitting bored for two hours in a meeting. After all, he could continue his relationship with God through prayer and Bible study rather than church meetings. This way of thinking is sadly missing the point of both what Biblical Christianity is and the importance God places on fellowship with other Christians. As in "normal life", when it comes to God, just because something is more enjoyable doesn't mean it is more beneficial.

In 1 John 1, John writes:

"(v3) We proclaim to you what we have seen and heard, so that you also may have **fellowship with us**. And our fellowship is with the Father and with his Son, Jesus Christ … (v6-7) If we claim to have fellowship with him and yet walk in the darkness, we lie and do not live out the truth. But if we walk in the light, as he is in the light, we have **fellowship with one another,** and the blood of Jesus, his Son, purifies us from all sin."

Here John writes that one of his purposes in proclaiming the gospel was that believers would be brought into fellowship with one another. He also declares that one of the primary signs that we are "walking in the light" and thus belonging to God is that we will be in fellowship with one another. The reason Jesus died on the cross was not just to restore fellowship between man and God, but between man and man. Again, I want to emphasise that this fellowship must be practical and literal as well as spiritual and pictorial.

The early Church, as we have read, was devoted to fellowshipping with one another. The word "devote" means "to endure, remain steadfast, to stick faithfully to". This was their mind-set towards fellowshipping with each other. The Greek word for fellowship here is "koinonia" – it is used 17 times in the New Testament. It was a fairly common Greek word used to describe anything from corporations to the most intimate of marriage relationships. From the usage of the word, we can conclude that fellowship is a word denoting an interdependent relationship, i.e. dependent on more than one individual.

In seeing the Church we have to see and understand our need for fellowship. Many people see Christianity as something that is intimately personal. They see it as purely being about their relationship with God. There is a huge emphasis on the receiving of Jesus as your "personal Saviour" and how God wants you as an individual to be blessed and prosper etc. While all of this is true it is only one side of truth. To ignore the corporate side of faith, the coming together to fellowship with other believers, is to miss out not only on huge chunks of scripture, but on a huge part of why we were created. There can be no Christianity without community.

Adam was created in God's image. He was sinless, lived in a perfect environment, had an intimate relationship with God and had authority and dominion. And yet despite all that, God still said, "it is not good for the man to be alone" (Genesis 2v18).

Adam needed fellowship with another human being. Indeed Adam could not fulfil the divine mandate to "be fruitful and increase in number" (Genesis 1v28) without that human fellowship. It is the same with us. It doesn't matter how close we are to God, it is not good for us to be without Christian fellowship. If God says it is not good, it is not good! We cannot fulfil our divine destiny without it.

Although worship is an intensely personal experience, it is a corporate experience too. Whenever worship is mentioned in the book of Revelation, it is in the context of believers gathering together around the throne singing songs of praise to God. Those who dislike fellowship now had better skip heaven! In that place there will be "a great multitude that no one could count, from every nation, tribe, people and language" (Revelation 7v9).

In Acts 28, upon arriving in Rome, some believers travelled to fellowship with Paul. Verse 15 tells us "at the sight of these men Paul thanked God and was encouraged". Even the apostle Paul needed the encouragement that comes from fellowshipping with other Christians. How much more do we need that encouragement? Those who don't see the point of attending church or don't feel like they are "getting anything out of it" fail to consider that their presence may provide a source of encouragement to people in the meeting who need encouraging.

The Power of Meeting

There may be no greater reason given for the power of meeting together than that found in Matthew 18v20 "for where two or three **come together** in my name, there am I with them" – Jesus Christ. The word for "come together" is the Greek work synago meaning "to assemble together". It is where the word synagogue comes from, meaning the gathering or congregation. In other words, Jesus is saying "whenever there is an assembly of Christians; whenever you gather together; wherever there is a congregation meeting in my name – I am there, personally present." There can be no greater reason to get to Church than that!

People can sometimes try to appear spiritual by saying things like "I don't need a Church service to draw close to God". Of course, our personal and private devotion is essential, but it is not spiritual to say you don't need a church meeting. In fact it is pride and arrogance and a denial of what God says we need in Scripture.

James talks about our need for each other in his epistle. "Is any one of you sick? He should call the elders of the Church to pray and anoint Him with oil" (James 5v14). Why? Why can't I pray for myself if I'm sick? I don't know, but perhaps God is teaching us this whole idea of mutual dependence and showing us our need for one another. In verse 16 he says, "confess your sins to each other and pray for each other so that you may be healed". It is in community, in relationship, in fellowship with others that we find healing. Healing is not just a physical thing but can also be psychological, emotional and spiritual. There are many Christians who are hurting and broken. It is only in authentic and loving communities that healing can come, never in isolation and separation. God doesn't waste words. He tells us to pray to one another, confess to one another and call for one another. This can only be done in fellowshipping with the Church.

Today, through the wonder of television, radio and the Internet, Christians no longer need to leave their home in order to receive some kind of Christian input. From the comfort of your living room you can receive wonderful teaching and experience the best church services from all over the planet within a few clicks. There is no doubt that for people who are housebound and unable to get to church, this can be a huge blessing. For those of us who attend a local church on a regular basis, Christian television and websites, for example, can be a great addition to our walk with God, especially for those who feel they may not receive great quality teaching in their own church community. However, the emphasis here has to be on "addition" and not "replacement". The growing trend for "internet church", or the idea that watching a church service on TV is the same as physically attending a Church service, is to fail to see the Church as the assembly that God designed it to be.

The Word has to become flesh in our lives (John 1). There has to be a literal meeting together, a physical touching of the body of Christ, relationships with real flesh and blood pastors and brothers and sisters.

In his description of the armour of God in Ephesians 6, Paul writes about "the shield of faith, with which you can extinguish all the flaming arrows of the enemy" (v16). In the culture of the day, Paul's readers, used to the military presence of Rome, would have understood the analogy of a soldier's armoury immediately. What is interesting is that, under attack from "the flaming arrows of the enemy", a Roman soldier's shield wouldn't have been enough to protect him. Instead, soldiers would assemble together in a testudo formation, drawing so close to the others in the unit that they could link their shields together. Some soldiers would lift their shields to provide aerial cover; others would link them so that the back and sides were covered. As they came together and linked shields they were almost impenetrable to every kind of missile. An observer would see an assembly of shields, as each member of the unit covered each other. In this formation they could move together and still be protected. There was so much strength in this coming together, that even horses and men could ride over them and they would remain perfectly safe underneath! However, if any soldier decided to break ranks by detaching his shield from the others, he would be easy prey for the enemy.

Paul tells us that this is what faith is like. We are in a real battle with a real enemy and we need the faith of one another. Our own individual faith is not enough. There has to be a physical coming together, a place where we meet and touch and connect with other Christians so as not to be easily taken out by the enemy. We cannot survive on our own. We know that there will be terrible times in the last days (2 Timothy 3v1) and that there will come a day when people who kill Christians will think they are doing God a service (John 16). Perhaps that is why we are told not to forsake meeting together "all the more as the day approaches", because more and more we are going to need each other.

When Peter and John were persecuted in Acts 4, the first thing that they did upon their release was go "back to their own people" ... and then they all "raised their voices *together* in prayer to God" (v23-24). No doubt this time of fellowship with the church brought them healing as they recovered from their ordeal and recharged their strength, faith and energy to carry on serving Jesus.

Conclusion

We have seen that the most basic aspect of Church is that we physically meet together regularly with other Christians for fellowship. We have to understand the need for this and the importance God places on it in the scriptures. Yes, we can have our own private devotional time with the Lord, but let us not forget "when Jesus had called the Twelve *together*, He gave them power and authority" (Luke 9v1). It is as we meet together that we are equipped and empowered to be all that God wants us to be.

However, Church is much more than just a meeting. Not only must we be in the "same place", but we must also be "together" in one place (Acts 2v1). The emphasis here is not just on our physical meeting together, but also on our spiritual unity. This is what we will look at in the next chapter as we look at another aspect of the Church: God's building.

LIVING STONES AND TEMPLES OF GLORY

"But Christ is faithful as the Son over God's house. And we are his house, if indeed we hold firmly to our confidence and the hope in which we glory."

(Hebrews 3v6)

Throughout the Old Testament one of the most common descriptions of the place where people would gather together to worship was "The House of God". This was a description used first of the Tabernacle in the wilderness and later of David's Tent. More commonly the Temple would frequently be referred to as The House of God. God is the master builder and He has never stopped building His House, but as we come into the New Testament Church Age we have a different perspective as to what the House of God is.

That the House of God is the Church is pretty clear throughout the New Testament. Paul says in 1 Timothy 3v15 that the Church is "God's household" and 1 Peter 4v17 confirms this. But as prophesied way back in the Old Testament, God's House under the New Covenant is not bricks and mortar; "the Most High does not live in houses made by man" (Acts 7v48). The Church, the House of God, is people. Indeed, the writer to the Hebrews tells us that "we are His house". The Church now becomes the fulfilment of Jesus' promise in John 14 "we will come to him and make our home in him". Not only must we see the individual impact of this truth but also the impact it has on us corporately, too.

Living Stones

"As you come to him, the living Stone – rejected by humans but chosen by God and precious to him – you also, like living stones, are being built into a spiritual house to be a holy priesthood, offering spiritual sacrifices acceptable to God through Jesus Christ." (1 Peter 2v4-5)

These verses emphasise again that God's House is, firstly, people and, secondly, a spiritual house. It is very important to see this, particularly for leaders. God never calls us to devote our attention and finances primarily to building buildings. Some pastors may point towards their building as a sign of the growth and health of the Church, but when Jesus' disciples tried to point His attention towards the splendour of the Temple, Jesus was not as easily impressed: "I tell you the truth, not one stone here will be left on another; every one will be thrown away" (Matthew 24v2). Buildings will rot and rust and collapse, but the people we are called to help build will last for eternity. Of course, buildings can help facilitate what God is doing and there is nothing wrong with having nice buildings, but our first priority is to build people. It is the spiritual health of the people that is important.

We also see from this passage that it is a "spiritual house". Whilst Church can be a place of fun, laughter and fellowship and a tool for outreach and social reform, we must remember that Church is not meant primarily to be a social club, a place of lots of activity or one devoted purely to social action. It is a spiritual house, offering spiritual sacrifices to God.

Now it is very important in this passage that we see both the corporate and individual aspects of the Church. Corporately, we are being built into a "house", but individually we are "living stones". That is vital to understand. You, as an individual, are a living stone (notice that Jesus is The Living Stone, so we are little Christs, little anointed ones). Together, we are becoming the House of God. In order for stones to become houses, one thing must happen – they must come together.

Paul helps explain this a little more clearer in Ephesians 2v21-22:

"In him the whole building is joined together and rises to become a holy temple in the Lord. And in him you too are being built together to become a dwelling in which God lives by his Spirit."

A number of years ago I was ministering in the nation of Zambia. One day I was looking out of the window of the room I was staying in and I saw a man constructing a building by hand, using stones. It was interesting to observe the process that this man undertook. He would pick up each stone one at a time and spend a few moments observing it. Some of the stones he would throw over his shoulder, as they were obviously no good to him. Other stones he would apply cement to and attach them to the building he was erecting. I sat there wondering why some stones were considered valuable and others worthless. What was he looking for? It gradually dawned on me that this man had no tools to chip or shape the stones, so what he was looking for were stones that would easily connect to the other stones. Stones that couldn't connect were deemed unusable. It was stones that fitted together with other stones that became part of the building. Thankfully, God in His mercy does have tools to chip away at us and shape us and mould us into vessels He can use. Even the misfits among us can become a habitation of God! But nevertheless the principle is still the same. Unless we are willing to be connected to other living stones we will never become the House of God.

Paul says that the whole building is "joined together" and "built together". The phrases "joined together" and "built together" can also translate as "to be closely joined and knit together". When a garment is knit together, each loop and fragment of wool is interlocked with the other. The Greek phrase "joined together" literally means "bound or welded together". It is a covenant word. Paul is speaking of us entering into a covenant relationship with each other. This is what David and Jonathan did in 1 Samuel 20. They were both bound together in a covenant of friendship. They swore a solemn oath to show each other "unfailing kindness like that of the Lord". It was an oath of love, that they would love each other as they loved themselves. It was an oath to honour each other, protect each other and serve each other. It would not be a fickle promise, but one that would last a lifetime and even beyond that to each other's extended family and descendants. This is perhaps what Paul had in mind when he saw the Church as God's building. Individual stones who have entered into covenant with other living stones to be faithful, to honour, to serve, to love, to be kind. It is a covenant to speak well of each other (1 Samuel 19v4) and to become "one in spirit" (1 Samuel 18v1) with each other.

Unity and Separation

A few years ago my wife and I bought a brand new house. Before we moved in, the builders warned us to expect movement. Sure enough, over the next few months, a few cracks began to appear as is common in quite a lot of new buildings. These cracks were only surface deep and with a little paint and Polyfilla were soon covered up. Imagine the scenario if the bricks that made our home decided they no longer liked being connected together and separated. Pretty soon we would no longer have a home, but a pile of rubble! Of course, bricks can't decide that because they are inanimate objects, but "living" stones can and sadly often do. When living stones decide that they don't like being connected to the other stones, the Bible calls it "division" and the House of God ceases to be the House of God, but a mess!

Jesus said this Himself in Matthew 12v25: "… a household divided against itself will not stand". Whenever there is division, the Church ceases to be the House of God. Division is characterised by criticism, jealousy, complaint, selfishness, cliques, isolation, lack of submission, lack of honour and lack of love - common traits in many churches, sadly. That is why many churches are no longer habitations of God's glory and presence. Where there is no unity He cannot bring blessing (Psalm 133).

In Acts 2, the early Christians were not just "in one place", but they were "together". Just because people are in one place, doesn't mean that they are together. Togetherness is both a mind-set and a heart attitude. It is something that I firstly decide to be; and then God, by His Spirit, enables me to be, by changing my heart.

It is helpful to recognise that unity is something God works in us. When the Master builder comes with his hammer and chisel and starts to chip away at our selfishness, impatience and carnality, our hearts are changed and are more inclined to love and honour. The Holy Spirit, according to Ephesians 4v3, brings about unity. That is why, as leaders, if we desire a united church, we must create an atmosphere for the Holy Spirit to work in people's lives. A prayer meeting might actually be more beneficial to creating unity than a BBQ. Many leaders try and organise unity and it doesn't work. Biblical unity is not social, but spiritual. Unity built solely around social and friendship activities is only surface deep and can easily be broken. It is in the many hearts, beating as one, that there is true unity. This is only brought about as people are filled and changed by the Holy Spirit.

The famous rivalry between Jacob and Esau became so fierce that Esau made a vow to kill his brother (Genesis 27v41). Later, circumstances would bring them back together. As they meet in Genesis 33, instead of Esau bringing a knife he brings a warm embrace, a kiss and tears of love. How had Esau's heart been so dramatically changed? In the previous chapter, while Esau is on his way to meet Jacob, Jacob is alone with God, having an encounter with His presence. Could it be, that as Jacob met with God, God changed and softened the heart of his brother? As the church creates an environment where people can meet with Jesus - a culture of prayer and Holy Spirit encounter - hearts that are full of bitterness, and areas of conflict and lack of forgiveness, may be touched and changed.

We must make a conscious decision to maintain the unity created in us by the Holy Spirit. Unity takes effort. Paul tells us to "make every effort to keep the unity" (Ephesians 4v3). We do this by "keeping the bond of peace". Peace and love are the cement that holds us together as God's building. Without them, we will divide. With them, we can keep connected no matter how greatly our relationships are tested.

Perhaps the clearest practical advice for keeping the unity is found in Colossians 3. It would be helpful for us to read and meditate on the full implications of these words in our daily lives and church communities:

"Therefore, as God's chosen people, holy and dearly loved, clothe yourselves with compassion, kindness, humility, gentleness and patience. Bear with each other and forgive one another if any of you has a grievance against someone. Forgive as the Lord forgave you. And over all these virtues put on love, which binds them all together in perfect unity." (v12-14)

We have to literally wear compassion like a garment, being gentle, patient and forgiving. We have to show kindness and humility. We sometimes have to put up with those we struggle to fellowship with, by being bound together in love. In scripture this is always a mindset and an action, never just a feeling.

In Ephesians, Paul tells us that one of the ways we either build or destroy the House of God is by how we speak to each other. That is why he tells us to make sure that we let no "unwholesome talk come out of your mouths but only what is helpful for building others up" (Ephesians 4v29). "Sharing your opinion" or "giving people a piece of your mind" may make you feel better, but it can actually destroy what God is trying to build.

The importance of unity, the power of connection and the danger of separation are themes that run throughout the scriptures. The churches in Colosse and Laodicea, in particular, were those where division appeared to be creeping in. Paul's goal therefore, the thing to which he "struggled towards" (Colossians 2v1) was that "they may be united in love" (v2). It is interesting that this was the culmination of Paul's vision for the church. His end goal was not necessarily a large church or prosperous church but a united church.

This was also the theme of the prayer of Jesus in the Garden of Gethsemane when He prayed for all believers. His prayer was that "all of them may be one" (John 17v21). Perhaps most significant about Jesus' prayer was that many of the things we often pray for Jesus never mentions, whilst the one thing we think is not that important, or presume we already have, is the focus of His prayer. It is also challenging to note that our example for unity is the Trinity itself "that they may be one as we are one". It is incredible to think that Father, Son and Holy Spirit have dwelt in totally unity since before time began and have never once had an argument or disagreement! This is what Jesus prayed we would experience with each other.

Ezekiel's vision of dry bones (Ezekiel 37) is a very well-known portion of scripture, particularly loved by Pentecostals and Charismatics because of the emphasis of the Holy Spirit coming, breathing upon and infilling those who have been slain. What must not be ignored, though, is the process by which this "revival" took place. Firstly, there was a "coming together, bone to bone" and then "tendons and flesh appeared on them and skin covered them". Many Christians desire the breath of

God's Spirit, but first there has to be the connection, the coming together with other believers. There also has to be that flesh and blood outworking of our faith with other people, the willingness to touch skin and live out our lives in community and real life relationships. In doing this we position ourselves to be filled with God's power and glory.

Temples of Glory

One of my favourite places in the world to visit is Fountains Abbey in North Yorkshire, a former monastery that once covered 70 acres. Although most of it is now ruined, it is still a breath-taking sight. It blows me away to think that, for over 400 years, from 1132 to 1539, it was a fully working monastery where monks lived lives of prayer, fasting, study, worship and service. It was called Fountains Abbey because "at that time and afterwards so many drank of waters springing up to eternal life as from the fountains of the Saviour." (William of Newburgh, twelfth-century Augustinian canon).

I find the story of the first monks arriving at the site incredibly inspiring. After a dispute in their previous abbey, 13 monks were expelled and arrived in the valley of the river Skell in the middle of winter. The environment they saw was more fitting for wild beasts than people. Gradually though, the men went to work, using stone to construct that incredible structure that would house 24-hour prayer and worship for centuries. If you go to the site today, you will see stone and rock scattered around, but in the Middle Ages, when those stones were connected and joined together they became a habitation of glory.

In the same way, Paul tells us that as we as living stones are joined together and built together, something incredible happens. We "rise to become a holy temple in the Lord ... a dwelling in which God lives by His Spirit" (Ephesians 2v21-22). The living stones become a holy temple. Those once divided now become a dwelling place for the glory of God. But we only "become this" in the process of joining together.

The glory that comes from connecting with each other is a powerful promise in scripture. Paul says it is unity that enables us to attain to the whole measure of the fullness of Christ (Ephesians 4v13) and to know Him (Colossians 2v2). Jesus said our unity would stand as a testimony to the world that He was who He said He was (John 17v23).

In John 15, Jesus teaches us the lesson that our fruitfulness is determined by our connectivity. We bear fruit and fulfil our destiny, not by striving, but simply abiding, connecting and remaining in fellowship with the vine and, consequently, our fellow branches (v5).

Conclusion

As an individual I am a brick. What use is a brick? Yet, cemented with other bricks, in love and peace and covenantal relationship, I form a building - God's House, a habitation of glory!

This is the wonder of the Church.
Remember, Church is the multifaceted wisdom of God! It is important that we see all the facets. The Bible not only shows us that we are God's House, but that we are in God's House! We will look at this aspect of Church in the next chapter.

4

ABBA'S HOUSE

"Do not let your hearts be troubled. You believe in God; believe also in me. My Father's house has many rooms; if that were not so, would I have told you that I am going there to prepare a place for you? And if I go and prepare a place for you, I will come back and take you to be with me that you also may be where I am."

(John 14v1-4)

Growing up in church and attending Sunday School from a young age, I have to admit to having been a little scared of heaven. The descriptions given were always so vague and mysterious that I was actually unsure I wanted to go there! However, Jesus takes away any fear or confusion regarding our eternal destination by simply calling it His Abba's House. Heaven was the place where Jesus' Daddy lived and that was where He came from and where we are going.

The phrase "House of God" appears throughout the Bible and can have different connotations. Here Jesus is specifically talking about Heaven. He speaks of Heaven as a literal place, as His Abba's House. Paul said in 2 Corinthians that if this "earthly tent is destroyed we have a building from God, an eternal house in heaven, not built by human hands". We can rest assured that our loved ones who have gone to be with the Lord are safe in Abba's House. We can also have a peace, even in the face of death, knowing that there is where we are going too.

The House of God has another aspect too, in that - and this is the wonder of the gospel – we, as individuals, are the House of God. Christ lives in us! Hebrews 3 tells us "we are His house". Jesus said in John 14 "Anyone who loves me will obey my teaching. My Father will love them, and we will come to them and make our home with them." Not only are we going to heaven, but the moment we receive Christ heaven comes to us! We are a mobile House of God and carry the atmosphere and culture of Heaven wherever we go.

The third aspect of the House of God, or Abba's House, is the Church. This is what we will focus on in this chapter. Whenever God's people gathered together in His Name and in His presence it was called the House of God. Whether that be the Tabernacle, David's Tent, the Temple or the New Testament Church, whenever we meet not only are we the House of God (as we saw in the last chapter), but we are entering the House of God. 1 Timothy 3 confirms this by saying that the Church is God's House (v15).

Let's look a little further at Abba's House.

The Blessings that are in the House

The Bible is a book full of blessings. Some of these blessings you can claim as an individual believer, but there are some blessings that specifically relate to the House of God. That is why people miss out when they say they don't need to attend a church meeting. Yes, there are some wonderful things that God can do in the secret place, but there are also some blessings that are only found in the House.

1. Abba's House is a place of good things

"Blessed are those you choose and bring near to live in your courts! We are filled with the good things of your house" (Psalm 65v4)

When we come into Abba's House we position ourselves to receive the good things He has in store for us. Sometimes people tell us that something is "good" – a good movie, a good restaurant, a good band – but when we experience it for ourselves we find it may not be to our taste, or not as "good" as they made out. When God says something is good, it really is good! He says His House is full of good things. Abba's House is a place where we receive His Word ... and where we pray, fellowship and praise – all good things! It is a place of joy, life, healing and peace – all good things! The Psalmist here speaks of those who don't just "visit" Church on a Sunday morning, but who "live" in the House of God, a heart attitude of devotion to the Church we make our spiritual home. Those who live like this will be "full" of the good things of the House. Not just a taste or a crumb but the fullness of blessing is ours.

2. Abba's House is place of abundance and feasting

"They feast on the bounty of your house, you let them drink from your delicious streams" (Psalm 36v8) – New Jerusalem Bible

In Abba's House there is always abundance. He gives life that is abundant. He gives grace that is extravagant. When we come into the House of God we are not coming to a religious service, we are coming to a feast! We come to feast on the Meat of His Word. We come to feast on the Bread of His Presence. We come to feast from the Lord's Table. We come to feast on Jesus, who is the Bread of Life.

The beloved in the Song of Songs said that He had taken her to the House of Wine (literal translation of 2v4). In Abba's House there is always an abundance of wine – speaking of joy, blessing, the promises of the New Covenant, love and the presence of the Holy Spirit.

When the prodigal son had been brought into the house, the older brother "heard the sound of music and dancing" (Luke 15v25). There is a unique sound in Abba's House and it the sound of celebration! There is no condemnation in Abba's House. It is a place where prodigals see a "Welcome Home" banner. The moment we enter the House of God, we are not greeted with a list of the sins we have committed that week. Instead the moment we set foot in His House we receive the embrace and kiss of Abba. We receive a robe of righteousness, the ring of son-ship and the sandals, which are the good news of peace.

When he was in the pigsty, thinking of home, the prodigal son said, "my father's hired men have food to spare" (Luke 15v17). What a wonderful thought that in Abba's House everyone has enough! If the servants not only have their needs met, but have enough left over, how much more the sons of the house?

3. In Abba's House, grace always triumphs over law

"Jesus answered them, 'Have you never read what David did when he and his companions were hungry? He entered the house of God, and taking the consecrated bread, he ate what is lawful only for priests to eat. And he also gave some to his companions.'" (Luke 6:3-4)

These verses are found in all three of the synoptic gospels, implying their significance. Jesus is recounting the story of how David, in his need, went to the House of God in 1 Samuel 21. David is on the run from Saul and goes to see Ahimelech the priest. David is so hungry that he does something that breaks God's own law; he eats bread that the law disqualified him from eating. Yet Jesus doesn't criticise David for what he did. As far as Jesus is concerned, this kind of behaviour is perfectly acceptable in Abba's House. In Abba's House, grace is more powerful than the law and there is enough bread for all, regardless of whether the law disqualifies us or not.

How many times do we come to Church and somehow feel that we are disqualified from enjoying everything God has for us? Christians somehow feel that their sin disqualifies them from taking communion, their lack of faith disqualifies them from receiving a miracle, or their lack of midweek prayer and bible study disqualifies them from worshipping with joy and freedom. All of these things may be true; it was true that the law banned David from eating that bread. But in Abba's House there is a higher law at work: the law of grace. It is the truth that in Christ Jesus everything that would disqualify us has been removed and nailed to the cross with Him (Colossians 2v14). The only restrictions are the manmade ones that we place on ourselves. In Christ, there is nothing to stop us enjoying everything God has for us. We are all priests in Abba's House. In Abba's House even those on the run get to enjoy the Bread of His Presence.

4. In Abba's House we see Jesus

"One thing I ask from the Lord, this only do I seek: that I may dwell in the house of the Lord all the days of my life, to gaze on the beauty of the Lord and to seek him in his temple." (Psalm 27v4)

To "gaze" literally means to have a revelation of. Perhaps the greatest blessing about coming into the House of God is that we get to see Jesus! When you are going to the home of someone you love for a meal, you may be excited about the quality of the food or the pleasant atmosphere, but more importantly you are excited that you are going to see them and spend time with them. Sadly, many Christians today are so distracted and excited by the external comforts of the house that they miss the most important thing of all – seeing Him.

In Abba's House, Jesus is revealed. During the Word, during worship, during communion and even in our fellowship with each other, we see Jesus. We have a revelation of His beauty, His glory, His goodness and His holiness. Psalm 93 tells us that holiness adorns His House. In His House, the veil is removed and we see Him face to face.

5. Abba's House is an awesome place

" *When Jacob awoke from his sleep, he thought, 'Surely the Lord is in this place, and I was not aware of it.' He was afraid and said, 'How awesome is this place! This is none other than the house of God; this is the gate of heaven.'"*
(Gen 28v16-17)

Many Christians are asleep to the reality of the awesomeness of the House of God. Like Jacob, they make the mistake of taking the normality of their surroundings at face value. Jacob assumed he was nowhere special because there was nothing outwardly spectacular about it, but God was there all along! It was when this realization dawned on Jacob that he could declare "this place is awesome! This is Abba's House!"

Many Christians focus purely on the outward aspects of a church: the comfort of the building, the quality of the coffee, the relevance of the preaching and the excellence of the music. In their absence, Church can become boring and routine to them. They may cast an envious glance at other churches that appear to have what their church does not. Some move from church to church, following where they perceive God to be moving to feed their need for a spectacular service, in which manifestations and spiritual gifts occur.

Jacob had none of these things. It was a boring, ordinary place, he thought - so boring he fell asleep (that has occasionally happened in some of my meetings!) However there was a greater reality than that which was visible. In the spirit realm, angels were present. A door was opened and he was in the presence of God Almighty. On waking, this revelation altered his perspective.

We need to be able to see what is happening in our own church, not just other peoples. Whenever we meet together, even in the most boring, mundane, ordinary place, we are in Abba's House. We are on Holy Ground. We have "come to Mount Zion, to the city of the living God, the heavenly Jerusalem. You have come to thousands upon thousands of angels in joyful assembly, to the church of the firstborn, whose names are written in heaven. You have come to God, the Judge of all, to the spirits of the righteous made perfect, to Jesus the mediator of a new covenant, and to the sprinkled blood that speaks a better word than the blood of Abel." (Hebrews 12v22-24) It isn't just a meeting – we are in Abba's House! That makes it awesome! The presence of God is a reality not a feeling.

Abba's House is a gate, which gives us access to the realm of Heaven. When we enter, a door is opened for us to access healing, miracles, provision, strength, grace, forgiveness and whatever else we may need. The gate gives access the other way, too, meaning heaven can come to us. The Holy Spirit can be poured into us. By being like Samuel and finding a place in God's House (1 Samuel 3) we position ourselves to encounter God and hear from heaven.

Once Jacob received the revelation of Abba's House, he decided that this was a place he would come back to and tithe to (Genesis 28v21-22).

A Passion for the House

Seeing all the blessings that are available in Abba's House should create within us a passion for the House of God.

This is something we see clearly in the life of Jesus. In Luke 2 there is the well-known account of Jesus, at the age of twelve, being taken to Jerusalem for the Feast of Passover. The first thing we notice is that Mary and Joseph took Jesus to the House of God. I thank God that throughout my childhood my parents always took me to church. The idea of being anywhere else on a Sunday would have been a totally alien concept to my brother and me. From a young age we were encouraged to have a passion and devotion for the House of God.

After the feast is over, Mary and Joseph return home only to discover that Jesus is not with them. After a frantic search they find Jesus "in the temple courts". To the question of why he had stayed behind, Jesus replies, "Didn't you know I had to be in my Father's house?" Notice that Jesus called the temple His Abba's House. Even after the feast, He was determined to remain in His Abba's House, listening to the teaching and answering questions – receiving and imparting into the House. Jesus seemed bemused that Mary and Joseph should wonder where He was. It was the most normal thing in the world to Jesus that if you loved God and belonged to God, you would be in His House.

Jesus never lost His passion for the House of God. Many years later He would return to the temple and famously turn over the tables of the moneychangers. It was on this occasion that His disciples "remembered that it is written: 'Zeal for your house will consume me.'" (John 2v17). This is a quotation from Psalm 69. The burning, fiery passion and zeal that Jesus had for His Abba's House was so clearly evident that His disciples actually recognised that He was living and modelling scripture. Our love for the House of God should be more than a belief system. It should be a way of life.

In the Bible, David is known as the man after God's own heart. From the Psalms, it is clear that a major passion in David's heart was for the House of God. Indeed, David would say in Psalm 23, his most famous Psalm, that he desired to dwell in the House of the Lord all the days of his life. Elsewhere, he would say:

"Yahweh, I love the beauty of your house and the place where your glory dwells."
(Psalm 26v8) – New Jerusalem Bible

Do you love the House of God? If you love God, then you are going to love His House. Many people today are passionate about their thing – their ministry, their vision, their dream. Our unique, God-given passions and desires, whilst wonderful, must never replace our all-encompassing passion for the House of God.

In both Ezra and Haggai, God had to rebuke His people. They were so busy building their own houses that His house was left abandoned. We all lead busy lives, whilst trying to fulfil our individual divine callings, but God clearly expects our priority and our passion to be His House. Everything else is secondary.

"I rejoiced with those who said to me, 'Let us go to the house of the Lord.'"
(Psalm 122v1)

For David, it was exciting to be able to enter God's House. How many of us have lost that excitement? Has church just become part of our weekly routine? I believe that one of the keys to regaining our passion is to remind ourselves that it is Abba's House. We are entering the place where He dwells! It is a place of unconditional love, where all things are possible. How exciting is that?

"But I, by your great love, can come into your house;" (Psalm 5v7)

David recognised that it was only because of God's love that he could enter God's house. We, too, must recognise that it is an absolute privilege to be able to enter God's House. None of us deserves to be in God's presence and yet he puts out the welcome mat especially for us. Sometimes we say things in church like "God is welcome here", as if He is a guest in our house! No, He is the One who welcomes us into His House! To invite someone into your home is a sign of friendship, a gesture offered by God to us all.

The Promises over the House

We can claim the following prophetic promises if we make the House of God our home.

1. *"A fountain will flow out of the Lord's house and will water the valley of acacias."* (Joel 3v18)

> God promises that in His House, there is a fountain. As we come into God's House, all those who are thirsty can drink from this fountain. It is a fountain of cleansing, of healing, of grace and of life. The river of His delights (Psalm 36) flows throughout His House and all who are thirsty can come to the waters.

2. *"We have a great priest over the house of God …"* (Hebrews 10v21)

> In the House of God, Jesus serves as our High Priest. He is a High Priest who lives to make intercession for us. We can rest secure in the knowledge that this High Priest always has us on His heart and mind. He daily carries our burdens. Jesus is a High Priest in the order of Melchizedek. When Abram encountered Melchizedek in Genesis 14, the one who was both king and priest came bringing to him bread and wine. When we are in someone's house, it is usually that person who serves us and not the other way round.

We often think that we come to God's house to give to Him, but we must remember that our humble king always comes to serve and not be served. In Abba's House, we sit at the table and allow our High Priest to serve us the bread and wine of His covenant.

3. *"Christ is faithful as the Son over God's house."* (Hebrews 3v6)

In Abba's House we come under the canopy of Jesus' Lordship. In that place there is protection, provision and covering under the shadow of His wings. All those in the House are safe and secure in the knowledge that Jesus is watching over the House. The gates of Hades themselves shall not prevail over it.

Conclusion

In this chapter, we have seen the wonderful blessings that are available in Abba's House. We have seen the examples set by Jesus and David in having a passion for the House of God. We have seen the wonderful promises that we can claim if we choose to follow suit.

In the next chapter, we look at the dangers of leaving the House and how our relationship to the House is the key to our lives flourishing - or not.
In closing remember that all those in the house are blessed. As the Psalmist said in Psalm 84, "Blessed are those who dwell in your house; they are ever praising you."

5

THE DANGER OF DISCONNECTION

"From one man He made every nation of men, that they should inhabit the whole earth; and he determined the times and places where they should live."

(Acts 17v26)

If we truly believe in the sovereignty of God over our lives and that He loves us, leads us, and that He has a plan for our lives then it cannot be coincidence that the church that we are a part of has been ordained for us by God. If God cares for us enough to give us the right career and the right spouse, surely He will also give us the right church to be a part of. If we can trust God to provide our daily bread and other necessities, surely we can also trust Him to provide us with the right spiritual home. I am firmly under the conviction that if our lives are submitted to the Lordship of Jesus and the leading of the Holy Spirit, then the church that we are a part of has been chosen for us by God.

Proverbs 27v8 says, "Like a bird that flees its nest is anyone who flees from home." When God has planted us in a spiritual home, we must be very careful about leaving that place. When God plants us somewhere, it doesn't mean that we will necessarily stay there forever. The only place we will truly be permanently at home is in heaven.

People can move churches for a variety of good and healthy reasons. But there can also be a very real danger in "fleeing the nest", in running away from the place where God wants us to be. Sadly, I have seen many people leave their spiritual home because they were running away from something or because they thought that the grass was greener elsewhere. Many times this has resulted in heartache and sorrow. Let's look at a few reasons why people can "flee the nest".

Famine in the House

The beginning of the book of Ruth tells us the story of a man called Elimelech and his wife Naomi. They lived in a town called Bethlehem. At some point in their lives, the Bible tells us that there was famine in the land. The name Bethlehem means "House of Bread". How ironic that there was no bread in the house of bread! In a desperate measure to feed his starving family, Elimelech leaves the house and goes to live in Moab. Naturally this sounds like a good, sensible thing to do. However it is important to understand that when Israel entered the Promised Land each tribe was given land as their inheritance by God. Bethlehem was the place where Elimelech's family had been planted by God's divine design. In leaving Bethlehem, they were leaving their inheritance, they were leaving their family home, they were leaving the place of God's promise, and they were even leaving the covenant nation itself and going to live among the Gentiles.

What was the result? Outside of the house where God wanted them to be, they were also outside of God's will and God's protection. It was in Moab that Elimelech and his two sons died and Naomi was left alone. When Naomi returned, her testimony was "I went away full, but the Lord has brought me back empty" (Ruth 1v21). The irony, again, is that although there had been famine in Bethlehem, in hindsight, Naomi had been full. And in leaving to find food, she had actually come away empty.
One of the major reasons often given for people leaving churches, especially smaller

churches, is that "I am just not getting fed there". When we go to church expecting bread and there is no bread, it can feel like we are in a famine. There can then be a great temptation to leave, because we feel like we are spiritually starving. In that situation, we can be so desperate for some kind of spiritual stimulus that we will go anywhere, as long we are being fed and satisfied. We will happily go to Moab for food, if it can provide a church service that meets our needs and that of our family. We have to understand, though, that Bethlehem was more than just a place where they lived, it was the place they had been spiritually planted by God. In the same way, church is much more than just meetings, no matter how full or empty they may seem to be. There can be times when God tells us to leave a place that is in famine, but we have to be very careful that we have heard from God and we are not just leaving because we feel that we have no choice.

Sadly, I have seen many Christians over the years leave a church because "they weren't getting fed". Often they will say things like "I had no choice! I couldn't stay in that dead church any longer! I had to get away!". Perhaps, Elimelech looked round at his hungry children and felt like he had no choice. Tragically his decision to get away cost him everything, including his life and that of his sons.

Like Naomi, many Christians find that in hindsight there was more bread in Bethlehem than they realised. Years later, they look back in regret, as the decision to leave left them empty. The famine would one day be over and bread would return to Bethlehem. If Naomi's family had simply waited for the season of famine to be over, they would have had all their needs met. Instead, the only thing Naomi brought back with her was bitterness (1v20). How many times do people become bitter with the church and angry with God, when taking the decision to leave the place they'd been planted in brought about their misfortune?

There are many Christians today who have a genuine hunger for God, but feel as though their needs are not being met in their existing church and that everywhere around them there is famine. The good news of the Bible is that God is able to feed His people even in a time of famine. Whether it was the ravens or the widow at Zarephath, God made sure that Elijah was sustained during a time of famine. The sons of Israel found that as long as they were in right relationship with Joseph (a type of Jesus-figure in the Old Testament) then they would have enough to eat during a time of famine. When there was famine in the time of Isaac, God specifically told him "stay in this land, and I will be with you, and will bless you" (Genesis 26v3). The result was Isaac reaping a hundredfold harvest, because he stayed where God wanted him to be, even during famine. Isaac's father Abram had made the mistake of leaving the Promised Land during a time of famine (Genesis 12) and it nearly cost him his wife.

I know from first-hand experience that God can sustain you in a time of famine. When I was in my early twenties, the church that I belonged to experienced a spiritual famine. It seemed that the church had lost all sense of direction and purpose. There were no salvations or healings and the church services were dry and unsatisfying. Many people, including most of my peer group, left. To make matters worse, the church that the rest of my family attended was going through a time of Holy Spirit renewal. It felt like I was in famine. There were times when I was desperate to leave. After seeking God I was utterly convinced that this was where God wanted me to be. I attended every meeting, no matter how dull it appeared to be. I kept giving, I kept serving, I kept honouring and I kept loving. At the same time, I knew that if I wasn't being fed during services, I had to let God spiritually sustain me. I was constantly reading the scriptures, developing a stronger prayer life, devouring Christian books and on evenings when my church didn't have a meeting, attending churches where I could receive input. After a few years, the famine in our church lifted (different seasons are simply a part of life) and we entered a new time of blessing and growth. I came out of that time with a depth of character and a new closeness to God that I had never had before, because I had looked to Him and not meetings for my spiritual sustenance.

When your church is going through a famine, it can be one of the hardest and most difficult things to cope with. I am not saying stay there indefinitely, only to please make sure you have heard from God before you leave. It may be that God just wants you to trust Him enough to feed you during famine. The testimony of God's providence in famine may be the greatest testimony of all. The story of Moses and the burning bush is proof that things can still be on fire even when surrounded by a wilderness!

The Grass Is Greener

Another common reason why people leave their church is because they think another church makes a more attractive proposition. The tribe of Dan had been allocated a portion of land along the west end of the strip between Ephraim and Judah. Although a small portion of land, it was extremely fertile. Possibly unsatisfied with this portion of land and facing opposition from the Amorites, most of the tribe decided to leave and find somewhere else to live. In Judges 18 we find that they had not yet found a place to settle, so they sent out spies to explore the land and find somewhere suitable. There was no sense of God's leading or direction, they were simply looking for somewhere good. They eventually decided on Laish because "they were prosperous", "the land was very good" and it was "spacious".

Like the tribe of Dan, some Christians like to "spy out the land" instead of settling where God has put them. They are constantly looking for a church that is bigger and better and more attractive. Other Christians will join a church because they are not being used in their own church. They go in search of more interesting or more influential ministry opportunities. Someone on the church payroll may be tempted to leave for a better-paid role in a more prestigious church.

The decision the Danites made was a disaster, as they finished up falling into idol worship (Judges 18v30). When the kingdom eventually split, Jeroboam established false worship in Dan (1 Kings 12v29-30). Dan became part of the northern kingdom, eventually destroyed by the Assyrians. It was no surprise that this tribe would end up in idol worship, as the decisions they had taken already showed a desire to overrule God's sovereignty and an eagerness to make decisions outside His will.

We must be very careful when we leave the place that God has called us to. The truth is that wherever we go there will be opposition, criticism and trouble. There is no perfect church free from strife and problems. At least if we know that we are somewhere God has called us, we are safe in the knowledge that we are in His will and subsequently under His protection.

They Hurt Me

One of the most heartbreaking realities of the Christian life is that sometimes Christians hurt other Christians. Whether that is through words or deeds, whether it is accidental or on purpose, there is probably not a believer on this planet who doesn't carry the wounds of being hurt by one of their own. When a church has hurt us, the automatic reaction is simply to leave. This happened to a lady in the Bible called Hagar. In Genesis 16 the Bible tells us "Sarai mistreated Hagar" (v6).

So, what did Hagar do? She ran away from the person that was hurting her. It is worth pointing out that Hagar, at that point, had been impregnated by Abram at the suggestion of Sarai. Those who were in authority over her had used her. Again, many Christians leave a church because they feel they have been used.

The most natural thing in the world when we feel used and abused by our leaders is to want to walk away. Again, when people in the church are attacking us, mistreating us or pulling down everything we are trying to do for God, everything within us just wants to leave. Before we leave a church, a good test of whether it is God's will or not is to ask ourselves if we are running towards or away from something. If we are running away from strife, hostility or broken relationships, we should first have heard God tell us that He definitely wants us to leave.

When God found Hagar, she was in a desert. Running away from hardship leads to barrenness more often than fruitfulness. She could not have safely given birth in the desert. God asked her the question "where have you come from, and where are you going?" Hagar could not honestly reply that she had been told by God to leave the house. Her reply was "I'm running away". God responded, "Go back to your mistress and submit to her" (v9). Hagar recognised that the One speaking to her was "The One who sees me" (v13). He knew all about the pain and hurt she was carrying, yet told her to return regardless - and not with a bad attitude, either, but to submit to those who had hurt and used her.

The baby Hagar was carrying could only be born in Abram's house (v15). Sometimes, the thing God wants to birth through us will be born in the place of our greatest trial and pain. God was more concerned about what Hagar was carrying than her temporary emotional happiness. The development of our character concerns him more than our comfort. Our comfort is temporary - our character lasts for eternity. Character is often formed during conflict, because that is when we learn true honour, love, grace, patience, submission and forgiveness.

God would bless Hagar, her son and her descendants (v10-11), but He could only do it in the place where He had planted her.

I Don't Need The House

Luke 15 relates the well-known story of the Prodigal Son. We are all aware of the state that he ended up in before he came to his senses, working on the pigsty and being so hungry that he longed to eat the pigs' leftover food. What many miss is how he ended up there. Yes, we all know that he wasted his father's money on prostitutes and wild living, but his downfall began way before that. His downfall began the moment he left his father's house.

The story begins with the younger brother asking his father for "his share of the estate". Many have speculated on the younger brother's motives in doing this, but at no point did the father object to this request or seem reluctant in any way to grant the desire of his son. In fact, the father was so generous that he not only gave some of the inheritance to the son who asked for it, but he also gave an equal share to the one who didn't.

It is here that things start to go wrong for the younger brother. We know from the discourse the father later had with the older brother, that the younger brother could have stayed in the family home and enjoyed all the blessings of his inheritance there (v31), but instead he decided to take the blessings his father had given him and leave the house. Perhaps he decided that now that he had all the gifts and riches his father had to give, he simply didn't need the house anymore. Perhaps he thought he had outgrown his father's house and needed to "be released" to do his own thing. I am sure that his intention was not to end up in a pigsty, but to enjoy the freedom that wasn't available whilst he was submitting and serving in the house. He probably had the best intentions. I doubt that he intended to hurt his father. He merely thought that he didn't need the house anymore.

The younger brother would soon become the prodigal son, however. He would find that the restrictions of being in the house were actually his greatest protection from the dangers of the world. Outside the protection of the house he would live a wild life, for where there is no revelation the people cast off restraint (Proverbs 29v18). Outside of the provision of the house he began to be in need, as there was no longer a place he could be fed. Outside the parenthood provided by the house he found that he was no longer treated like a son, but a slave. Sons cannot be sons unless they are in the house.

We can learn some great lessons from this story. The first is that our Heavenly Father is willing to lavish us with his blessings and gifts. Nowhere in the Scriptures are we condemned for asking for anything from our Father. Our Father delights to give good gifts to His children and Jesus died so that we could have our share of the inheritance now (Ephesians 1v18). However, we must be very careful that we don't receive the Father's blessings but reject the Father's house. The two always go hand-in-hand. Sadly, I have witnessed many of God's children - all too eager to desire the anointing, the blessing and the favour that God gives - decide that they no longer need the covering, protection and provision that is found in the house of God. Some want to be free to do their thing with the ministry God has given them without the need to submit to a local church. Others feel that as long as they have the blessing of the Father, they no longer need to be part of a spiritual community. The younger brother would come to the realisation that simply by being in the house he would be blessed anyway, but by receiving the Father's blessing and rejecting the Father's house, he would end up with nothing.

We never outgrow our need for the Father's house. He gives both an inheritance and a home and we need both. Every Christian I have known who decided that they didn't need the House of God has always lost the presence of the Father.

It is interesting to note that both Jesus and the prodigal son left their Father's house.

The result, of course, was very different. There is not necessarily anything wrong with moving churches, but we must be very careful how and why we leave. A comparison between Jesus and the prodigal son might be beneficial:

- Jesus was sent, the prodigal son went. Jesus was sent on a mission that He had been asked to do by His Father. Since before creation, Jesus had been recognised as the Lamb of God who would take away the sins of the world and now He was being sent to fulfil that mission. If our ministries are not recognised and used in the house we are in and we are not being sent out to fulfil that ministry elsewhere, we are following the model of the prodigal son and not the model of Jesus.

- Jesus leaving the House would result in sacrifice; the prodigal son leaving was just so that he could have fun. Whenever we move into something new for God, although there is excitement and passion, there is usually a sacrifice, a cost that we are leaving something behind and paying a price in following God's path. If we are too keen to get away and leave, perhaps it's a sign we were never planted in the first place.

- Jesus would remain under the covering of His Father, the prodigal son had a life of "wild living" – he was not interested in any submission or covering. We must make sure that we go nowhere without the full blessing and covering of those sending us. Perhaps, the prodigal son thought it was Ok for him to leave because no one stopped him, but that is a wrong understanding of spiritual authority. Don't ever take the Father's silence for the Father's permission.

- Jesus would return to His Father's house. If we ever physically move church, there should never be a spiritual "cutting of ties". We are part of that spiritual family and although all children eventually leave, they are always welcome back home. If we have left and relationships have ended badly and we carry around that un-forgiveness and baggage, we have again followed the model of the prodigal son and not that of Jesus.

A Wrong Attitude To The House

In contrast, the older brother stayed in the house and served in the house. Perfect son? No! His attitude towards the house was also wrong. The older brother served because he wanted to get something out of it (Luke 15v29). When he didn't feel that he was getting what he felt he deserved, he became bitter. Many Christians will serve in the House because they want recognition, honour, a title or a future leadership position. When that doesn't come, they can get angry and bitter with the church. The older brother then became jealous over the attention his younger brother was getting (v30). Again, Christians can become bitter and jealous because other people are being used - their gifting recognised whilst their own are overlooked.

Sadly, the older brother not only missed out on everything the Father wanted to give him (v31) but he also ended up outside the party (v25-26). When we fail to celebrate with those God has raised up or we feel that, somehow, the church owes us something, not only do we miss out on the blessings of the House, but we can end up on the outside of what God is doing. It is possible, like the lost coin in Luke 15v8-10, to remain in the house, yet be as lost as those in the pigsty. "He who hates his brother is still in darkness" (1 John 2v9). Bitterness can easily destroy us. William Penn said, "It would be better to be of no church than to be bitter toward any".

The Right Attitude - Planted In The House

"The righteous will flourish like a palm tree, they will grow like a cedar of Lebanon; planted in the house of the Lord, they will flourish in the courts of our God. They will still bear fruit in old age, they will stay fresh and green." (Psalm 92v12-14)

"I am like an olive tree, flourishing in the house of God." (Psalm 52v8)

God has placed is all in a spiritual house. Unless we have been released by that house to move into something else or we have heard clearly from God to move, we must remain planted in the house through every season. As we plant ourselves in God's house (meaning to be devoted to that house) we flourish. God's house, when we are rightly aligned to it, should be a place where we flourish. It is place where we bear fruit, pass the test of time and stay spiritually alive and vibrant. Those planted in the house will be like a palm tree (thriving in difficult conditions), a cedar of Lebanon (strong and sturdy) and an olive tree (fruitful and life giving).

In Exodus 12, the children of Israel applied the blood of the lamb to the doorposts of their house. Then they had to stay in the house until the angel of death had passed over. There is no safety for those outside the house but for those in the House there is total protection and safety.

Jesus told the following parable in Luke 11:

"When a strong man, fully armed, guards his own house, his possessions are safe. But when someone stronger attacks and overpowers him, he takes away the armour in which the man trusted and divides up his plunder." (v21-22)

In God's House, Jesus is the strong man. There is no one stronger than Jesus. No one can overpower him. Although the thief comes to steal, kill and destroy, there is protection in the House. As long as we are in the House we are protected by Jesus and no one can touch those who belong to Him.

Conclusion

When Jesus finds us on the dusty road of life, beaten up and injured by sin, the world and the devil, He lovingly picks us up and bandages our wounds, whilst pouring in the oil and the wine of His love (Luke 10v34). However, He doesn't just leave us by the side of the road. He leads us to a house, where we can stay and be taken care of by His servants until He returns (v35). In seeing the Church, we must see the importance of being in the House He has placed us. Remember, that a lily is clothed in glory (Matthew 6v28-29), not by striving, but by simply remaining planted in the right environment.

Over the past couple of chapters we have examined the Church as the House of God. What makes a house different to any other building is that a family inhabits it. In seeing the Church we must also see it as the Family of God. That is what we will look at in this next chapter.

6

FAMILY: A PLACE OF BELONGING

"Consequently, you are no longer foreigners and aliens, but fellow citizens with God's people and also members of his household"

(Ephesians 2v19)

The truth of the gospel is that because of the death of Jesus, we are now united, not only with Him but also with each other. To the nation of Israel, a foreigner or an alien was very much isolated from the community, outside the duty of care and considered separate from those who belonged to the household of faith. But Paul here tells us that that is no longer the case with us. We no longer need to live our lives as strangers, as wanderers, as isolated individuals; because of Jesus we have become part of a family; because of Jesus there is now a place in which we belong.

It is called the Church.

As we look through the scriptures we can see that every major dispensation of God began with a family. When God created a man to rule and reign over His creation, God commissioned him to start a family (Genesis 1v28). When God chose to destroy the human race because of its wickedness, He chose to save, not just one man, but an entire family (Genesis 7). When God decided to set apart for Himself a special nation on earth to be His people, how did He begin? With Abraham, Sarah and Isaac – a family. It was Isaac's son, Jacob, who became Israel and from his children came a nation. It all began with a family. When God wanted to anoint a king who was a man after His own heart, where did He look? He told Samuel to go to the house of Jesse. The king would come from his family. When Jesus was born of Mary, God made sure that Joseph didn't divorce Mary as he had originally intended. It was very important to God that Jesus grew up as part of a family. In one of the most significant moments in Bible history, the Holy Spirit being given to the Gentiles, who were the first people to receive Him? The family of Cornelius (Acts 10v2).

Is it a coincidence that every one of these major moments in Biblical history happened to families? Could it be that the family is right at the heart of God's plan and agenda?

Psalm 68v6 tells us "God sets the lonely in families". No matter how strong our relationship with God, we are all susceptible to feelings of loneliness and we all desire relationship with each other on a spiritual as well as a social level. God sees our need and understands our need and His solution to this is to place each one of us in a spiritual family. This is what the church is. In seeing the Church we must see it as more than a meeting place or an organisation, but as a family. A place where we belong, a place we call home, a place where we both give and receive love and friendship. Our need for family is an innate God-given desire. Children grow and flourish best in a family environment and as adults there is a strong desire within most of us to have a family of our own. Being part of a family gives us a security that is found in knowing that there are others looking out for us. It gives us a reason to live that is bigger than just ourselves.

Although God provides us with an earthly family, He also provides us with a spiritual one. Jesus Himself recognised that the connection He had with His spiritual family, was far more real than the connection He had with His earthly family (Matthew 12v49). Blood is thicker than water, but Spirit is stronger than blood. For those of us who may not know the love that comes from being part of an earthly family, we don't need to be discouraged. In the Church, God has provided us with a spiritual family that we can be a part of. For those of us who have wonderful earthly families, we must see the need of also belonging to a spiritual family too.

In Luke 8 we read the account of a man who was possessed by a legion of demons. This man was no longer in his right mind and had literally come under the control of devils. This is interesting as it gives us a little insight into how Satan seeks to hurt us. One of the things it says is, "he had been driven by the demon into solitary places" (Luke 8v29). I used to think that this man was living in the tombs because he had become a danger to society. But that was not the case. It was actually one of the tactics of Satan that man would live in isolation and separation from the rest of the community. Perhaps Satan kept this man away from his family because he knows that freedom and healing takes place where there is the love of a family.

Satan knows the great power that there is in family. The Bible tells us that "one man may chase a thousand, two may put ten thousand to flight" (Deuteronomy 32v30). Quite simply we are more powerful when we are together. No wonder Satan seeks to keep us in solitary places, away from the family of God. Although there can be times when we need to be alone for special seasons of seeking God, isolation must never be a lifestyle. When it does, we must be very careful that we are not being influenced by Satan, as this man was. Interestingly, what was the command of Jesus to this man once he had been set free? "Return home and tell how much God has done for you." (Luke 8v39). Jesus immediately sent this man back to his family. The sign of this man's bondage was that Satan sent him into solitary places. The sign of this man's freedom was that Jesus sent him back into a family.

Ecclesiastes 4v12 is a favourite verse to quote at a wedding. It reads, "Though one may be overpowered, two can defend themselves. A cord of three strands is not quickly broken." At a wedding people often use it in the context of the need to have a third person in the relationship – God. However, there is another interpretation to this passage. If we view us and God as the two, we need that third person – our brother and sister in Christ - to make us strong and complete. Either way, the danger in isolation is obvious - one can be overpowered. But God doesn't want us to live life alone. Not only does He give us His Spirit, He gives us the Church, He gives us brothers and sisters in Christ. As we look through the New Testament we can see that our fellowship with each other is as important as our fellowship with Him. We need that third strand of being a part of the family of God. John Wesley said, "The Bible knows nothing of solitary religion".

When Cain murdered his brother Abel, part of the punishment was that he would be "a restless wanderer on the earth" (Genesis 4v12). The curse that fell on Cain was that he would no longer be part of a family, he would no longer have a place he called home and he would no longer have the love and security of being in relationship with brothers and sisters. Sadly, many Christians have actually chosen this for themselves. They don't see their need to be part of a spiritual family. What was Cain's response? "My punishment is more than I can bear.... I will be a restless wanderer on the earth, and whoever finds me will kill me." (v14). Cain knew that his security and safety was found in family. Interestingly the first thing that Cain does after this is have a son and build a city. Cain was trying to create his own family and build his own home. Although this may have worked in the natural, he was still destined to live as a "restless wanderer" because the original family unit he had been a part of was in God's presence, as well as in the presence of each other (v16). As vital and important as our natural families are, we must also see our need - and God's plan - for us to be part of a spiritual family, one where we are in the presence of God and each other.

Satan hates the family and is always trying to attack it and destroy it. We can see this clearly in society as well as in the lack of family we see in many churches. But God's desire is for the family. It is important to recognise that God created the family before He did the Church. Or rather, the family was the first form of the Church. When Adam and Eve fell, not only was their relationship with God damaged but also their relationship with each other. Adam and Eve had the first dysfunctional family, with mistrust and accusation entering their relationship and later jealousy and hatred coming between their children. Today we still see the effects of the Fall in families all around us. But the Church is meant to model to the world what family should be like.

Cities of Refuge

Mentioned in numerous places in the Old Testament were certain cities, which were designated as "cities of refuge". Cities of refuge were not man's idea, but God's, and He gives clear instructions regarding them in His Word. Cities of refuge were designed for people who had accidentally or unintentionally committed a murder to be safe from retaliation by relatives of the murdered person. If you were the person who had committed such a murderous act, outside the city of refuge you were in constant danger from those looking for revenge. You had no protection or safety and were destined to a life "on the run". However, once you entered a city of refuge you instantly found protection and safety. For those who lived in the city already, you were commanded by God to protect the guilty person who had entered your city of refuge (Numbers 35v25). Cities of refuge, therefore, became a place of safety and created an obvious image of protection from pursuit and a renewal of a life that would otherwise be doomed. They became a place of salvation and acceptance for the guilty, a kind of family for those who had to flee from their own family.

Why is there so much written in the Old Testament about these cities of refuge? Because I believe that each church family is meant to model the attributes and characteristics of a city of refuge. Before we come to Christ we are all guilty and destined to live a life of guilt, shame and fear, haunted by the spectre of death. But the moment we enter the Church, we have found a family, we have found a safe place. The family of God is meant to be our greatest place of protection. Whilst the Church itself doesn't save us, it is the method God uses to save the guilty and condemned. We no longer need to run; we have found a home; we have found a family, and we have found a place to belong. People could live in a city of refuge for as long as they liked until the High Priest died. Praise God that we have a High Priest who lives forever (Hebrews 6v20), therefore we can "dwell in the house of the Lord forever". (Psalm 23).

Once we have entered a city of refuge, we then become part of that family and consequently have a responsibility to treat others seeking refuge in the same way that we have been treated. One of the amazing things I find about the cities of refuge was the way God commanded them to accept and welcome anyone who came there for protection. Remember, we are talking about people who had committed manslaughter here, people who had actually been responsible for the death of a human being. Perhaps we would be tempted to let justice have its way. Perhaps we would think that they didn't deserve protection, that we didn't want people with that kind of past living in our city - but God commanded them to accept, welcome and protect all who came to them. In seeing the church as the family of God, acceptance is a huge word. I know that when I am with my family, I am accepted. Other people in this world may judge me, hate me, criticize me, but among my family I am accepted just the way I am. It doesn't matter what mistakes I make; it doesn't matter what personality foibles I have that annoy others; my family love me with an unconditional love. I may have had a bad day, but the moment I enter my house I know I am among family that love me, accept me and want the best for me.

Thank God that Jesus loves us as we are and not as we should be. He loves us even in our sin and our weakness. Yet we often place a higher standard on each other than God places on us. We demand moral perfection and a higher level of spirituality than we ourselves have. In Church life there will be those who are hypocrites, those who struggle, those who are weak, and those who are lukewarm. Just as in our natural families there will be people with all kinds of issues. The call is always to love and accept. We are not called to judge or point out people's faults or demand something of each other that God never demands of us. God's love is, of course, transformational. He doesn't leave us in our sin, but takes us out of it. Nevertheless, the gospel is not "be good and God will love you", but "God loves you: now be good". Inclusivity precedes transformation, it doesn't follow it. Similarly, we often don't accept people because of their behaviour. We should accept people, faults and all, because that is how God treats us. As people are included in our family, the power of God's love transforms them to His image and likeness. Romans 15v7 simply says, "Accept one another then, just as Christ accepted you".

Does excellence get in the way of family?

Paul says the following in 1 Timothy 5v1-2:

"Do not rebuke an older man harshly, but exhort him as if he were your father. Treat younger men as brothers, older women as mothers, and younger women as sisters, with absolute purity."

Paul here is writing to a young leader and he is trying to get Timothy to see the church as the family of God. He is trying to get him to see that the members of his congregation are members of his spiritual family. I wonder if we have lost some of that in the church today.

One of the big emphases in many churches today is on doing things with a spirit of excellence. Many churches have this as one of their core values and priorities. Perhaps in the past, churches had a "that'll do" attitude when it came to music, building decor or even the kind of coffee served afterwards. Thank God that leaders now want to make sure that we give our best to God and want to present God's house as a place of excellence and want the music etc to be of a high standard.

There is an inherent danger in this. If I want excellent music in my church, I need excellent musicians. If I want an excellent Welcome Team or media presentation, I need people with the gifting to do it. Most churches aren't necessarily filled with gifted and talented individuals. What do we do then? Do we bypass the family and bring in outsiders who are more gifted? Some do. Do we replace those who we don't think are good enough and bring in others who come up to a higher standard? Again, some do. I have to go back to the Bible and come to the conclusion that this is wrong. We can choose many things in life, but you can't choose the family we are born into!

What makes a family a family is not excellence, but love. My wife, for the record, is an excellent cook, but suppose one day I came home with this attitude: "Darling, I have decided to get a new wife to cook for me. I am going to replace you because there is now a culture of excellence in this house and you aren't good enough!" Yet this is how many leaders treat the church. If someone is not good enough they are replaced. This is not family. Of course people need to be used in their appropriate gifting, but that doesn't mean people can be hired and fired based on their performance. People can be encouraged to be better and even moved into something different, if appropriate, but to make people feel as though they're not good enough or that they could never be used is not family. A child doesn't need to play football like Pele or sing like Frank Sinatra to make their parent proud. They are proud simply because they are. That's family. Church is never meant to be a TV reality show or talent contest where people are fired because they are not good enough or voted home because someone is considered better. It is a family where all are loved, all are valuable, all are accepted, all are needed and all contribute.

Many Christians in our churches feel like second-class citizens who can never compete with the highly gifted people who are positioned on the stage or make up the important leadership positions. Others are constantly worried that somehow they are not good enough or have to come up to this incredibly high standard that they know they can never reach. Others are living in fear that one day they will be replaced when they make a mistake or someone better comes along. This may be how a record company or movie studio works, but not how family works. It is not how the gospel works either, as God is the God who chooses "the foolish things of the world to shame the wise; God chose the weak things of the world to shame the strong. God chose the lowly things of this world and the despised things – and the things that are not – to nullify the things that are" (1 Corinthians 1v27-28). Our churches must be fear-free zones where people have the confidence to be themselves without fear of rejection, scrutiny or prejudice.

I want my son to know that he doesn't have to reach some great high standard of excellence to be part of our family. He is loved, accepted and welcomed and always will be. He doesn't have to perform to belong. No one better will replace him. I want to create a culture where he is secure in the love of a family and where he is free to dream, take risks and be himself. Anyone who has children will desire the same, because that is how we are in families. Have we failed to see the church as the family of God?

In a family, people are free to fail; they are born into belonging; they know they are loved enough to risk losing; they are valued regardless of their virtues. Our churches should have the same culture.

The "most excellent way" according to the Bible is not perfect people under pressure to put on a perfect performance. The "most excellent way" according to the Bible is love (1 Corinthians 12v31). A love that protects, trusts, hopes and perseveres – the love of a family.

Brothers and Sisters

"Keep on loving one another as brothers and sisters." (Hebrews 13v1). The kind of love that the New Testament church had for one another is a very specific type of love. The love language of the New Testament Church is one of family. They called each other brother and sister. Why? That is what they were. Sometimes, in church it is helpful to call people "brother" and "sister" because we can't remember their real names! The early Church actually treated each other as if they were brothers and sisters. Again, they did this because that is what they were. The Church was a family long before it became an organisation or a meeting.

If we only see Church as an organisation that we are loosely connected to, or a meeting we attend, the results are obvious. If upset or offended, I will leave. If I see a more attractive church down the road I will go there. I certainly have no obligation to help you or give to you, because you are just someone I happen to sit next to on a Sunday morning.

Seeing the Church as my family changes everything. I can get upset and offended with my family if I want to, but they are still my family. We are bound together. I could decide to cut ties, I could decide to walk out, but it doesn't change the fact, nothing can, that they are my family. I am morally obliged, even if I don't feel like it, to love and care and provide for my family. In the same way I am commanded to love my brothers and sisters in Church. I am commanded to forgive. I am commanded to serve, honour, provide and be in right relationship with them. They are my family.

Peter puts it like this: "Live in harmony with one another; be sympathetic, love as brothers, be compassionate and humble" (1 Peter 3v8). To love as brothers draws out of us feelings of intense loyalty and camaraderie. The bond of brothers is not something that is easily broken. Proverbs 18 tells us "there is a friend that sticks closer than a brother". We can have many friends in Church, but God desires that we be as close as brothers, that there is a trust, an honour, a protection, sympathy, compassion and humility present in our relationships.

Ruth was a Moabite who married into the family of Elimelech by marrying his son. When Elimelech died, as well as her husband and her brother in law, Ruth was literally left with no one other than her mother-in-law, Naomi. Naomi decided to return to Israel, but exhorted Ruth to go back to her own people and re-marry. This was Ruth's get out clause! As a single woman, a widow and a foreigner Ruth wouldn't have had any rights at all in Israel. Although life would have been tough in Moab, she would at least have had a chance of meeting another husband, but Ruth recognised that Naomi was now her family. She wouldn't abandon her family when it was tough. She wouldn't just walk away because it wasn't convenient. She wouldn't live a life to please herself and get her needs met. She would honour the commitment she had made to her new family.

Ruth would decide to stay with Naomi and she would make the famous declaration, "Where you go I will go, and where you stay I will stay. Your people will be my people and your God my God. Where you die I will die, and there I will be buried. May the Lord deal with me, be it ever so severely, if even death separates you and me." (Ruth 1v16-17). The name Ruth means "friend". Even though she had no blood ties to Naomi, she chose to recognise her as family and would therefore befriend with an unconditional, life-long friendship that only family members can make.

Oh that we had more Ruths in the church! Those who would see each other as family and recognise that that is what we are in Christ! That we would make that vow to stick with each other, in good times and in bad! That we wouldn't leave and walk away and start a new family, even though that might sometimes be the easier option.

Of course, we know the end of the story: how Ruth ends up marrying Boaz and becomes part of the family lineage of Jesus Christ. There is an interesting exchange between Ruth and Boaz after Boaz tells her she has a place of work in his fields. When Ruth asks, "why have I found such favour in your eyes that you notice me?" Boaz responded, "I've been told all about what you have done for your mother-in-law since the death of your husband." (Ruth 2v11). It was Ruth's commitment to family and the value she placed on staying with her new family that got the attention and favour of Boaz. Likewise, I believe that there is something that our kinsman redeemer, Jesus, finds beautiful and attractive about our love, passion, devotion and commitment to our spiritual family – something that causes Him to bestow favour upon us.

A New Identity

When Jesus died and rose again He enabled us to become part of His family. Hebrews 2v11 tells us "both the one who makes men holy, and those who are made holy are of the same family. So Jesus is not ashamed to call them brothers". God here is not speaking in metaphorical terms; it is an absolute reality and truth that we part of God's family. We have been born again, born of God, born God's children (John 1). God is really our Father and Jesus is really our brother. That cannot be argued with or disputed. It is truth. In the same way, every other Christian has become our brother or sister. This is not a metaphor or a nice picture, it is truth. It is an undisputed biological fact that Matthew Murray is my brother, we have the same DNA, the same family name and the same parents. It is also an undisputed spiritual truth that if you belong to Jesus you are also my brother and sister. God's desire is for this to become reality more than it is doctrine.

Seeing the Church as the family of God changes the way we view ourselves and the way we view each other. In a family there are no superstars, just people who love and accept each other and are united by a common bond. In the same way, it doesn't matter what our position or place in society is. Whether we are a pauper or a millionaire is irrelevant, the moment we enter the Church, we all become one in Christ Jesus. We are all brothers and sisters, we are all children of God.

The place Jesus loved

One of the most special places for Jesus in the gospels was a place called Bethany. Bethany was a place Jesus would visit on many occasions. Perhaps most significantly of all it was the place Jesus would stay in the days leading up to his crucifixion (Matthew 21v17). What was it that drew Jesus to Bethany? We don't know for sure but we do know that at Bethany there was a family. This family comprised of Lazarus and his two sisters – Martha and Mary. The Bible simply says "Jesus loved Martha and her sister and Lazarus" (John 11v5). Jesus loved this family. Perhaps it was the need to be around a loving, caring family that attracted Jesus so much. Like any other family, this family had its share of highs and lows. There were moments of great worship and moments of great confusion. There were arguments, a little jealousy, times of sickness and bereavement, and yet it was a family - and Jesus was there. Where Jesus can find family He will be present. He came into the home of this family (Luke 10v38). His presence will always grace us when there is family. Where there is family there is an atmosphere for miracles (John 11). It was in Bethany that He blessed His disciples after His resurrection. Where there is family there is blessing.

Conclusion

"We ought always to thank God for you, brothers and sisters, and rightly so, because your faith is growing more and more, and the love all of you have for one another is increasing." (2 Thessalonians 1v3)

Paul made a point of thanking God for his brothers and sisters in Christ. Why don't we do that today? What a privilege to be part of this wonderful, spiritual family called the Church of Jesus Christ!

In this chapter we have looked at the importance of having "Philia" – a brotherly love for each other. We will continue the idea of treating one another as family by looking at the gospels and seeing how Jesus taught us to treat our brothers and sisters.

7

THE WAY OF THE MASTER

"Now when Jesus saw the crowds, he went up on a mountainside and sat down. His disciples came to him, and he began to teach them."

(Matthew 5v2)

We are looking at seeing the Church as the family of God, at seeing the local church where I fellowship as my spiritual home and the fellow members of the congregation as my brothers and sisters. In understanding this, we are led to an important question: if family surrounds us, how should we treat one another? How should the family of God behave with each other? If the world will know that we are Christians by the love that we have for each other, then love must look like something. Like what? What should the family of God look like?

In Matthew chapters 5-7, Jesus teaches what has become known as "The Sermon On The Mount". Many scholars describe this teaching as Jesus' Kingdom manifesto as He describes in detail what our lives should be like as people who are God's children and part of God's Kingdom.

The Sermon on the Mount begins with "The Beatitudes", a list of eight attitudes that those in the Kingdom are to possess. These attitudes lead to a life of blessing, fruitfulness and abundance. Rather than laws that we have to obey in order to escape punishment, they are principles that if followed open up doors to blessing. Most people when teaching on "The Beatitudes" teach them as being internal characteristics. Poverty of spirit, meekness, hunger for righteousness etc. are qualities of the heart. Whilst there is no doubt that this is the case, I believe that there is another application to these verses. I believe that not only are "The Beatitudes" internal characteristics, but that they are to be outward manifestations too.

Immediately after "The Beatitudes", Jesus talks about "salt" and "light". Salt is something that is applied to something else. When it comes into contact with things it brings flavour and preservation. Light is always visible and noticeable. So "The Beatitudes" are not just attitudes of the heart, but actions that come into contact with those around us and shine out of us wherever we go. Notice that when talking about light, Jesus talks about two different kinds of light. He speaks about a city shining on a hill, which refers to us demonstrating "The Beatitudes" to the world. But Jesus also speaks about a lamp that shines within the house. The house is always a picture of God's House. The Church; therefore "The Beatitudes", are meant to be qualities that we demonstrate to each other too.

In asking how should the family of God treat each other, perhaps the best way to answer this question would be to look at "The Beatitudes" and ask ourselves do we live like this towards each other? Do we follow the way of Jesus in living out this kind of lifestyle among our brothers and sisters?

Blessed are the poor in spirit

The original Greek language that is translated as "poor in spirit" literally speaks of being a beggar. It speaks about being poor and helpless. In other words to be poor in spirit means to recognise that we have a need.
Admitting that we have a need is usually the last thing we want to do as Christians.

We are constantly told from the pulpits that when we come to Christ He meets all of our needs; and because we firmly believe that those that are in Christ are totally satisfied, to admit to another Christian that we have a need is often seen as a sign of immaturity, lack of faith or spiritual weakness. If we do have a need we are to take it to God, as "My God shall supply all my needs...." (Philippians 4v19). To actually go to another Christian and say "I need help" would be the last thing most Christians would do.

Yet to see the Church as the family of God begins with admitting that we are all poor and helpless beggars, in need of God and in need of each other. In fact to attend a church at all is to admit that I have a need. I need love; I need fellowship; I need a family; I need a place to belong, a place I can call my home. To attend a local church means admitting I need a pastor; need teachers; I need people to be accountable to. People often say that Christians are hypocrites because we go to church and pretend that we are perfect. They are missing the point. If I were perfect, I wouldn't need to go to church. The very fact I set foot through the doors of a church is a confession that I am a beggar and I can't do this on my own.

Some Christians have the attitude that they don't need the church. Instead, they have the attitude that the church is in need of them. They approach the pastor and tell him about what they can do, the call that is on their life, the ideas that they have to improve the church and the talents and gifting that they possess. People like this have the mindset that they are the answer to all the problems in the church and if only they were recognised and used, the church would be so much better.

Actually, Jesus says: those who have the true authority and power of the Kingdom are those who start by admitting that they have a need. They approach their pastor and their brothers and sisters with humility, saying "I need this church", "I need your love and encouragement", "I need your leadership", "I need your prayers", "I am a spiritual beggar in need of a family and a place to call home". Bonheoffer said, "I need the Christ in you and you need the Christ in me". It is admitting that we need each other that releases the Kingdom into our lives.

In John 13, Jesus famously washes the feet of His disciples and then encourages us to "wash one another's feet" (v14). There are two aspects to this. The first is to do what Jesus said, to wash each other's feet, to serve one another, love one another etc. however, there is also another aspect. If we, as a spiritual community, are to fulfil this command, then not only must I be willing to wash other people's feet, but I must also be willing to allow other people to wash my feet too.

How many times are we like Peter, who refused to allow Jesus to wash his feet (v8)? Why not? I believe the simple reality was that Peter had dirty feet! Walking the dusty roads of Israel would have left his feet dirty, smelling and not very pleasant to look at. Now Jesus asks to wash Peter's feet. In order for that to happen Peter would have to admit to Jesus that his feet needed washing. Not only that, but he would have to take off his sandals and expose the very dirt and dust that he had covered up. He would also have to place his feet in the hands of someone else and allow them to do the washing and the cleansing for him.

Jesus' response to Peter is very important "unless I wash you, you have no part with me" (v8). Jesus here is teaching that all relationship is based on vulnerability, on exposing our needs to one another and placing our trust and faith in each other. This is a very scary place to be in and one that requires absolute openness on our part, a nakedness of soul. Allowing other people to wash our feet is often the last thing we want to do, yet Jesus says that this is how we become part of each other: this is how family is formed.

How many times have we come to church dry, empty, needy, run down, spiritually bankrupt and been asked "How are you?" What is often our response? "I'm doing great brother / sister! Isn't God good?! Bless God! Never been better! Hallelujah!" Whilst sometimes this can be a confession of faith, it is usually a confession of pride, in not wanting to admit our needs, as well as a confession of fear in not wanting to expose our weaknesses.

The truth is that every single Christian has dirty feet. Even those cleansed by Jesus pick up dust on our walk with Him through this world. In seeing the Church as the family of God, there has to be vulnerability in our relationships with one another where we are willing to expose our needs and allow other people to wash us with prayer, words of encouragement, love and friendship.

The Bible shows us that when we confess our faults to one another, healing can take place (James 5v16); that it is only when we bring our sins out of the darkness and into the light that we can be forgiven (1 John 1) and only when we allow other people to wash us that we can be refreshed.

I have tragically known Christians die of terminal illnesses that were unknown to the church. They didn't want to bother the church by asking for prayer. How many of us are struggling with all kinds of issues instead of just going to our brothers and sisters and saying "I need help"?

How many times have we been listening to a sermon and thought "I hope so-and-so is listening, they really need to hear this"? We are so good at picking up on what we think other people need. All the while, the Word cannot wash us because we are not willing to admit that we are the ones with a need, we are the ones who need help.

Our relationships with each other must begin in that place of being poor in spirit, recognising I actually need a relationship with the local church and with my brothers and sisters in Christ.

"Blessed are those who mourn"

The original Greek word "mourn" is usually used in the scriptures in the context of grieving over someone or mourning at the death of a friend. "Blessed are those who mourn" is actually funeral language! So how does this outwork itself in our relationships with each other? Who is meant to be dead and buried? I would suggest that we are. My paraphrase would be "Blessed are the dead". The call of Christianity was always "come and die" before it was "come and be blessed". Jesus told us plainly "Whoever wants to be my disciple must deny themselves and take up their cross and follow me." (Matthew 16v24)

When we come to Christ our spirits come alive, but there is always a call to crucify our flesh and to allow the cross to put to death our soul life. Sadly, for many, self is still very much present, and this is never more evident than in our relationships with each other. How many of us struggle to submit to and obey spiritual authority because it offends our ego and is a battle against our own will? How many of us are quick to give people our opinions on what the church should be doing? How many of us, the moment someone does something to us that we don't like, get offended, upset or angry? Our flesh has been pricked and we don't like it!

When we come to the cross, a death has taken place. Self has been crucified. "It is no longer I who live, but Christ who lives in me" (Philippians 1v6). Dead men can't give their opinion. Dead men don't have a will of their own. Dead men can't be offended. Dead men have taken their offence and upset with them to the grave.

Nothing provokes the flesh more than being in relationship with other Christians. In the reality of living out our faith with each other, there is a daily conflict between us and other people. Mature Christians learn to daily visit the cross where they deposit their offences, opinions and stubborn self-will on the altar and leave them there, allowing the fire of God's Spirit to consume it all. Then as dead men walking, we live our lives with each other not with a sensitive flesh, but with a sensitive spirit, alive and aware of other people's needs, other people's desires and other people's opinions.

"Blessed are the meek"

The blessing given to the meek is that they will inherit the earth. This in part refers to the receiving of a ministry on earth, a title or position within the church. There is nothing wrong with desiring to want to be used by God. The Bible even tells us "Whoever aspires to be an overseer desires a noble task." (1 Timothy 3v1) Sadly we often go about this all wrong. We think that in order to be used by God, we have to be noticed by man. Therefore we love to show off our gifting and we love to promote ourselves. We strut around among our fellow Christians displaying our ministries and anointing. We can't help but tell everyone we meet about what we can do and what we have done for God. Our identity has become so wrapped up in our ministry and what we do for God, rather than the identity that we have as His children.

To be meek simply means to be content with who we are. This doesn't mean that we lose our zeal and passion in wanting to be used by God; it simply means that we are content to be hidden, we are happy to serve in the shadows and we are trustful that God will do the promoting. A friend of mine says, "Self-promotion takes something beautiful and makes it ugly". The wonderful truth of God being God is that He is able to speak to other people about me without me having to speak to other people about me!

Above all, we must make sure that we never take the sword of ministry - we must always wait for it to be given to us. So many people have simply rushed into ministry through selfish ambition and have wrecked lives, including their own and their families. When people talk about their desire to "do something for God", they often mean in public. The meek are those who never lose the inner fire to want to advance God's kingdom, yet at the same time are content with who they are and what they are doing in the here and now. They are happy to allow God to open the right doors and put more faith in His favour than in their networking and advertising skills.

"Blessed are those who hunger and thirst after righteousness"

Those who hunger and thirst after righteousness are those who ache for the salvation of the world and long for God's kingdom to be established in the lives of those around them. Rather than being selfish and self centred, these people see the needs of those around them. They hate any form of injustice, oppression or lack in any way. When this hunger and thirst becomes salt and light, it will lead them to action to try and meet the needs of those around them and bring wholeness and completeness where there is need.

Sadly, many of us are so caught up with our own worries and cares that we have become numb to the cries of our brothers and sisters around us.

In the Old Testament God established a law that would protect the rights of widows. If a man died and left behind a wife but no children to take care of her, it was the responsibility of the dead man's brother to marry his brother's widow and have children with her. This way the dead man's family name could continue and his widow would be protected. God was showing us that it was the duty and responsibility for each man to take care of his brother.

Sadly, one of the oldest attitudes man has had is "Am I my brother's keeper?" (Genesis 4v9). I look out for me and mine; I can't be expected to take care of my brother's family too. Deuteronomy 25 tells us what is to be done to the man who refuses to marry his brother's widow. "His brother's widow shall go up to him in the presence of the elders, take off one of his sandals, spit in his face and say, "This is what is done to the man who will not build up his brother's family line." That man's line shall be known in Israel as The Family of the Unsandalled. (v9-10)

The unwillingness to provide for your brother was clearly seen as something incredibly shameful and dishonouring. Yet how many of our churches could be known as "The Family of the Unsandalled", where everyone is concerned about their own needs and rights and there is no hunger and thirst to see right done in the lives of those around us.

God expects us to meet the needs of our brothers and sisters in Christ. He says it is our duty and responsibility to do so. We are our brother's keeper! How many times do we pray to Jesus for Him to meet the needs of those around us, when He expects us to "give them something to eat" (Matthews 14v16)? If we have the resources we also have the responsibility to act. The only difference between the sheep and the goats, according to Matthew 25, was in what they did and didn't do.

British revivalist Leonard Ravenhill said, "I want to see a fellowship where your burdens become my burdens; your grief over your children becomes my grief. When we really bear one another's burdens; where we really love each other and let the world see that we are the followers of the meek and lowly Jesus who cared only to do the will of His Father."

Those who hunger and thirst for righteousness, Jesus tells us, "will be filled". This is a wonderful promise! Jesus knows that we have needs and he longs to meet our needs, only He does so in a way that we don't expect. We focus intently on having that need met – we pray, we fast, we declare it in Jesus' name! Yet Jesus says, "If you want to be filled, focus on others". In the Kingdom, the way to be blessed is to be a blessing to others, the way to get our needs met is to meet the needs of others, the way to be satisfied is to give ourselves away. There are so many books today on "How to Be Blessed", "How To Prosper", "How To Be A Success". The answer can be summed up in one word – others! Pour yourselves out on others. Live to allow the righteousness of God to be established in the lives of your brothers and sisters in Christ. In so doing, God will make sure that your life is filled to overflowing.

Blessed are the merciful

In the Old Testament, God's glory was above the Mercy Seat in the tabernacle. God's presence and glory always dwell where there is mercy. A more literal translation of the word mercy in Matthew 5 is "compassion". In our relationships with each other in the family of God, Jesus expects us to have compassion towards each other.

Paul rebuked the church at Philippi because "everyone looks out for their own interests" (Philip 2v21). True love is not self-seeking (1 Corinthians 13v5). Love always looks outwards and has a genuine concern and compassion towards others. This is what Paul meant when he told us to "carry each other's burdens" (Galatians 6v2).

The Bible tells us over and over again that God loves humility. God always blesses the humble, promotes the humble and honours the humble. True Biblical humility is not thinking less of yourself, it is thinking of yourself less. It is losing yourself and being caught up in others, having a love and empathy for them.

My family has experienced something of the love of God, displayed through the

Church over the past few weeks. Just over twelve weeks ago my brother Matthew was ministering in the United States when he got very sick and was admitted to hospital. After tests he was diagnosed as having malaria, picked up whilst doing missions work in Africa. At first we weren't too concerned, knowing that malaria is a treatable disease and that he had the finest health care in the world available to him. We then received bad report after bad report. Firstly, the doctors informed us that the strain of malaria he had contracted was the most serious form of the disease and was potentially fatal. Then after tests to find out how much of the malaria was in his bloodstream, they discovered that 50% of his blood was infected with malaria parasites (5% is considered extremely serious). Finally Matthew's major organs, his heart, liver and kidneys, began to shut down. For Matthew's wife, Becky, and son, Josiah, this was an incredibly frightening time, whilst the rest of us, on the other side of the ocean, felt helpless and afraid as doctors told us there was little chance of survival and to prepare for the worst.

Becky posted the relevant information on social media sites and amazingly the Church did what it does best – come together in a crisis. Messages of love and support began to come from Christians all over the world, and more importantly people began to pray. Not token, religious prayers, but prayers of genuine love and compassion. Christians prayed and fasted throughout the night for someone they had never met, but had compassion for. Some Christians even flew out to be at Becky's side and support her through this time of hardship.

Little by little, doctors were amazed as God performed a miracle. Prayers were answered as the parasite levels in Matthew's bloodstream began to rapidly fall and his vital organs began to function as they should. As I write this several weeks later, Matthew is alive and well, a walking miracle of God's healing power, as medically the situation was hopeless.

What was more encouraging than the miracle (I know that God answers prayer) was the compassion that the Church showed our family in a time of great need. This is what the Church should do as we see ourselves as part of God's great family.

In contrast, I have read this week of another ministry scandal. Yet another public ministry has fallen due to immorality. Even sadder than this situation are all the Christians saying "I told you so!", "I never liked him!" and taking obvious glee from his downfall. Whilst we never excuse sin, where is the love and compassion that we are to show towards a fellow brother in Christ?

I am also reading through the pages of an internet ministry created to publicly expose "false prophets" and point out the doctrinal errors and faults in various well-known ministries. Whilst I don't agree with every ministry in the world, God has never called anyone to pull down other people's ministries. He has called us to lift up Jesus! He has called us to show love and compassion to one another and to be merciful towards each other. This is the way of the Master! Didn't Jesus condemn the Pharisees? Yes - but He also shed His blood for the Pharisees. You can only criticize what you love and are willing to lay down your life for.

Blessed are the pure in heart

The importance that Jesus places on having a pure heart is incredibly challenging. It shows us that we can do the right thing, but with the wrong motive. This is certainly true of our relationships within the local church. For example, someone can serve in the background in the local church (the right action), but can do so simply because they want to be noticed by people (the wrong motive). Someone can be involved in public ministry, but desire to be praised by man. Some give financially to the church in the hope that this will afford them influence with the leadership. Jesus speaks very strongly against people who seemingly do the right thing, but with the wrong motive.

In our relationships with the local church, our hearts must be pure. That means that there is no hidden agenda or ulterior motive in what we do. Jesus warned His disciples against "the yeast of the Pharisees and the yeast of Herod" (Mark 8v15). Whilst the yeast of the Pharisees is speaking of the spirit of religion, I believe that the yeast of Herod is speaking about a political spirit that can so easily manifest in our churches and gatherings. Herod was a master political manipulator who plotted and schemed to make sure he was aligned with the right people and who always made sure that he said and did the right things to keep himself in favour with those who had influence in Rome.

Those with a political spirit seek to make the right connections, in order to fulfil their ambitions. They will praise the pastor and leadership, telling them what a good job they are doing and how wonderful they think they are. Whilst every believer should encourage their leaders, those with a political spirit flatter them in order to garner future favour. Though incredibly generous and hospitable, they will only open their home or give their time or money to those in leadership or those in the church that have influence, connecting with those who are seemingly well-connected in order to further their agenda.

Leaders who possess a political spirit will network with other leaders, but only with those who they hope to profit from e.g. a preaching date in their church or financial support. They make a big show of boasting about their connections, giving the impression that they are important in order to open doors.

The political spirit is abhorrent to God. Those who truly see God and know God will go out of their way to praise and love and be generous towards all God's children, even those who can do nothing for them in return. Those who truly see and know God have a pure heart in their relationships with others. There is no hidden agenda or motive or desire in their encouragement of leaders or hospitality towards others.

They don't look to be part of the "in crowd". They treat everyone the same and never lean on their relationships, so as to try and open up doors or have influence in the Church. They love just because. They serve just because. They give just because. They encourage just because.

Blessed are the peacemakers

The New Testament tells us, over and again, the importance of maintaining peace with one another. Romans 14 tells us "make every effort to do what leads to peace and to mutual edification" (v9). 2 Corinthians tells us "live in peace" (v9). Ephesians 4 tells us that unity is maintained "through the bond of peace" (v3).

Some believers are incredibly aggressive and forceful in the way that they speak to other Christians. They feel it is their God-given right to tell you their opinion on Bible passages or church practices. They love to argue over doctrine and to debate with people over scripture. Some people are very critical and love to point out faults in other church members, especially anyone in public ministry. Some Christians are very loud and "in your face" and constantly have to be the centre of attention.

Peacemakers are not like this. Peacemakers are happy to be quiet and in the background and are happy for others to be in the spotlight. Peacemakers don't always have to give their opinion on everything. Peacemakers are happy to admit that they might be wrong. Peacemakers are happy to admit that they don't know everything. Peacemakers can look on faults without feeling the need to pass judgement. Peacemakers don't feel the need to defend themselves and their argument.

The Bible tells us that "love covers" (1 Peter 4v8). When Noah became drunk and lay naked in his tent, his son, Ham, immediately told his brothers about it. His delight in exposing his father's wrongdoing brought a curse upon him and his family (Genesis

9v25). In contrast, Shem and Japheth honoured their father. Walking in backwards, they covered their father's nakedness. As a result, they received favour and blessing.

Carnal Christians love to expose faults and failures, or go out of their way to expose weaknesses in an argument. Peacemakers notice faults, but are happy to keep the peace by loving, covering and honouring. Any rebuke is done gently and privately and with the aim of restoring the person concerned. Peacemakers are never smug or superior.

"Blessed are those who are persecuted"

We know that if we are to live for God, then this world will hate us and persecute us. As difficult as this is to understand, most Christians can accept this, but we struggle to accept persecution by our own brothers and sisters. This is the type of persecution Jesus is talking about. He refers to the persecution of the prophets who were persecuted by their own people. Tragically, we don't have to have been in Church long before somebody will mistreat us. We have all been hurt or mistreated by other Christians at some point in our walk with God. Some people hurt us without realising. Bizarrely, some Christians actually hurt us on purpose, deliberately wounding us with their words, judgemental opinions or wrong actions.

How we respond when other Christians hurt us is incredibly important. We can become hard, angry or bitter. We can carry hurt, offence and un-forgiveness for years. Alternatively, we can do what Jesus says and "rejoice". We can only do this when we are willing to let go of the hurt and forgive those who have mistreated us.

"Therefore, if you are offering your gift at the altar and there remember that your brother or sister has something against you; leave your gift there in front of the altar. First go and be reconciled to them; then come and offer your gift."(Matthew 5v23-24)

Jesus is telling us that it is meaningless to bring worship to God until we are in right relationship with our spiritual family. If we carry un-forgiveness or bitterness towards the Church our worship will not be accepted. Jesus tells us in Matthew 18 that it doesn't matter how many times we are hurt or how many times we are offended, we must always choose the way of forgiveness. It is never acceptable to walk away from our spiritual family because we are offended. The power in Jesus' statement to forgive our brother up to seventy seven times is not that we keep forgiving, but that we are willing to keep placing ourselves in a position where we can be hurt. Many forgive, but reject the relationship because they don't want to be hurt again. But Jesus says, not only are we to forgive those who hurt us, but we are to remain in relationship even at the risk of being hurt again. If we are to be part of the family of God, we are going to be hurt time and time again. But Jesus says that's ok. Better to know love and pain than only know loneliness and isolation.

Jesus frequently instructs us to forgive those who have hurt us. My negative reaction towards those who have wronged me may be equally sinful in the eyes of God, as their wrong action was.

Many Christians know the importance of forgiveness, but don't know how to forgive or feel that they couldn't possibly forgive certain people. Forgiveness always begins with a decision, a choice, and an act of will. The Greek word to "forgive" is the word "aphiemi" which means "to send away, to dismiss, to let go, to release". This is how forgiveness starts. I am reminded of the scapegoat in the Old Testament narrative. The priest would lay his hands on the scapegoat and impart the nation's sins into it and then release it into the desert. At first the scapegoat would still be visible, but gradually it would get further and further away until it eventually disappeared from view, symbolising that their sins had been taken away. Similarly, when we forgive the hurt and pain may still be there, along with feelings of anger and betrayal, but it starts with that initial step to release that person from what they did and to let go of the offence that we have held onto. Bit by bit, God will heal the hurt and take it away, but we must make that first step to hand our feelings over to God.

Saint Francis of Assisi said: "You should not let a single person in the world, whatever sin that person may have committed, come before your eyes and depart without having found mercy with you. And should that person not ask for mercy from you, then you must ask it of him. And were that person to come to you a thousand times, continue to love them so as to lead them back to the right path. Always have compassion, for all of us have sinned."

Conclusion

Jesus Himself gave us the supreme example of how we should treat one another in the Church. Jesus came, not in the form of a mighty deity, but as a baby born in a manger, totally trusting and dependant on others to meet even his most basic of needs. Jesus never lived for Himself, but always had the attitude "not my will, but yours be done" (Matthew 26v39). Jesus never promoted Himself or brought attention to Himself, but always pointed people to the Father and made sure that He was honoured and exalted. Whenever Jesus was confronted with need, He always met that need. Jesus always showed compassion to everyone He met. Jesus' relationships with people were always pure and transparent. He never did anything merely to please people or join the in-crowd, rather He deliberately spent time in relationship with those who could do nothing for Him.

Jesus was the Prince of Peace, bringing peace towards all He met. He never carried offence or un-forgiveness in His heart, but cried out, "Father forgive them" (Luke 23v34) to those who had just crucified Him.

Let us follow the way of the master when it comes to our relationships with our brothers and sisters in Christ.

8

WHAT IS THE MOST IMPORTANT COMMANDMENT?
(The answer may surprise you!)

"Hearing that Jesus had silenced the Sadducees, the Pharisees got together. One of them, an expert in the law, tested him with this question: "Teacher, which is the greatest commandment in the Law?""

(Matthew 22v34-35)

Before we get into this chapter it is important to understand the religious culture of the time that Jesus lived in. In our day it may be a little unusual - perhaps even considered a little rude - to interrupt the pastor and ask him questions, but that was quite a common part of the culture of the day. It would have been accepted and even expected that when in the presence of a rabbi you wouldn't just listen, but also ask questions. Certainly, when religious leaders and rabbis got together there would be discussion, debate and questioning. The question that is asked of Jesus was not a particularly unusual question. The question "what is the greatest commandment in the law?" was quite a common discussion point. At this point in their history the Jews had so many laws (both those found in the Torah and those that were manmade), that it was often debated amongst scholars which one was the greatest. Note, they were not asking "which is the most important?" as all of God's Word was seen as having equal authority and importance, but rather which is the greatest. In other words "what is the summarising principle of the law or the Old Testament?" Or to put it another way "Jesus, if you could sum up all the commands and requirements of God in one command, what would it be?"

Jesus responded with two scriptures. The first was Deuteronomy 6v5 "Love the Lord your God with all your heart and with all your soul and with all your strength." The second was Leviticus 19v18 "Do not seek revenge or bear a grudge against anyone among your people, but love your neighbour as yourself. I am the Lord."
Jesus takes these two scriptures, which would have been very familiar to them all, and links them together. Jesus said that the whole of the Old Testament hung on these two scriptures. The Greek word "hung" is the same word used for hanging people on a cross during crucifixion; it was something that was permanent and final. Jesus is saying that these two scriptures are now linked together for eternity. Jesus said that the second scripture – love your neighbour - was "like" the first scripture, love God. The phrase "like it" means "of the same nature". So in reply to this question, Jesus is stating that our love for God is clearly linked to our love for others.

In the five books of the law (the first five books of the Bible) there were 613 commandments, or separate laws, that God gave to His people. 613 laws is a lot to remember, so in Exodus 20 God takes 613 laws and sums them up in 10 – the Ten Commandments. If remembering the Ten Commandments is too difficult, well, Jesus here takes the ten and sums them up in two – love God and love people.

What if, however, you were to take the two commandments and sum them up in one? Which one would it be? Would it surprise you to know that the New Testament does exactly that? You may be a little surprised by which one it is!

*"You, my brothers and sisters, were called to be free. But do not use your freedom to indulge the flesh; rather, serve one another humbly in love. **For the entire law is fulfilled in keeping this one command: "Love your neighbour as yourself.""***

(Galatians 5v13-14)

Here is Paul writing to the churches in Galatia. Follow the process here – God has 613 commandments in His Word. He takes those 613 and sums them up in 10. Jesus takes those 10 and sums them up in 2 – love God and love people. Here, Paul takes the 2 and sums them up in 1. Remarkably, though, Paul says the 1 command that sums up all the others is not Deuteronomy 6v5 – love God – but rather Leviticus 19v18 – love your neighbour. This is not a discussion about which law is most important. Paul is not saying that loving God is not important, in the same way Jesus wasn't saying that the two commands He quoted were in any way better or more important than the others. The question being asked is what is the root command, the one that sums everything up, the one that all the others flow out of? Paul says it is this – love people.

Now any true theologian worth his salt will tell you that you can't just take one Bible verse in isolation and create a doctrine around it. However what Paul says in Galatians 5 is not just found here, it is found elsewhere. Look at Romans 13v8-10:

*"Let no debt remain outstanding, except the continuing debt to love one another, for whoever loves others has fulfilled the law. The commandments, "You shall not commit adultery," "You shall not murder," "You shall not steal," "You shall not covet," and **whatever other command there may be, are summed up in this one command: "Love your neighbour as yourself."** Love does no harm to a neighbour. Therefore love is the fulfilment of the law."*

Once again, when the New Testament sums up the whole of God's laws, commands and requirements, it doesn't mention loving God at all; it clearly states loving people. This is perhaps the thing we all miss. Whenever I ask the question in churches, which is the greatest of the commandments, everyone always answers "Love the Lord your God with all your heart etc". When I mention the "love your neighbour part" everyone mumbles in agreement thinking, "yes, we know Jesus said that too, but that was just an additional thing, an afterthought almost; the greatest commandment is loving God". The rest of the New Testament shows us, though, that this whole "love your neighbour" thing is much more than an afterthought. This is the whole heart of the Bible and the summarising of all the commandments.

This is all very confusing. Why does Paul say twice that the greatest commandment is loving our neighbour? Why no mention of Deuteronomy 6v5 and loving God? Perhaps the answer is pretty simple and not confusing at all. Perhaps what Paul is saying is that the way we keep Deuteronomy 6v5 is by keeping Leviticus 19v18. Or in other words, the way we show our love for God is by loving others.

John, known as the apostle of love, puts it like this; "Dear friends, since God so loved us, we also ought to love one another. No one has ever seen God; but if we love one another, God lives in us and his love is made complete in us." (1 John 4v11-12) What John is saying here is that as we show love to people that we can see, we are actually showing love to the God we cannot see. Or to put it another way, as we love mankind, who are actually made in the image of God, we are showing love to God Himself. This is what Jesus Himself said in Matthew 25v40 "whatever you did for the least of these brothers of mine, you did for me".

Many times in our church sermons we place a huge priority on people's relationship with God. We encourage people to pray, read their Bibles, worship, have a passion for God etc. In comparison, we spend much less time encouraging people to love one another, serve one another, encourage one another etc. As individuals, we often mistakenly believe that as long as I am in right relationship with God, it doesn't matter whether I am in right relationship with my brothers and sisters in the family of God. Yet to Jesus, the two were inseparably linked. To the apostles, being in right relationship with God was only shown by being in right relationship with people. The Bible is clear – you cannot have one without the other. John put it as strongly as saying that if we are not in right relationship with each other we are still in darkness (1 John 2).

"Thy kingdom come"

" If you really keep the royal law found in Scripture, "Love your neighbour as yourself," you are doing right." (James 2v8)

Leviticus 19v18, this whole idea of loving our neighbour, loving each other, is described by James as "the royal law". Loving each other is the law of the Kingdom. Wherever there is love, there the Kingdom is manifest. Where there is no love, God's Kingdom cannot be demonstrated.

I have seen the royal law lived out in the life of my sister-in-law, Becky. In 2009, Becky visited a tiny village called "Bumala B" in the West of Kenya. It was a place filled with poverty, illiteracy and an ignorance of the gospel of Jesus Christ. The land was bad and unproductive. Alcoholism and witchcraft were embedded in its culture. Friends of mine who are evangelists had sought to change it by holding gospel crusades. Many of the villagers had come to Christ and small churches had been planted around the area. However, Becky wanted to do more than just tell people about the love of God - she wanted to demonstrate it. Alongside the gospel crusades, Becky would feed the poor and demonstrate the love of God in practical ways, in particular feeling a burden for the children of Bumala, many of whom were orphans.

This led to the building of the "King's Children Home" which opened in December 2012 and now houses children from all over the village who are literally the poorest of the poor. These children are being clothed, fed, educated and most importantly of all, being loved. They are being taught the Christian faith and I can testify from first-hand experience that these children know how to pray, how to worship and how to love one another.

The result? A village has literally been transformed. The Bumala B village of today is very different to the one that Becky first visited in 2009. The whole spiritual dynamic of the community has changed as churches are packed and the name of Jesus is now honoured. The Kingdom of Heaven has literally invaded this tiny community in Kenya. If you were to ask Becky how she did it, the answer would be one word – love.

I have often walked into churches and felt in the atmosphere dishonour, division and tension between church members, worship team members or members of the leadership. Those church services can be some of the hardest to minister in. I have also walked into churches where you can feel the love they have for one another. Sometimes, this sense of love has moved me to tears. It's like walking into heaven on earth. It is in these meetings that miracles and healing seem to flow with ease. Why? The royal law is being demonstrated, so the King can manifest His Kingdom.

If we truly want God's Kingdom rule to be manifest in our lives, churches and communities, it comes one way – love.

What is love?

God's love is not a feeling or an emotion; God's love is a verb. God demonstrated His love by doing something, by sending His Son to die. True love always demands a demonstration. When Jesus asked Peter if he loved him, the response to Peter's answer of "yes, Lord" was "show it by doing something", taking care of and feeding others (John 21). Although love can be shown through our words, it has to be more than that. James tells in James 2v16 that merely using words is not enough; we have to do something to actually show people the love of God. How many times are we guilty of just shaking hands with someone on a Sunday morning and saying "God bless you" with no thought to actually discovering what that person's needs are and doing everything within our power to meet that need?

In the famous parable of the Good Samaritan in Luke 10, Jesus concludes the story by saying "which of these three do you think was a neighbour?" The answer was obvious "He that showed mercy" (V37 – Amplified). It was not the ones who noticed but walked by, but the one who showed love, who demonstrated love. And the punch line to the whole thing "Jesus told him, "**Go and do** likewise". There is always a going and a doing in response to the love of God.

According to 1 John 4, our loving one another makes complete the love of God. It is both the incredible privilege and the incredible responsibility of the Church to bring to completeness the love of God, which was initially demonstrated by the sacrifice of Jesus on the cross. The meaning of this word "complete" is "to bring to its intended goal". We have to understand the ultimate goal of Jesus dying on the cross. It was not just to forgive you of your sins and give you a ticket to heaven. The goal of God's love at the cross was to "bring many sons to glory" (Hebrews 2v11). It was to raise up a family of brothers and sisters called the Church, who passionately and purposefully demonstrate the love they have freely and unconditionally received by freely and unconditionally loving others. In doing this, they not only complete the love of God but they show forth the Kingdom of Heaven on earth.

Family

I'll never forget the story that an elderly guest preacher told one Sunday at our Church. The name of this pastor was Gordon White and he told of how, when he was in his late teens, he was asked to take on the pastorate of a small village church. One of the members of his congregation was an incredibly ancient old lady who had been in the church for decades. This lady was so weak and old and frail, that once Church was dismissed, they would never know whether she would still be alive by the following Sunday. In winter especially they would have to keep a careful eye on her, never knowing whether she would make it through the winter months.

This woman had been a widow for many years and the only family she had was her only son. This son was a drunk who had lived a wild and rebellious life of heavy drinking, womanising, crime, violence and general un-godliness. The dear lady had had her heart broken many times but always prayed that one day her prodigal son would come home.

Early one morning, Pastor White received a telephone call from the local police. They regretted to inform him that this lady's son had been killed in an accident and would he go and bring some kind of comfort to her during this distressing time. His heart sank, knowing that this news had the capacity to kill the woman on the spot.

As he drove to the house, he prayed for the words to use to soften the blow. However, the police had arrived ahead of him and he admitted to being slightly relieved that he wouldn't have to be the one to break the news. He found the old lady sitting very quietly, gently rocking back and forth. He seated himself alongside her. No words were exchanged for a long time, as the old lady stared straight ahead, seemingly oblivious to his presence.

Eventually she spoke. "He was a bad man, wasn't he, Pastor?" The Pastor knew that this was no time to lie, so he softly responded by saying, "He was sister". There was another long pause before she spoke up again: "It was the drink that killed him, wasn't it?" Again, he knew he had to be truthful: "Yes, it was the drink that killed him." The old lady looked him straight in the eye and with a trembling voice cried, "But he was my boy and I loved him anyway!" She let out a great cry, like that of a wounded animal, and began to sob.

I remember hearing that story and being moved by the unconditional love of a mother. It's this kind of love that seems to exist only in families. When family works best, there is an unconditional love, an "agape" kind of love. A love that says "I will love you and keep loving you, no matter what you do or how far you go. Why? Because we are family. The only motive this dear old lady had in loving the wicked and rebellious drunk was that he was her boy and they were family. Loving came naturally to her even if it seemed unnatural. She couldn't help but love. This is how families treat one another. The Greek word "agape" literally means to cherish, to prize, to highly esteem. It is used time and again in the New Testament to describe God's love for us and to describe our love for one another.

There is no greater description of the love that we are called to have for one another that in Paul's letter to the Corinthians:

"Love is patient, love is kind. It does not envy, it does not boast, it is not proud. It does not dishonour others, it is not self-seeking, it is not easily angered, and it keeps no record of wrongs. Love does not delight in evil but rejoices with the truth. It always protects, always trusts, always hopes, and always perseveres." (13v3-7)

Conclusion

In seeing the Church as our family, I hope that we can see the simple truth that "these three remain: "faith, hope and love. But the greatest of these is love" (1 Corinthians

13v13). Church has to be a place where we love each other. We love each other not as a cliché, but in a very real, practical sense. We love with an unconditional love that says, "I will not let you go".

In the flesh we may feel that this is impossible, but praise God there is Love Himself, Jesus Christ living inside of us doing the loving. "The fruit of Spirit is love" (Galatians 5v22).

In the Kingdom, love always operates alongside honour. Families soon break down when there is a lack of honour, as they do when there is a lack of love.

In seeing the Church as a family it is vitally important we see the need to honour. This is what we will look at in the next chapter.

9

WHERE IS THE HONOUR?

"Yet you have made him but a little lower than God (or heavenly beings), and You crowned him with glory and honour"

(Psalm 8v5 – Amplified version)

One of the most humbling things I find when it comes to God is the way in which He honours mankind. The Psalmist here declares that God has chosen to crown us with glory and honour. We, who are nothing compared to the greatness and majesty of God, have been honoured, crowned and celebrated by heaven. This verse is not necessarily talking about the redeemed, but all people of the earth. Although there is no doubt that God's children receive greater honour, there is a sense in which God honours all humans, simply by the fact that we are created in God's image and the ones Jesus shed His blood for.

Because the divine principle is "as you have freely received, freely give" (Matthew 10v8), every human being has a debt to honour God and to allow honour to flow from within us to others. None of us deserve any honour from God, but He freely gives it. Likewise honour should be so integral to our identity that it freely flows from us to all.

In respect of the family, honour has to be a foundational principle that abides in every home. The Bible is very clear about this. God commands children to honour their parents and wives to honour their husbands. Likewise husbands are to treat their wives with honour and parents are to honour their children. The command to honour is the only one that contains a promise "that you may live long in the land" (Exodus 20v12). On the other hand "anyone who curses his father or mother must be put to death" (Exodus 21v15). I believe that this divine principle operates in all our family relationships – where there is honour, there is life; where there is a lack of honour, there is death.

Sadly in many homes today there is a lack of honour. How common is it to find men who show no honour whatsoever to their wives? Likewise, how common is it to find wives who constantly belittle and pull down their husbands? I have been in homes where children scream abuse at their parents and show blatant disrespect; and I've observed parents who will swear at their children and declare over them, "You are lazy!", "You are useless!", "You're no good!" A quick look at the television or glance at social media will see people pulling apart politicians, protesting about those in authority or mocking and ridiculing celebrities. In short, honour has disappeared from our culture. It has departed from our culture because it has departed from our families. This is a tragedy. Where there is no honour, there is always chaos.

We only have to look at the marriage of David and Michal to see what happens when dishonour creeps into a family. In the account in 2 Samuel 6 where David is dancing before the Lord, his wife looks at him and "despised him in her heart". This inner lack of honour would later manifest itself in her words of mockery, complaint and accusation to him. The result was "Michal daughter of Saul had no children to the day of her death" (v23). Whether this was divine judgement or from a lack of intimacy with her husband we don't know, but we do know the Biblical principle – homes, relationships, families where is no culture of honour - are barren places.

On the other hand, God gives the amazing promise in Exodus 20v24, that where honour is put into operation "I will come to you and bless you". Homes that want the presence and blessing of God are homes that honour.

What has all this to do with the Church? Everything! If we see the Church as the family of God, we must all see the vital need to fill our churches with a culture of honour.

The need for honour

In Mark 6v1-6 there is the account of Jesus preaching in the synagogue in his hometown. It's fair to say that it didn't turn out to be the greatest service in the world - and I am sure that wasn't down to Jesus' preaching! What scares me is not that Jesus **didn't** do any miracles there, but that He **couldn't** do any miracles there. There was something in the hearts of the people that day that limited the power of the Omnipotent One. Many people point to it being the lack of faith the people had (v6), but notice what Jesus said before, that "Only in his hometown, among his own relatives and in his own house is a prophet without honour" (v4). Their lack of faith was the result of their lack of honour. The root cause of the closed heaven over that gathering was the absence of honour in their hearts - not necessarily a lack of honour for God or His Word, but no honour for the guest speaker that day. The result? They were cut off from what God wanted to do. We can see the challenging truth: God cannot work in a place without honour.

Conversely, there are plenty of positive examples of how heaven is opened when people show honour. In the last chapter of the book of Acts, Paul is stranded on the island of Malta where he sees an incredible healing revival. After the father of the chief official is healed "the rest of the sick on the island came and were cured" (Acts 28v9). It's an amazing demonstration of the power of God, with Paul seeing a 100% success rate in praying for the sick. Could it be that this release of God's power upon the Maltese people was down to how they treated Paul and his friends? "They honoured us in many ways" (v10). It is the same link between the miraculous and honour that we see in the life of the Shunammite woman in 2 Kings 4. Her honouring the man of God, and opening up her home to him, made way for the miraculous power of God to invade her life and home.

Heaven is full of honour. Revelation 5 tells us that the angels around the throne ascribe "honour" to the Lamb. When we demonstrate and show honour in our churches, we are filling them with the same atmosphere that permeates heaven. In doing so we are giving an invitation for a demonstration of the power of God's Kingdom.

Who we honour

In our churches there are five levels of honour that need to operate. These are – the honouring of leadership, the honouring of each other, the honouring of diversity, the honouring of the least of these, and the honouring of our enemies.

<u>The Honouring of Leadership</u>

"The elders who direct the affairs of the church well are worthy of double honour" (1 Timothy 5v17). The Bible clearly states that those in a position of Church leadership or authority have been put there by God and act as His delegated authority. God takes it very seriously when we show a lack of honour to his delegated authority. Sadly, we live in a culture where people undermine those in authority, denigrate, mock, criticize and give their opinion on how they are doing things wrong and how things should be done differently. It is a disaster when this kind of culture invades the local church.

Our sense of self-importance can result in a struggle to honour others, because we think it means devaluing ourselves. We argue that we are all equal. Leaders aren't any greater than us in God's Kingdom, so why should they get special treatment? Though true that, as God's children we are all equal, God does demand and expect special honour to be given to those in leadership. This counterbalances the fact that they will be judged more severely than others. In Exodus 12, we find Miriam and Aaron showing a lack of honour towards their brother Moses. God heard them grumbling against Moses and took it very personally and seriously. In his discourse, he emphasised the fact that Moses was his servant and therefore should have been treated with honour. The result was that Miriam was struck with leprosy and for a time had to be separate from the rest of the camp.

David is a good example in the Bible of a man who showed honour to leadership. Before David became king himself he had to serve under two other leaders – Samuel and then later Saul. Samuel and Saul both treated David very differently.

Samuel treated David well, recognising his calling and releasing him into it. Saul was very different. Jealous of David, he treated him badly. Seeing David as a threat to his position, he spoke against him, used and abused him and even tried to kill him. Yet in spite of this, David always showed honour to both Samuel and Saul. He never spoke against Saul. Even when he had the chance to kill him, he refused to touch the Lord's anointed (1 Samuel 26). On the one occasion he showed a small sign of disrespect to Saul, by cutting off the corner of his robe, he was conscience stricken (1 Samuel 24). When David eventually found out about Saul's death, he mourned as if he had lost a close friend and took revenge on the one responsible (2 Samuel 1).

The greatest test that David had in his ascension to the throne was not how he treated Samuel, but how he treated Saul. Many Christians mistakenly think that if a leader treats them badly, or is in error or blatantly acts incorrectly, that they are well within their rights to attack them, criticise them or point to their shortcomings in public. What they fail to see is that God will always give us a Samuel and a Saul to honour. How we honour Saul can determine if the door to our own destiny opens or closes.

Honouring each other

Honouring leadership is an essential part of honour. If we can't do that, we can forget knowing the fullness of God's blessing and holy presence in our lives and churches. However, honouring leadership is the most basic form of honour. Honour has to be shown to everyone in the Church, not just those who hold a ministry position.

Paul tells us in Romans 12v10, "honour one another above yourselves". It is easy to see the faults and failures in our brothers and sisters in the family of God. We condemn each other, criticize each other or point out people's weaknesses and mistakes. This is the attitude that Ham, Noah's son, had when he pointed out his father's nakedness to his brothers in Genesis 9. Because of his lack of honour, Ham and his descendents were cursed. Shem and Japheth who covered their father's nakedness, showed both love (love covers a multitude of sins) and honour. In doing so they received honour. Let us have this attitude. As Saint Jean De Chantal said "in our neighbour we should observe only what is good".

In our relationships with everyone in the family of God, we must see people as they are - our brothers and sisters who are made in God's image, people God loves and Jesus died for. That way we can show "proper respect to everyone" (1 Peter 2v17).

Honouring Diversity

If we honour our leaders and we honour each other, we are doing well. But this doesn't mean the honour principle is operating fully in our lives. In the Church there is a diversity of ministry gifts, as well as styles and backgrounds, races and ages. To truly be people of honour, we must show honour to all. Honour is not honour if it only reaches to those we like or prefer or are comfortable with. That is pride, not honour, because we are celebrating something that is like us. True honour is a canopy that covers all.

Jesus said in Matthew 10, "anyone who receives a prophet because he is a prophet will receive a prophet's reward". I interpret this verse to mean that when we honour someone's ministry gift, we are able to benefit and receive from that person's ministry. Sadly, some can only honour the ministry that they enjoy the most. Some people love teaching ministry and therefore can only honour teachers. If an evangelist is preaching, they are immediately put off because they consider that ministry too basic and not deep enough. Others love to sit under the ministry of a fiery evangelist, but fail to appreciate the pastor of their local church. Others may honour the spectacular prophetic ministries that are in the Church but fail to come under the authority and fatherly mantle of an apostolic ministry. God has given His Church diverse ministry gifts because we need them all. We may all have our own preference, but unless we are willing to recognise all the gifts that are in operation in the Church we cut ourselves off from receiving the ministry that God wants to pour into our lives. Maybe the ministries we enjoy least are the ones we need the most, because they highlight the areas of our walk with God that we are lacking in.

Likewise, there are so many different streams of churches and I think that this is a good thing because they are all needed. We make a big error when we put down another church because it doesn't fit our style, or they put a different emphasis on something that we do. Many times we fail to see God move in our cities because churches divide over their diversity instead of coming together and being complete. There must also be honour shown among the different age groups in the Church. Traditional churches and youth churches were never God's intention. God's intention has always been that the different generations honour each other (not just tolerate) and come together as part of His family.

Honouring the least of these

To truly be a person of honour, honour must flow down to those who, in society's eyes, are below us. Kingdom honour lifts them up so that they worship alongside us. In the time of Jesus, everyone honoured the Pharisees. What set Jesus apart was that He honoured everyone. He honoured women, children, tax collectors, sinners, prostitutes, lepers, the sick and the needy. Those who the culture of the day would ignore or mistreat, Jesus showed honour, concern and respect to. How different would our church culture be if, as the family of God, we extended honour to those who are not yet part of the family, e.g. the poor, the addicts, the broken, the abused? How different would life be if we treated those who weren't part of our family as if they were family, in the hope that they would become family?

This is what James meant when he said:

"My brothers and sisters, believers in our glorious Lord Jesus Christ must not show favouritism. Suppose a man comes into your meeting wearing a gold ring and fine clothes, and a poor man in filthy old clothes also comes in. If you show special attention to the man wearing fine clothes and say, "Here's a good seat for you," but say to the poor man, "You stand there" or "Sit on the floor by my feet," have you not discriminated among yourselves and become judges with evil thoughts?"

(James 2v1-4)

The Bible is pretty clear: unless honour includes all, we are not honouring. Who knows what might happen if we show honour to those we would normally bypass? Hebrews tells us, "Do not forget to show hospitality to strangers, for by so doing some people have shown hospitality to angels without knowing it." (13v2). You just never know who you are showing honour to!

<u>Honouring our enemies</u>

Finally, the greatest test that we are a person of honour is that we can show honour to those who mistreat us. Many Christians, the moment someone speaks against them, will leave the church upset or offended. Perhaps God has allowed that person to mistreat us as a test, to reveal to us whether we are person of honour or not. Anyone can honour those who honour us, but what about those who mistreat us and despise us? A true person of honour is even able to honour those who persecute them. People will mistreat us in life – being a Christian doesn't remove us from this - in fact, it can make it more common. It is most painful when it is a fellow Christian – but honour, honour, honour! Always honour! If there is always a flow of honour out of our lives, there will always be a flow of blessing into our lives.

How do we show honour?

To honour means to respect, to regard, to value and to esteem. It has to be outworked through four areas: our words, our giving, our service and our obedience.

<u>Our Words</u>

How people speak to others is a good indication of whether that person is a person of honour or not. People of honour are not rude, argumentative, aggressive or forceful in the way that they speak. People of honour are polite, gentle and respectful. People of honour speak life-giving and life-imparting words of blessing, not words that cut, wound and pull down. People of honour freely praise people, both publicly and privately. They don't wait until someone's funeral to honour them, but do it every chance they get. A church that honours uses the words "thank you" often. "Thank you" is a phrase that is used too little in the Church and as a result people often feel undervalued and underappreciated. All those who serve in the Church, whether it is on the pulpit or behind the scenes, should receive constant thanks from those they are serving.

Our Giving

The giving of finance is often linked with honour in the Bible. The Queen of Sheba gave great riches to Solomon, not because he was short of cash, but because she honoured him as a great king. Proverbs 3v9 tells us that we show honour to God with our wealth. If we are to be people of honour we will give our finances to our local church. This is a sign that we recognise the church and honour it as the family we belong to. We can and should give to other ministries around the world, but it starts by giving to our local church. The excuse that we don't get anything out of our local church is to misunderstand the honour principle. We give our finances to something to honour what God has said it is, not what we perceive it to be.

Giving is not just restricted to finance. Giving also involves our time. Jesus showed honour to people by having time for them - "the disciples were surprised to find him talking to a woman" (John 4v27). He even had time for the little children who were brought to Him (Matthew 19). When the disciples wanted to send the crowds away, Jesus refused to do it (Matthew 14). We must never think we are too good for people, or too busy for people. Jesus made time for everyone; we show honour by doing the same.

Our serving

Those we honour we will serve. Honour has to be more than lip service. It has to be something that is outward in practical ways too. When Elisha showed honour to Elijah, he put himself in a position to receive the prophet's mantle. If we honour the church, we will serve the church. If we honour leaders, we will serve our leaders. If we honour each other, we will serve each other. If we honour other churches and ministries we will support their events and not just our own (a helpful reminder for church leaders!). If we honour the poor, we will serve the poor. If we honour our enemies, we will serve our enemies (ouch!)

<u>Our obedience</u>

This is mainly in relation to the honouring of leaders. We can easily use words of honour towards our leadership, but then blatantly go against what they ask us to do. Let us never be like Judas who gave the kiss of honour, but had the heart of a betrayer. True honour whether it is towards God or towards others, always contains an element of godly fear, reverence and respect

Honour and the heart

"The Lord says: "These people come near to me with their mouth and honour me with their lips, but their hearts are far from me." (Isaiah 29v13)

We can say and do all the right things and still not be a person of honour. Ultimately honour is an issue of the heart. It is a genuine respect for people, a genuine value and appreciation of others, not something that we fake. One of the sad observations I make in churches is that people get jealous when others are used instead of them, or they are bypassed for promotion to a more prominent position. Jesus said these words: "Whoever speaks on their own does so to gain personal honour, but he who seeks the honour of the one who sent him is a man of truth; there is nothing false about him." (John 7v18). A true man of honour, Jesus said, is someone who wants others to be honoured, wants others to be used, and wants others to succeed.

Someone who just wants honour for themselves is not a person of honour at all.

Jesus also had this to say on the subject of honour: "When someone invites you to a wedding feast, do not take the place of honour, for a person more distinguished than you may have been invited." (Luke 14v8) Jesus is instructing us never to seek honour. Many get upset because they are looking for honour (no one thanked me, I am not appreciated in that church, no one acknowledges my gifting etc). The divine principle is that honour is not something we seek, but something we give. When we give honour, God who is the source of all honour will make sure honour comes back to us.

In this context, I don't believe the opposite of honour is dishonour. If honour is to value, prize and esteem something, then I believe the opposite of honour is "to treat something as common". This was the mistake they made with Jesus when they saw him as simply the carpenter's son. They missed out on all He had to give, because they failed to see all that He was. In the context of our churches, we fail to show honour many times - not on purpose, but because we have become so familiar with each other. We must never do this. We must intentionally show honour to each other, even "outdoing each other in showing honour" (Romans 12v10 – ESV). I once heard a preacher say, "God will often send us what we need in a package we don't want so we don't receive it; or in a package so familiar we don't recognise it"

A story about honour

A few years ago I was asked to speak at an evangelistic service in a town close to where I live. After I had agreed, the leader of the meeting told me that there were certain things I couldn't do. I wasn't allowed to preach; I could only share testimonies; I wasn't allowed to read scripture; I wasn't allowed to pray for people at the end. I knew straight away that if I kept these wishes then my ministry would be greatly restricted.

I had heard of another evangelist who had shared at the same meeting a few months previously and so I called him to see what he had done. Gleefully, he boasted of his disregard for the wishes of the leadership. He had preached a full sermon with Bible scriptures and had called people out for prayer, laying hands on them and having a good Charismatic ministry time. I enquired as to the result. He replied, "They chucked me out and told me never to come back!" He wasn't too discouraged, believing he was being persecuted for the gospel!

I then had a choice to make. Did I do what I wanted to do, or did I honour the leaders of the meeting? I decided to take the way of honour. I did exactly as I'd been asked, told a few stories, and then handed over. To my surprise, the leader of the meeting had been quite moved by what he had heard. He said, "If it is ok with this young man, I am going to ask him to share a few thoughts from the scriptures and then lay hands on people. If you would like this, let's go into the spare room next door." Around 70% of the people followed us and I was given full liberty to minister as I saw fit. People gave their lives to Christ, were healed, filled with the Holy Spirit and encountered God in wonderful ways.

I learned a great lesson that day. In insisting on doing things "his way", the other evangelist had closed the door to heaven's touch. By showing honour, even if it wasn't easy, I had made a way for God to break in. When you show honour, God will ultimately honour you - either in this life or at the Judgement Seat. Sow honour, receive honour.

Conclusion

In seeing the Church as God's family we must see our need for Church to be a place of honour. I once heard a preacher say the following:

- Honour elevates
- Honour stands at attention
- Honour bows in respect
- Honour serves with passion
- Honour looks past offences
- Honour believes the best
- Honour is both a lifestyle and a language

In continuing to look at the Church as the family of God, we will now look at the role of spiritual fathers and mothers and our need for them.

10

I AM A FATHERED SON

"Elisha saw this and cried out, "My father! My father! The chariots and horsemen of Israel!"

(2 Kings 2v12)

What I want to look at over the next two chapters is one of the most misunderstood, neglected and controversial areas in the Word of God, due to its potential to be abused, its difficulty in being outworked and general ignorance of its importance. For make no mistake about it, I believe that when in operation in our lives and churches it can be one of the most valuable, important, necessary and rewarding aspects of our Christianity. I think it is especially important for any young Christian who has a desire to go into ministry or some kind of service in the Kingdom.
I am talking about the need to have a spiritual father and / or mother.

We are looking at the Church and the importance of seeing the Church as the family of God. As we look at the Bible we can see the immense importance God places on the role of the father in the family - so much so, that He gave Jesus an earthly father in Joseph, though it was not biologically necessary. One of the biggest attacks Satan has made on the family in society has been to reduce or even remove the role of the father. Yet most social science studies speak of the benefit of having a close relationship to a father and the wholeness that it produces later on in life. That is not to condemn any woman who has to raise her children without a husband, as God can give grace and empowerment in that situation. However, the Biblical as well as the social ideal is that children will be raised having and knowing a father.

This is not only true in society, but also true in the Church. And yet if you were to ask the majority of Christians who their spiritual father was, they would look at you blankly. If a pastor began to teach on this subject, he would immediately be accused of trying to create a cult or enforce controlling leadership. Sadly, it isn't only a modern audience who fails to understand this concept. Paul would write in 1 Corinthians 4v15:

"Even though you have ten thousand guardians in Christ, you do not have many fathers"

What was Paul's solution to this fatherless generation? "In Christ Jesus I became your father."

When it comes to those who are in leadership over us, I think there are three basic categories that they can fall into.

Firstly, there are those who are simply "leaders". They have been placed above us and they instruct us and direct us and yet we have no close relational connection with them at all. We have to obey them, follow them and serve them as this is what the Bible instructs us to do, and yet the relationship we have with them is purely technical; it doesn't go any deeper than the surface. I am sure we have all had, or do have leaders in our lives like this.

Secondly, there is the phrase Paul uses here "guardians". The meaning of this word is a teacher, a supervisor a trusted advisor, someone who looks after us. A modern day word would be "a mentor". A leader who is a mentor obviously has a much closer connection to the person they are investing in than a leader who is a leader in name only. A mentor or guardian is there to instruct us educationally and connect with us relationally. There seems to have been an increased awareness in the Church in recent times on the need to have a mentor. I think this is good and beneficial. We should all have several mentors in our lives.

However, we must also see that the term "mentor" is not a Biblical term at all. When we speak of apostolic ministry and kingdom ministry, the Bible speaks not of mentors but of fathers and sons. A spiritual father does all that a mentor does, but there is also a much deeper connection - a spiritual connection. The major ministries of the New Testament, Paul and Jesus Himself, both recognised the need to be spiritual fathers to younger disciples. The Old Testament ends with the prophet Malachi saying:

"See, I will send the prophet Elijah to you before that great and dreadful day of the Lord comes. He will turn the hearts of the parents to their children, and the hearts of the children to their parents; or else I will come and strike the land with total destruction." (Malachi 4v5-6)

God is a multigenerational God and in these last days there is going to be a renewed understanding of the need for fathers in the Church. The hearts of older men are going to be turned to younger believers who they will adopt as sons and daughters, and the hearts of younger believers will be turned to those God gifts to them as spiritual fathers.

(I should point out that, although I am speaking specifically in this chapter about the need for a spiritual father, there is of course an important role for spiritual mothers in the church, too. Deborah, for example, was known as a mother in Israel (Judges 5v7), and Paul saw himself as having the characteristics of both mother (1 Thessalonians 2v7) and a father (1 Thessalonians 2v11) in his dealings with the Church). Many of the principles we will look at in this chapter are relevant to both spiritual mothers and fathers.

Pastor Cleddie Keith is a spiritual father to countless number of men and women around the globe. I once heard him make this statement: "I am a fathered son". It is such a simple and yet profound statement. Pastor Cleddie has understood that it is one thing to be son; it is another thing to be fathered. This can be true of our relationship with God and it can also be true of our relationships with our leaders. How many of us would say that we were sons and daughters of the house and yet we have never truly allowed ourselves to be fathered?

Elijah and Elisha

As an example of a father/son relationship in the Bible, one of the clearest examples is the relationship between Elijah and Elisha. That Elisha saw Elijah as a spiritual father can be seen in his cry "My father, my father" as Elijah ascended to heaven. It could be argued that this was just a term of respect, but looking closely at their lives, I think that their connection was much stronger than that. There are several lessons we can learn about spiritual fathers and mothers and their sons/daughters through their relationship:

1. Their connection was God ordained

"The Lord said to him (Elijah)....anoint Elisha son of Shaphat from Abel Meholah to succeed you as prophet" (1 Kings 19v15-16). Note that it was not Elijah's idea to have Elisha as a spiritual son; it was something that God told him to do. Likewise it was not Elisha's idea to have Elijah as a spiritual father.

Let's face it, if you were looking for a spiritual father or mother, someone more pleasant and emotionally stable than Elijah would be your first choice! God ordained this. I am constantly asking God to show me who He wants me to be a spiritual father to; I don't just go ahead and pick the most gifted and talented to be with me. Likewise, your spiritual father or mother is not always someone who you would choose or who you would naturally like to be with. It's something that God shows you.

2. It was a spiritual connection

"Elijah went up to him (Elisha) and threw his cloak around him" (1 Kings 19v19). The prophet's cloak represented his mantle, his office, his anointing. The first interaction between the pair was this touching with the mantle. Straight away, we can see the connection Elijah and Elisha had was a spiritual one. It is a sad fact of life in the modern day church that we try and organise things on behalf of the Holy Spirit, instead of leaving it to the Holy Spirit. Unity is one example of this. Pastors often try and organise events to promote unity, but Biblically unity is a spiritual thing that is produced by the Holy Spirit. Likewise, the connection between a spiritual father or mother and son/daughter is something that you can't plan or organise; it is something the Holy Spirit produces.

I led an internship for two years and had one-on-one time each week with the interns. During that time I would try and impart into their lives and get them to open up to me. I was trying to organise and force a connection that could only be produced by the Holy Spirit. Those who didn't recognise me as a spiritual father would sit there in awkward silence, before eventually leaving the room. Those who perceived me as a spiritual father often didn't need that planned time anyway. We were already sharing our hearts and lives together anyway on a regular basis. The father/mother and son/daughter relationship in the Church should be supernaturally natural.

3. It wasn't a forced connection.

"Elisha then left his oxen and ran after Elijah. "Let me kiss my father and mother goodbye," he said, "and then I will come with you." "Go back," Elijah replied. "What have I done to you?" (1 Kings 19v20)

Notice that Elijah gave Elisha the option as to whether to follow him or not. We see elsewhere, that Elijah would often give Elisha the option to "get out" of this relationship. The moment you speak of having spiritual fathers or mothers in the church people get nervous and think you are trying to bring in "heavy shepherding" or controlling leadership. Of course this teaching can easily be manipulated into becoming just that. But being a spiritual son or daughter must never be something that is forced upon you. It should be totally up to you whether you follow your Elijah or not. Likewise, as fathers and mothers we can never force, control or manipulate those we see, or would like to see as spiritual children. We cannot force the yoke of submission on people; it must always be given willingly. Sadly there are those who don't want a spiritual father or mother or who don't see the need for one, so we must simply let them be and allow the Holy Spirit to speak to them.

4. It was a relational connection.

"Then he (Elisha) set out to follow Elijah and be his attendant." (1 Kings 19v21)

Some may wonder how this kind of relationship works. It's quite simple; it's all about relationship. Elisha physically set out to follow Elijah. Notice that this was something that Elisha had to intentionally pursue. Elijah wasn't there checking up on him and forcing the relationship to work. When Jesus called the twelve disciples (His spiritual children) their primary calling was to "be with him". (Mark 3v14).

A spiritual father/mother and son/daughter relationship doesn't come through preaching/teaching or a discipleship course. It comes from being together, from having relationship together. Jesus took the twelve nearly everywhere He went. Not only did they minister together but they ate together, laughed together and travelled together. This is how you get a spiritual father, by taking time out of your schedule and intentionally spending time with the person God has called you to have that relationship with.

The role of a son

There are three important things we must do if we are to be spiritual sons and daughters. We must serve, learn from and stay with the men of God who we desire to be our spiritual father.

1. Serve

Many times spiritual sons can be a burden and hindrance to pastors, because they demand their time and attention. In the sincere desire to relate better with their leaders I have known people say to their pastors, "I am going to spend one whole afternoon with you a week", thinking that this is what the pastor wanted. In their zeal they had given no thought to the pastor's busy schedule or limited free time. Yes, we must spend as much time with our spiritual fathers and mothers as possible - that is how the relationship works, but we must never be too demanding or forceful. The best way to create this balance is to do what Elisha did. He didn't force himself upon Elijah, but gave himself to serve him. The first thing we read of Elisha was that he became Elijah's attendant. I love that Elisha had no hidden agenda in wanting to be with Elijah; he wasn't after a position or title, he never asked to be his successor. In fact you never read of Elisha asking his spiritual father for anything until he was asked what he wanted. Instead Elisha simply served Elijah and tried to make his life and ministry as easy as possible.

One of the most important jobs of a spiritual son or daughter is to serve their father or mother. Timothy was another spiritual son. Paul would say of him, "you know that Timothy has proved himself, because as a son with his father he has served with me in the work of the gospel" (Philippians 2v22). Elisha obviously did such a good job serving Elijah, that he was known as the man "who used to pour water on the hands of Elijah" (2 Kings 3v11). Many people want the "double portion" that Elisha received, yet are not willing to serve an Elijah. If we want what he had, we must be willing to do what he did. He served Elijah faithfully for many years, all the while being prepared for his own successful prophetic ministry.

It is a spiritual principle that if we cannot be faithful where we are, we will never be successful where we are going.

2. Learn from them

Elisha would have a very different ministry from that of Elijah, and the two certainly had very different personalities. Do not make the mistake of looking for a spiritual father or mother who is like you. Someone very different might be what you need the most. However, one thing is for sure, as spiritual children we are here to learn from our spiritual fathers and mothers. In 2 Kings 2 we read of Elijah's last ever miracle, the parting of the Jordan River. Interestingly, we also read of Elisha's first ever miracle. What was it? The parting of the Jordan River, in exactly the same way as Elijah had done it. No doubt as a true spiritual son he had been constantly observing the life and ministry of Elijah and learning from it.

Paul, confident in his role as a spiritual father, could write to the church in Corinth and say, "I urge you to imitate me" (1 Corinthians 4v16).

3. Stay with them

One of the most moving parts of scripture for me is 1 Kings 2, when God reveals to Elisha that this was the day Elijah would be taken away. Rather than rejoicing that this grumpy old prophet was going and Elisha could finally have his own ministry, Elisha is actually very distressed by the news. As Elijah travels from place to place he keeps urging Elisha to stay there, but on each occasion Elisha declares "as surely as the Lord lives and as you live, I will not leave you". Elisha was clearly not in a hurry to leave this relationship and was determined to stay with Elijah until the very last possible moment. When they were finally separated, it was the horses and chariots of fire (representing God's presence) that separated them. Apart from the odd exception where people can minister together for a lifetime, generally even very close father/mother and son/daughter relationships are separated. There comes a time when the spiritual son or daughter is now ready to have their own ministry and have spiritual children of their own. The job of a good spiritual father or mother is to recognise this and release them into it, but as spiritual children we must never be in a hurry to leave our spiritual father/mother. We must determine not to leave because of boredom or frustration or ego (thinking we don't need them), but to stay until God Himself brings the separation.

The role of a father

Why do we need a spiritual father or mother? Of the several reasons we have touched on, I want to highlight three: to be a source of impartation, wisdom and a prophetic voice.

1. A source of impartation

The root Hebrew word for the word "father" actually means "source". We see a little hint of this in the words of Jesus: "If you then, though you are evil, know how to give good gifts to your children..." (Luke 11v13). Fathers are meant to impart into their children everything that they are able to. When we have a close relationship with a spiritual father or mother an impartation takes place. Impartation doesn't only happen from the laying on of hands at an altar; it also takes place through osmosis as we relationally connect with our spiritual fathers. This was seen clearly in the life of Elisha, as the other prophets observed, "the spirit of Elijah is resting on Elisha" (2 Kings 3v15). Of course God as our Heavenly Father is the ultimate source of every good and perfect gift (James 1v17), but God also gives us men as spiritual fathers and mothers who are to be a source of wisdom, direction, gifting, prayer, anointing and whatever else they carry and are able to impart into us.

2. A source of wisdom

In life there are times when we need wisdom, and what a blessing to have fathers and mothers in the faith that we can go to for their wisdom, advice and counsel. In 1 Kings 12, Rehoboam made a huge mistake of ignoring the advice of the fathers of the nation and instead listening to the young men who had grown up with him. This failure to take on the wisdom of the elders led to him loosing the vast majority of his kingdom. We make a huge error if we think we don't need the wisdom of spiritual fathers and mothers, or if we are quick to dismiss that wisdom once it is given because we think that we know best.

The opposite of a Rehoboam would be Moses who, Exodus 18v24 tells us, "listened to his father-in-law and did everything he said". This saved Moses from burn out and also released others into their ministry. While all advice should be Holy Spirit filtered, we must all recognise the need to allow our spiritual fathers and mothers to be a source of wisdom to us.

3. A prophetic voice

One thing we see perhaps more clearly in the Old Testament (although it is there in the New Testament as well) is the prophetic role that the father played in the lives of his children. This is seen most powerfully in the last days of Jacob who, in Genesis 49, prophesies over each of his children. These verses would be more than just the ramblings of an old man, but prophetic destiny that would impact not only his children, but generations to come. The prophetic words a father spoke over his children were so powerful that, once uttered, they could not be revoked (Genesis 27v37). One of the most important aspects of having a spiritual father or mother is having someone who can be a prophetic voice into your life. While ministry from itinerant prophets can be powerful, there is something even more powerful about prophecy when it comes out of relationship.

A prophetic voice doesn't only mean giving directional or predictive prophecies.

A spiritual father is someone who sees the greatness of God in our lives and calls it out of us and declares over us what they see in us that often we don't see in ourselves.

True sons?

The Bible tells us that when it comes to our status as children of God it is possible to be illegitimate sons. The book of Hebrews is pretty clear as to how to differentiate between true sons and false sons:

"And have you completely forgotten this word of encouragement that addresses you as a father addresses his son? It says,

"My son, do not make light of the Lord's discipline, and do not lose heart when he rebukes you, because the Lord disciplines the one he loves, and he chastens everyone he accepts as his son."

Endure hardship as discipline; God is treating you as his children. For what children are not disciplined by their father? If you are not disciplined–and everyone undergoes discipline–then you are not legitimate, not true sons and daughters at all. Moreover, we have all had human fathers who disciplined us and we respected them for it. How much more should we submit to the Father of spirits and live! They disciplined us for a little while as they thought best; but God disciplines us for our good, in order that we may share in his holiness. No discipline seems pleasant at the time, but painful. Later on, however, it produces a harvest of righteousness and peace for those who have been trained by it." (Hebrews 12v5-11)

This passage makes it very clear that true sons are those who will go through the process of discipline. This is true in our relationship with God, but also true of our relationship with our spiritual fathers and mothers. As we grow in our walk with God there will be times when our spiritual fathers and mothers have to rebuke us and discipline us. In fact, God our father often disciplines us through our spiritual fathers. Our response to this discipline determines whether or not we are true sons and daughters. There have been times when my spiritual fathers have had to rebuke me over areas in my life. At the time it is often the last thing you want to hear, but later, as the scripture says, you recognise the harvest it has produced.

The book of Proverbs contains such wisdom as "rebuke a wise man and he will love you" (9v8); "a rebuke impresses a man of discernment" (17v10); and "a man who remains stiff necked after many rebukes will suddenly be destroyed without remedy (29v1). It is clear that the foolish reject the rebuke and discipline of their fathers and mothers, but the wise accept and respond to correction. We can commit grave sins, but if we truly repent once our spiritual fathers and mothers confront us and are willing to go through a process of discipline, then there is no doubt that God can restore us. However, if we are defensive and have a "who are they to speak to me like that" attitude, we are not true children and God cannot do anything with us. If we respond to correction by walking away from that church, or we become bitter because we think we are being mistreated, it is a clear sign that we have an orphan spirit. Some Christians will leave a church the moment the pastor preaches a challenging or hard-hitting sermon. Orphans only want to hear encouragement and praise, but true sons and daughters understand that the true role of a father and mother is not only to "encourage and comfort", but also to "urge you to live lives worthy of God" (1 Thessalonians 2v11-12)

If Elisha is an example of a good spiritual son, his disciple, Gehazi, is an example of a bad one. When Elisha refused payment after healing Naaman the Aramean, Gehazi took it upon himself to claim the reward. His refusal to accept the "no" of his spiritual father cost him his ministry position, any future chance of succession and caused him to become leprous (2 Kings 5). One of the biggest tests to being under a spiritual father is when they say "no" to something we want them to say "yes" to. Sometimes we can't understand why they are saying no, or just firmly believe that they are wrong. Our willingness to accept their "no" when we say "yes" - or their "yes" when we say "no" - is a true test of our son-ship. No matter how successful we become in ministry, we must always make sure that there are people in our lives who are not afraid to say "no" to us.

Sons of the house

In seeing the church as the family of God, we must see our need to become fathered children by embracing the concept of a spiritual father. Once we have done this we become not just "church members" but "sons and daughters of the house". This brings two aspects into play in our lives:

1. Responsibility

When I lived at home with my parents, I didn't act like a guest in the house. I treated it as though it was just as much my house as theirs. As a son of the house I enjoyed all the benefits of the house, but it also meant I had certain responsibilities. I am sure we have all had the teenage experience of being asked to do the dishes, take out the trash or tidy our rooms. Our response? "It's not my job!" The counter-response? "As long as you are in my house, under my roof, as long as I am paying your bills.... it is your job! Get on with it!"

How many Christians treat the church as a place they visit on a Sunday morning? In seeing the church as a family, you must recognise that you are a son and daughter in the house. That means you have responsibility. If there is a piece of rubbish in my house I pick it up and throw it away, even if I didn't leave it there. I take ownership of that need because it's my house. Many Christians will not take ownership of things that need doing in the church. They state, "It's not my job! I don't get paid to do it. It's the pastor's job!" They are not true sons or daughters of the house. True sons and daughters of the house recognise their responsibility to meet the needs of the house. They take ownership of a situation where a need arises.

2. Blessing

If we are willing to do this - contribute to the family of God and come under a spiritual father or mother - we are positioning ourselves to receive incredible blessing. After years of faithfully serving Elijah, Elisha found himself in the right place to receive the prophetic mantle and have an incredible ministry of his own (2 Kings 2v13). All the other prophets observed the mantle falling, but only Elisha was close enough to Elijah to receive it. The blessing that God gave Abraham was passed down to his sons Isaac and Jacob. The Bible tells us that, as Gods children, there is an inheritance available to us (Galatians 4v5). The Bible principle is clear: mantles, blessings, anointing and inheritances are only ever passed onto sons and daughters.

The people I know with the greatest ministries have all served under a spiritual father or mother who they were in close relationship with for many years before they were released into their own ministry. I personally owe everything I have and am as a minister to both the grace of God and my spiritual fathers. Very recently I had a young man come up to me at the end of a conference and ask for my advice as he felt called to be an evangelist. My advice surprised him: "find a man of God who can be your spiritual father and serve him until he releases you." In my opinion it is the best way to a fruitful ministry and walk with God.

Conclusion

Some time ago I came to a crossroads in my ministry where I desperately needed to hear from God. Thankfully at that time I had the privilege of spending a week with Pastor Cleddie Keith as he visited the UK. As well as being a spiritual father to many, Pastor Cleddie is also known as a powerful prophetic voice. I was expectant that Pastor Cleddie would give me a prophetic word telling me exactly what to do. On the first day of the trip, Pastor Cleddie looked at me and said "Andrew..." (Here it was, the prophetic word that would show me what to do, but Cleddie simply said) "I love you and I'm proud of you". I felt a little awkward, but thanked him politely, inwardly disappointed that I'd not received what I considered a prophetic word. Over the course of the week I drove Pastor Cleddie hundreds of miles around the country. He would often speak directionally into the lives of other people who were travelling with us and in the meetings themselves he would give people powerful prophetic words. Me? Not a thing! The only thing he kept saying was, "I love you and I'm proud of you". He said this nearly every day.

At the end of the week I was so disappointed, no closer to discovering what I should do regarding the important decision I had to make. The following week, as I was spending time with God, I felt the Holy Spirit whisper into my heart: "Through that man I was showing you the heart of a father. You thought the most important thing I had to communicate to you was my will, but really it was "I love you and I'm proud of you". This revelation released me to embrace my identity. Once I had discovered who I was, the choice of what I was to do became pretty easy.

In our desire to serve God and be all that God has called us to be, we can mistakenly think that what we need most is a position or title in church or more knowledge or ministerial training, when perhaps our greatest need is for a spiritual father or mother, someone who will look us in the eyes and say "I love you and am proud of you".

In 1 Chronicles 25v6, the Bible says of those serving David's tabernacle, "All these men were under the supervision of their father for the music of the temple of the Lord". In our ministry and service are we under the supervision of a spiritual father or mother? Do we have a spiritual father or mother? Do we see the need for one? If the answer is no, maybe we should pray on this to God.

Once we have become sons or daughters, we are placed to one day become fathers and mothers. Only sons and daughters can be father and mothers. In the next chapter, we will look at how we become spiritual parents and the importance in raising up sons and daughters in the family of God.

11

THE SPIRIT OF ADOPTION

"Then God said, "Let the land produce vegetation: seed-bearing plants and trees on the land that bear fruit with seed in it, according to their various kinds." And it was so. The land produced vegetation: plants bearing seed according to their kinds and trees bearing fruit with seed in it according to their kinds. And God saw that it was good."

(Genesis 1v11-12)

The above scripture is the Genesis account of the third day of creation. I believe the book of Genesis contains powerful principles that give us an understanding of who God is and how He operates. I believe that the creation account in particular shows us some vital principles of how God always creates things.

A simple description of the third day of creation would be that it was on this day that God created the plants and trees. However, a closer look shows us that something much more significant was taking place. Not only did God create the plants and trees, but He also placed within them "seed". This meant that the plants and trees He created now had the ability to bear fruit and produce other plants and trees. There is a divine principle at work here. Whenever God creates something, He doesn't just give the object of His creation life, he also gives it the potential and the ability to reproduce that life. So, God didn't just create an apple tree on the third day. He created an apple tree that had seed within it, meaning that it had the ability to produce another apple tree. It was this that God said "was good".

God's creation of man was along a similar pattern. God didn't just create Adam. He also put seed in Adam, meaning that Adam now had the ability to reproduce. In fact it was the command (not the suggestion of God) that man "be fruitful and increase in number; fill the earth..." (Genesis 1v28). As trees and plants were created with the purpose of producing other trees and plants, mankind was created with the purpose of producing children, other human beings.

Everything in creation is a foreshadowing or type of an even greater spiritual reality. If natural seed produces natural children, then spiritual seed is meant to produce spiritual children. When God saved you, it was never His intention to just give you life. It was His intention to also place within you His seed, His nature, that you would produce spiritual offspring, spiritual children. As surely as man was commanded to "be fruitful and increase in number; fill the whole earth..." the Church has been commanded to "go and make disciples of all nations" (Matthew 28v19). Although all natural children are a gift from God, my son didn't appear one day on my front doorstep nor was he carried to us via a stork. I was involved in the creation process! Likewise, although God is the One who ultimately saves and sanctifies people, the process of discipleship doesn't just automatically happen. We have to be heavily involved in the process of producing spiritual children. This is what Paul meant went he said to the Galatians, "My dear children, for whom I am again in the pains of childbirth until Christ is formed in you" (Galatians 4v19). Paul's prayers, intercession and fatherly ministry played a huge part in these believers reaching the point of mature Christ-likeness.

In Galatians 4, there is a wonderful description of one of the roles of the Holy Spirit in our lives. The Bible says "because you are his sons, God sent the Spirit of his Son into our hearts, the Spirit who calls out, "Abba, Father." So you are no longer a slave, but God's child; and since you are his child, God has made you also an heir." The Holy Spirit is the Spirit of adoption. Paul calls Him elsewhere "the Spirit of sonship" (Romans 8v15). When we are born again, God literally adopts us as children. Being a child of God is not just a picture or a metaphor: it is a very real and literal thing. Being a child of God is not just a title we are given, it is something that we become. I have literally become a son of God. It is the Holy Spirit who acts as heaven's adoption agent, not only taking us and placing us in the Father as His son, but also revealing this fact to us. Without the Holy Spirit we cannot be adopted as God's children and even if we could be, we would be ignorant of this fact. Praise God for the Holy Spirit, the Spirit of Adoption, who reveals to us our nature as sons and daughters and God's nature as Abba, for in exactly the same way as the Holy Spirit, who is the source of miracles, enables us to perform miracles and as the Holy Spirit, who is the source of holiness, enables us to live holy, the Holy Spirit, who is the Spirit of Adoption, enables us to adopt spiritual sons and daughters.

The Spirit of Adoption is something that God wants to reveal more and more, especially in these last days when "He will turn the hearts of the parents to their children, and the hearts of the children to their parents" (Malachi 4v5-6). More and more we see a breakdown in society due to a lack of good fathers and mothers. Sadly, the same is also true in the church. Without the Spirit of Adoption, the land is "under a curse". To curse can simply mean to limit or restrict. To say that the Church is limited or restricted without the Spirit of Adoption is an understatement. If we only exist to sustain the life we have, the life of God will be taken from this earth when we are and there will be no influence of heaven left in our communities. In seeing the Church as the family of God, we must see that we exist for more than ourselves. We exist to impart the life that God has given us into others and through the Holy Spirit adopt and raise up the next generation of disciples and spiritual children.

The book of James tells us that "Religion that God our Father accepts as pure and faultless is this: to look after orphans" (James 1v27). Now, how do we practically look after orphans? What do orphans need? Do they need clothing, shelter, housing, education? Of course they do, but don't we all? What is the unique need of an orphan? They need a father and mother. God is showing us here that God expects His Church to be a place where the Spirit of Adoption is in operation. The Bible tells us that God doesn't place orphans in an orphanage but "He sets the lonely in families" (Psalm 68v6). In an orphanage, children can have all their needs met, except their greatest need, that of parents. That can only be found in family. Likewise, a worker in an orphanage, whilst they might care dearly for the children under their care, is still a hired hand, who clocks in and out at the start and end of their shift. A father and mother receive no payment for looking after their children. Likewise, they can't turn on and off the instinct to parent. It is a 24 hour, seven day a week, 365 days a year commitment from the moment that child is conceived right until the end of the parents life.

In the Church we must understand what new born spiritual babies need. We often make the mistake of thinking that the only thing a new Christian needs is teaching, ministry, prayer and a new-beginner's course. Whilst all of these things are important, they neglect people's ultimate need and desire, which is a relationship with a father and mother. If all we do is preach to, teach and mentor new Christians, we are making the mistake of thinking the Church is an orphanage and not a family.

Paul writes in Ephesians 3, "for this reason I kneel before the Father, from whom His whole family in heaven and on earth derives its name" (v14-15). The word family here is derived from the Greek word "pater" meaning "father". So a more accurate translation of this verse would be, "I kneel before the Father, from whom all His fathers in heaven and on earth derive their name". So, God has fathers both on heaven and on earth, who represent Him and demonstrate the love, care and nature of their Heavenly Father to others.

The need of the hour, Paul said to the Corinthians, was that they did not have many fathers (1 Corinthians 4v15). The way that Paul addressed that was to become their father (v16). That is why he addressed them as "my dear children" (v14). If we think about it, this is actually the whole point of ministry. Ephesians 4v11 lists the five different ministry gifts that Christ gives to His church. Verse 12 then gives us the reason for those gifts: "to prepare God's people for works of service." In other words, no ministry exists just for itself, to outwork the ministry that God has given it, rather each ministry exists to recreate itself, to reproduce spiritual sons and daughters "according to their kinds". Any ministry or church that fails to raise up sons and daughters is not a true New Testament ministry.

Let's look at how, as leaders and churches, we raise up sons and daughters.

Change of perspective

1. Seeing yourself as a parent

In certain Christian circles today, there seems to be a huge emphasis on leadership. We are told that the future of the Church depends upon its leaders and many hours and much money is spent on raising up leaders. As existing leaders we are constantly being told to improve our leadership skills. Whilst all of this is helpful, we must remember that the basic DNA of a leader is someone who has influence. The biggest influences in most of our lives, particularly in our formative years, were our parents. The greatest leader of all is God Himself and the ultimate revelation of who God is, is that He is our Father. Jesus told us to pray to "Our Father". Thus we see that leadership is not telling people what to do and dishing out orders. Leadership is not about having people under us, serving us, helping us fulfil our vision. Leadership is not about having a title or what we do from a platform. Leadership is parenthood.

I firmly believe that what the Church needs is not more leaders, but more fathers and mothers. We don't need better leaders but better spiritual parents.

If we only see the church as a business, then we will produce followers. However, if we see the church as a family, then we will produce sons and daughters. Raising up followers can be useful, but followers can suddenly turn around and decide to follow someone else. Sons and daughters tend to stick around until they are released. Followers are loyal to a title; sons and daughters are loyal to a person.

I urge today's leaders not to see themselves as corporate CEOs, but as fathers and mothers of a family. Please don't see the people under you as "staff" or names on a rota who help you do what you want to see done. See them as dearly loved children - like Paul did, like Jesus did.

For all mature believers in Christ, there must be a change in perspective as we start to see ourselves as fathers and mothers in the church. According to Matthew 6v32 and Matthew 7v11, the role of a father is to know the needs of our children and supply those needs: "your Heavenly Father knows that you need them"; "(you) know how to give good gifts to your children". In understanding this we soon realise that our purpose in life is to invest and impart into those we consider spiritual children.

2. Seeing those we influence as our children

I want us to observe here these words from the Apostle Paul, in what are known as his "pastoral epistles":

"To Timothy my true son in the faith:" (1 Timothy 1v2)

"Timothy, my son, I am giving you this command in keeping with the prophecies once made about you … " (1 Timothy 1v18)

"To Timothy, my dear son:" (2 Timothy 1v2)

"You then, my son, be strong in the grace that is in Christ Jesus."
(2 Timothy 2v1)

"To Titus, my true son in our common faith:" (Titus 1v4)

The language that Paul uses when speaking to Timothy and Titus is significant. He never says they are "like" sons to him. He speaks in very literal terms when he says things like "my true son", "my dear son" and "my son". Paul didn't refer to Timothy and Titus as his spiritual sons as a metaphor or nice turn of phrase. They were as much his children as my son, Judah, is to me. The only difference is that they were not biological children, but spiritual. The bond was just as real and as important. How had this happened? The spirit of adoption had hit Paul and he had literally adopted these two men as his own children in the Spirit. I believe that the spirit of adoption is an actual anointing and grace of the Holy Spirit that He wants to give to us, so that we see those whom we influence as our actual children and that they in turn see us as their fathers in the faith.

In speaking of Jesus, the prophet Isaiah declared "Here am I, and the children the Lord has given me" (Isaiah 8v18). It was actually prophesied that the Messiah would have children given to Him by the Father. Of course, Jesus never married and had no biological children, but He did have spiritual children who He said were given to Him by the Father (John 17v6). At the end of His time on earth, Jesus actually considered that the culmination of the ministry His Father had given Him was the impact He had had on His disciples (John 17v6-18). How many times do we consider the major parts of our ministry to be what we discuss in the boardroom or preach from our pulpits? Actually these are minor things in comparison with the most important work. The most important thing we need to be spending our time and energy and resources on, is in raising up spiritual sons and daughters.

The battle for a generation

2 Kings 6 is one of the most disturbing portions of scripture. It is the account of the famine that hit Samaria in the time of Elisha the prophet. In verses 26-29 a woman comes to the king with a complaint against her neighbour: "This woman said to me, 'Give up your son so we may eat him today, and tomorrow we'll eat my son.' So we cooked my son and ate him. The next day I said to her, 'Give up your son so we may eat him,' but she had hidden him."

Things had got so bad in the city that women were actually killing their own children in order to survive. The instinct to preserve our own life is at the core of all creatures, but these women's self-preservation was actually costing them the next generation. They were being fed, but the next generation was dying and no one cared.
The parallel with the Church is hopefully obvious. Many Christians see their only purpose in life as to take care of their own spiritual life. Many Christians come to church to get fed and that is it. Yet, all around us, the next generation is dying because of our selfishness. No one cares about impacting and investing in the next generation. The king of Samaria immediately tried to pin the blame on Elisha, but it was his own disobedience that had caused the famine. Woe to us if we think we can blame the church's youth pastor for a lack of mature spiritual young people in our churches. They don't need the latest trendy youth programme; they need fathers and mothers. Our disobedience in failing to release the spirit of adoption is costing us a generation.

Sadly, this selfish attitude can affect even the godliest leaders. King Hezekiah was one of Judah's most godly kings and yet when he received a prophecy that the Babylonians would destroy the nation in the time of his children, what was his response? "The word of the Lord you have spoken is good … will there not be peace and security in my lifetime?" (2 Kings 20v19). This may sound like an incredibly selfish thing to say, and it is, but don't be too harsh on Hezekiah, as most of us are exactly the same. As long as we are ok, our ministries are ok and we are blessed, all is well. There is no concern for the next generation being raised up and impacted.

In contrast, look at two heroines of the Bible, Shiphrah and Puah. These two women were the Hebrew midwives who defied Pharaoh's orders and let the Hebrew boys live after Pharaoh had ordered them killed as they were being born. These two women risked their own safety and even lives to preserve the life of the next generation. God so honoured these two women, that not only did He make sure their names were reordered in Scripture but that they had families of their own (Exodus 1v21). God takes how we treat the next generation very seriously.

A long term approach to ministry

"What is your vision for the next five years?" is a question I have sometimes been asked. At a stretch someone might ask "what is your vision for the next ten years?" I must honestly say that I have no idea what my vision is for the next five, ten or twenty years. I do have a vision for the next hundred years, though. Of course I am not going to be alive in hundred years, but my ministry can still be effective and have an impact, one hundred, two hundred years from now (if the Lord doesn't return). How? Through my spiritual children and their spiritual children and so on and so on. My ministry never began with me and will not end with me. It is a product of someone else's ministry. My job now is to release my spiritual seed into the next generation.

We are all just one link in the chain. What we do never began with us and God forbid that it should end with us. There is always someone behind us, but it is vitally important that there is someone after us. We cannot just be sons and daughters; we have to be fathers and mothers, too - else, no matter how great our ministry, it ends with us. The mantle of Elijah passed to Elisha. The tragedy of Elisha was that due to the disobedience of his spiritual son, Gehazi, the mantle was never passed on. Elisha died with the anointing still in his bones (2 Kings 13) because he had never been able to impart it into another. This is a pattern we see time and again in the Bible and in church history. Samuel was arguably the greatest prophet Israel ever had, but his failure to produce godly sons led to Israel asking for a king and the carnal Saul being appointed. We must always remember that it doesn't matter how big or successful our church is, if we do not leave behind godly sons and daughters we are only one generation away from rebellion or extinction.

Invest

As a new father I have learned pretty quickly that raising children calls for investment. There is an investment of finance certainly, but most importantly of all there is an investment of time. It is very easy to have children, but very difficult to be a father. The key to raising up sons and daughters has to be spending time relationally with those we adopt. Jesus knew the importance of this more than anyone. His command was clear when He said, "Let the little children come unto me … " (Mark 10v14). He spent time with the children, taking them in His arms and blessing them. Jesus was exactly the same with His disciples. Although the ministry of Jesus impacted large crowds, He invested a large amount of His time in raising up spiritual sons. In fact, there are occasions when Jesus dismissed the multitudes in order to influence the small group of men He considered to be His spiritual children, as evidenced in passages such as John 13v33 where He actually addressed them as "My children" and John 14v18 where He told them "I will not leave you as orphans" (incidentally this verse is another key scripture in showing us that the Holy Spirit is the Spirit of Adoption).

As we have already mentioned in the previous chapter, the disciples of Jesus were called primarily to "be with Him" (Mark 3v14). This would have been incredibly time consuming and emotionally draining for Jesus and in some ways His own ministry was restricted and limited because of it. Yet after Jesus' ascension the ministry of Jesus did not end. He had raised up spiritual sons who would continue the works He did and in fact go on to do greater works (John 14v12). They of course in turn would go on to have spiritual children of their own. And so the chain continues to our own spiritual fathers, who invested their time and energy into us. Now, are we going to break the chain, or are we going to invest our time in others?

Recently I met up with a pastor and leader from Kenya who had been a Bible college student placed at the church my brother and I attended as children. Even though I was ten years old at the time and my brother only five, we both remember him clearly to this day as he had made such an impact on us during the two years he was at our Church. The interesting thing is, we can never remember a single sermon he preached, but we can both remember the time he invested in us, just chatting to us and encouraging us. In fact, all of the men and women who have impacted me the most had one thing in common – they spent time with me as a friend. As a preacher, my ego tells me that people will remember every word I preach, but in actuality, my experience tells me that they remember very little. What they do remember is the time I spent with them. Families are based on relationship. My wife and I have spent countless hours spending time with the young people in our care, having driven them thousands of miles to events up and down the country, spent hundreds of pounds, cooked dozens of meals and opened up our home countless times. It has been time consuming, energy sapping and emotionally draining, but I have loved every minute of it! Many of these young people have grown to become some of the most polite, humble, spiritual and servant-hearted people I know and they are seeing God do great things through them. We are told that leaders should have followers, but I am not sure that is Kingdom. Kingdom people don't have followers but sons and daughters - and that means a lot of love and time.

Impart

One of my biggest heroes of the Bible is Manoah, the father of Samson. The reason I love Manoah so much is because of two verses in Judges 13. Manoah and his wife cannot have children. One day, the angel of the Lord visits Manoah's wife and tells her that God will do a miracle and she will conceive and give birth to a son. When she tells her husband about this encounter, I find his response very interesting. "Then Manoah prayed to the Lord: "Pardon your servant, Lord. I beg you to let the man of God you sent to us come again to teach us how to bring up the boy who is to be born." (v8). When the angel turned up again, this time with Manoah present, Manoah's request was to ask "what is to be the rule for the boy's life and work" (v12). What I love here is the importance Manoah placed on having the wisdom needed to nurture and bring up his son. Even though he wasn't a father yet, he was already thinking like one. Rather than just calling a party and celebrating the miracle of new birth, Manoah knew that this wasn't the end of his prayers, but actually the beginning of a new role that would last the rest of his life. How many times in church do we celebrate the miracle of someone being born again as if that is it, they've made it? We are right to celebrate salvation, but then we act as if that is the end of it, they are saved, God has answered our prayers, all is well. When my wife and I conceived, we knew that this was only the beginning, we now needed to care and protect and nurture this little life for the rest of our days. In the same way, salvation is only the beginning. We are now called to bring up this new child of God in all the ways of the Kingdom. In order to do this we need to pray for wisdom like Manoah did.

We do not have time to study the whole story of Jehoiada as found in 2 Kings 11, but it is well worth reading as he is a wonderful example of a spiritual father to Joash, the boy prince who he hides in the temple from the wicked Queen Athaliah. Athaliah is eventually overthrown and Joash is placed on the throne. There are some wonderful examples of how Jehoiada treats Joash that can help us impart into our spiritual sons and daughters.

Firstly, the reason Jehoiada protected Joash was because he saw him not as a child, but as a future king and leader. Babes in Christ can test our patience because of their immaturity and instability. We can quickly get frustrated and be tempted to give up in our discipling of them. Prophetic eyes, however, see beyond the temporary to the future destiny of those who may now be infants in the faith, but with the right investment can go on to be mighty in the Kingdom.

Secondly, we see Jehoiada as a prophetic voice in the life of Joash as he addressed him as king even before he was placed on the throne. As spiritual fathers we are there to speak out and declare the greatness of God in our spiritual children.

Thirdly, we see that Jehoiada even at the risk of his own life, did everything he could to protect and preserve the life of Joash, ordering armed guards to surround him and put to death any unauthorised person who tried to come near him. Jehoiada knew the importance of the task he had been given. In the same way that natural parents would do anything for their children, even laying down their lives if needed, spiritual parents would do anything for their spiritual children, even recognising that a good shepherd would lay down his life for his sheep (John 10v11).

Fourthly, we see Jehoiada presenting Joash with a copy of the covenant (v12), thus making sure that he had God's Word available to him at all times. Just like a good natural father makes sure his children are well fed, spiritual fathers and mothers feed their spiritual children with God's word, making sure they are encouraged, comforted and challenged (1 Thessalonians 2v11).

Finally, we see that Jehoiada continued to instruct Joash all the days of his life. In taking on the role of a spiritual father we must understand that it is not short term ministry. We are investing in people for the long haul and have a responsibility to watch over and instruct those in our care until the time they leave or God releases us.

Discipline

One example of a poor spiritual father in the Bible is the priest, Eli, who we read about in the opening chapters of 1 Samuel. We know from verses like 1 Samuel 2v22 that Eli's sons were involved in corruption and immorality and Eli was well aware of this. Because of their sin, Eli's sons would both be judged; however, it is also worth pointing out that God had very strong words for Eli himself, even though his own conduct seems to be above reproach. In fact, God has harsher words for Eli than for his sons. The accusation made against Eli was that "he failed to restrain" his sons (1 Samuel 3v13), similar to the fault of the great King David - a failure to rebuke and discipline his children. The Bible is very clear: "Whoever spares the rod hates their children, but the one who loves their children is careful to discipline them" (Proverbs 13v24). In our role as spiritual fathers and mothers we cannot afford to ignore sin or immaturity, but must be willing to discipline, rebuke, correct and constantly challenge our spiritual children to be all that they can be in God.

Release

When we have invested so much time and energy into our spiritual children, there can be a strong desire to hold onto them for as long as possible, especially if they are serving our ministry in some way! We may be reluctant to lose them and the help that they bring. Worst of all, if there exists within our spiritual children a real respect and submission towards us, it can be very tempting to try and control and manipulate them into doing what we want them to do. However, the Bible tells us that children are like arrows in the hands of a warrior (Psalm 127v4). The whole point of an arrow is not to be kept in a quiver, but ultimately to be released and sent. The whole point of having children is that ultimately they will leave home and start a family of their own. Likewise, the whole point of having spiritual children is that ultimately they will be released into their own ministry and destiny. Sometimes we can partner with them in that. Other times, we have to release them and watch them from a distance.

In the ministry of Jesus we see Him spending just three years with His spiritual children before releasing them into their ministry. Jesus wouldn't hang around to watch over them, on hand to step in if they messed up. On the contrary, Jesus would depart and leave the task of world evangelism entirely up to them, trusting that the Words He had spoken into them and the Spirit He had left with them to be enough. If you closely read Paul's letters to the churches, you find him often referring to his spiritual sons (like Timothy and Titus) in the context of sending them to such-and-such a place, or commissioning them to appoint elders somewhere else. Paul was clearly comfortable with the idea of releasing his spiritual sons into ministry and he trusted that they would do what they had been called to do.

We must guard against releasing our spiritual sons and daughters too early, as many have fallen into this trap and released immature leaders into the work of God, damaging both them and the Church. At the same time, however, we must ensure that we never hold onto people too tightly, but are always ready to release people into what God has called them to. Sometimes this can be very painful, as we feel like we are losing those God has given us. We never truly lose sons and daughters, but launch them into their God-given destiny and rejoice from a distance at all God does through them.

Sons and slaves

The tiny epistle of Philemon is one of the least read parts of the New Testament, but it has some interesting things to say about the spirit of adoption.

Philemon is a spiritual son to Paul, who in this letter writes to him about another one of Paul's spiritual sons, Onesimus. Philemon was a very wealthy man and a slave owner, whilst Onesimus was one of his runaway slaves. It is interesting that Paul adopted both the rich and slaves. True love is able to reach both into the highest and lowest places in life.

Paul writes to Philemon saying "this man was your slave, but now he's my son, which makes him your brother". Here we see that the spirit of adoption will embrace slaves as sons. The spirit of adoption will look past the chains that bind people and loosen people into their true identity as sons and daughters. Paul writes "In the past he may have wronged you … " The spirit of adoption sees beyond the past and allows room for people to change. Everything about Onesimus' life had changed since Philemon had known him. This is the transformational power of the spirit of adoption.

Paul writes that although Onesimus had once been useless, now he had become useful. Onesimus actually means useless, so there was a little play on words here. Paul spotted the potential of this runaway slave, though his master considered him "useless". Paul's spirit of adoption had led him to adopting this man as a son and now he had become not only a child of God, but someone who was useful, valuable and useable in the Kingdom. As a father, Paul spoke on behalf of Onesimus. He considered the value in this man, saying he had become "very dear to me". Paul was even willing to invest financially in him, offering to pay any debt he owed. Although Paul wanted desperately to keep Onesimus with him, as a true spiritual father he ended up releasing him back to Philemon where he belonged.

Although not confirmed by all scholars, a long-held Christian tradition is that this same Onesimus was the one appointed by the apostles to succeed Timothy as leader of the church at Ephesus. I certainly hope that this is true, as it would make a lovely ending to his story! Even if it isn't, there is no doubt that he was born again and we shall meet him in heaven. Quite a turnaround from the runaway slave. The difference? No doubt the message of the gospel, but also an apostle who carried the spirit of adoption and despite the chains he himself was wearing, loosened the chains of someone else by adopting them as a son.

How many lives are there who we can impact and transform through the Person of the Holy Spirit as He flows through us as the Spirit of Adoption?

Conclusion

Over the past several chapters we have looked at the challenging aspect of seeing the Church as the family of God. We have looked at how we should love one another and treat each other as brothers and sisters. We have looked at the somewhat controversial issue of having and being spiritual fathers and mothers.

We now move on to look at another aspect of the Church, which is seeing the Church as the Body of Christ. We will start by looking at a church in the New Testament which outwardly seemed great, but by failing to see this aspect of who it was, failed miserably.

12

THE CORINTHIAN PROBLEM

"I already gave you a warning when I was with you the second time. I now repeat it while absent: on my return I will not spare those who sinned."

(2 Corinthians 13v2)

The two letters that Paul writes to the church in Corinth contain some of the harshest and strongest rebukes that we find in the New Testament. Although Paul is known as an apostle of grace, who writes tenderly in the Pastoral Epistles, and majestically in the book of Ephesians; 1 and 2 Corinthians contain some fairly strong words of criticism. The church at Corinth was obviously full of problems and Paul was not afraid to try and bring correction to them. 1 Corinthians in particular sees Paul describe the members of this church as worldly (3v3), childish (3v1), mere men (3v4), arrogant (4v18), defeated (6v7), cheats (6v8), under judgement (11v31) and infantile (14v20).

As we read that list we can clearly see that the Corinthian church was far from the ideal church! So what was the problem with this church? I believe that as we study the book of 1 Corinthians, we can see that although Paul addresses many symptoms, there was an underlying root cause that was at the heart of the sickness prevailing in this church. I believe that it is a problem in many Christians and churches today and one that we have to be very careful to avoid ourselves.

The problem was not the problem

If you were to ask most Christians what would make their church better, most of them would reply better church meetings i.e. if the worship was better, if the preaching was better, if the fellowship was better, if there was more moving of the Holy Spirit then consequently the church would be better. Even most pastors spend the majority of their time and energy trying to improve the quality of their church services and programmes. If the Sunday gatherings were better and the midweek programme improved, then as a result more people would join, more people would get involved with what we are doing, and therefore all our problems would be solved. Would it surprise you to know that none of this is the case? In fact, if the quality of church services was a mark of the health of a church, the church at Corinth would be the greatest church in the New Testament. Obviously it was not.

Those who love the moving of God's Holy Spirit constantly say "what the church needs is more of the power of God in our meetings". "If there was more of a tangible sense of God's presence, a revival atmosphere, signs and wonders breaking out; then we would have the perfect church". In describing the Corinthian church, Paul says they "do not lack **any** spiritual gift" (1v7). Imagine a church where all nine spiritual gifts are in operation on a regular basis! We would certainly call that a revival atmosphere. And yet despite this, this church is still criticised more than any other New Testament church! Although having the manifest presence of God, and the demonstration of the gifts of the Spirit in our churches is vital, none of that is a guarantee that our churches are healthy.

Well then, some may say, perhaps this church was a little flaky, only interested in moves of the Spirit but they had neglected the teaching of God's Word. What the church needs, some argue, is better teaching. Good, solid, powerful Biblical teaching and preaching is a sure sign of a healthy church. And yet Paul says of the

Corinthians that they had been "enriched in every way...in all your speaking and in all your knowledge". This church clearly had sound Bible teaching that was both inspirational and doctrinally correct. And yet they still had huge problems! Although having great preaching and teaching is vital, again, that in itself is no guarantee of a healthy church.

Perhaps then this church had become self-satisfied, content and prosperous. Perhaps it had taken the message of prosperity to an extreme and everyone was so content with the pleasures of this world that they gave no thought to heaven and the things of eternity. Again, this is not true. Paul writes that they "eagerly wait for our Lord Jesus Christ to be revealed" (1v7). This church had a genuine desire for the coming of Jesus and subsequently a real focus on eternity and living for the Kingdom.

So what was the problem with this church? It was obviously not the quality and spirituality of their church meetings. Neither was it a lack of focus or spiritual devotion on their part. This is a very important lesson for us all. Church is more than meetings. We can have the greatest meetings in the world containing the best teaching and great moves of God's Spirit and yet still be a far cry from the church that God intends. Paul even said that these no doubt powerful meetings, full of revelation, prophecy and the miraculous "did more harm than good" (11v17). Likewise as individuals we can have a real love and hunger for Jesus and still be in serious error. There is a real danger that we can miss out on what God's church really is, just like the Corinthians did.

So what was the problem?

I think one of the clearest descriptions of the Corinthian problem is found in 1 Corinthians 11v18: "When you come together as a church, there are divisions among you". How ironic, in that they thought that they were coming together and yet they were really separate. Although their meetings were superficially powerful, in reality they were powerless, as it was simply a coming together of individuals instead of a united corporate body. This is something Paul mentions over and over again. He even begins the letter by saying "I appeal to you, brothers and sisters, in the name of our Lord Jesus Christ, that all of you agree with one another in what you say and that there be no divisions among you, but that you be perfectly united in mind and thought." (1 Corinthians 1v10)

The unity of the body is the one central theme running throughout the epistle. Paul goes on to address many issues in the church from sexual immorality, to spiritual gifts to the way they took communion, but the key thing he keeps taking them back to, and the main revelation that they need to get is this – you are part of a body. The health and the unity of that body is the most essential thing, far more important than your personal preferences and spirituality. The heart of the epistle is chapter 11 verses 27-34 where Paul gets them to look at themselves as being the Body of Christ. Throughout the epistle he keeps going back to this one theme, you are all the Body of Christ.

The Corinthian church failed to get this key revelation. They simply saw the Church as a group of individuals who met together to have a good service, get their needs met, and exercise their particular gifting and ministry. There was no recognition of the need to benefit others, be united with others and serve others. It was self-seeking rather than a body-building group. As such it receives severe criticism from Paul. And yet sadly, we see much of this in operation in the Church today.

What is communion?

For any church that takes communion on a regular basis, 1 Corinthians 11 is a familiar passage. I well remember, as a child, my pastor quoting the words of Paul each week before the bread and the wine were distributed:

"For I received from the Lord what I also passed on to you: The Lord Jesus, on the night he was betrayed, took bread, and when he had given thanks, he broke it and said, "This is my body, which is for you; do this in remembrance of me." In the same way, after supper he took the cup, saying, "This cup is the new covenant in my blood; do this, whenever you drink it, in remembrance of me." For whenever you eat this bread and drink this cup, you proclaim the Lord's death until he comes."

This was often followed by one of the most controversial and I believe mis-understood parts of Scripture:

"So then, whoever eats the bread or drinks the cup of the Lord in an unworthy manner will be guilty of sinning against the body and blood of the Lord. Everyone ought to examine themselves before they eat of the bread and drink from the cup."

(v27-28)

When this part of the passage was read out, you could almost feel the tension in the air, as we were warned to "examine ourselves" before we took communion. What were we examining ourselves for? Well, obviously to see if we had any sin in our lives. We were warned to let the cup pass us by if we had, as taking communion with sin in our life would result in severe punishment, for "that is why many among you are weak and sick, and a number of you have fallen asleep." (v30)

On occasion, as a boy, I would have a cheeky look round during communion and would observe one or two people refuse to take the bread and the wine. My curiosity was pricked "ah, they have obviously sinned this week! I wonder what they have done!" As I got older and began to fear the Lord, there were occasions when I would refuse communion due to some sin that I had committed that week and the fear that I would "sin against the body and blood of the Lord".

As I have matured though, I have come to realise what a bizarre misunderstanding of scripture the traditional interpretation of 1 Corinthians 11 is. Firstly, nowhere does it tell us that we are examining ourselves to see if there is any sin in our lives. Secondly, if we have committed sin that week, the whole point of taking communion is to remember the blood of Jesus that washes away our sin. Surely if we are convicted of sin, the answer is not to not take communion, but to take it! If we have sinned we need communion more than ever! We need to confess our sin, repent of it and receive the bread and the wine that testify of Jesus' sacrifice on the cross that enables our sins to be forgiven!

So if this passage is nothing to do with personal sin, then what is about? I believe the answer is fairly obvious. Paul says "For those who eat and drink without **discerning the body of Christ** eat and drink judgment on themselves" (v29). Other Bible translations talk about "recognising" or "appreciating" the Body of Christ. The Body of Christ, as Paul repeatedly tells us elsewhere is the Church. A closer examination of the way the Corinthians took communion shows us what the problem was. "So then, when you come together, it is not the Lord's Supper you eat, for when you are eating, some of you go ahead with your own private suppers. As a result, one person remains hungry and another gets drunk." (v20-21)

When the Corinthians took communion (which was part of an actual meal) they did so in a selfish, greedy way. They came together to get their personal needs met, they came to feed themselves. There was no concern that others were not being fed; there was no patience in allowing others to go first; there was no recognition that actually this is not about me, but about the Body. This was a private thing between them and the Lord and no acknowledgement of their brothers or sisters in the Body of Christ took place. In fact, Paul says that although they took communion, they "despised the church of God" (v22).

Paul had already written to them in the previous chapter about what communion is really all about, which is much more than a personal act of devotion to God and a personal act of remembering Jesus. The fact that there is one cup (10v16) and one loaf (v17) is a reminder that there is one Body. Taking communion, eating of the bread, which represents His body, means that we are now partaking of the Body of Christ. It is a recognition that I am not an individual, I am joining together with the Body of which I am a part.

Now we see what communion really is, we can see that the Corinthians were making a mockery of communion by giving no thought to the rest of the Body, which was the very thing that they were there to celebrate. "Examining ourselves" therefore is not to do with unconfessed sin, but to do with examining ourselves to make sure that we are recognising, honouring and appreciating the Body of Christ and the love and unity that we share together. It's not about making sure I am being fed, but about contributing to meeting the needs of others.

Now we see what "sinning against the body and blood" is all about. Don't let communion bypass you if you've told a lie that week, repent and get on with it! But do let communion bypass you if you are not in right relationship with the Body of Christ. Don't take communion if you don't honour and submit to your pastor, if you don't love your brother and sister, if you haven't forgiven that other Christian that hurt you and if you don't love and appreciate your local church, and aren't serving and contributing to the life and well-being of the Body. Otherwise, Paul's warning is very real "that is why many among you are weak and sick, and a number of you have fallen asleep". This may be a controversial view but I have seen it happen time and time again. A failure to discern and appreciate the Body of Christ has led to Christians having to go through some horrendous situations that were never part of God's plan for their lives. Please don't misunderstand me. I am not saying that God necessarily punishes people who take communion in a self-centred, individualistic way, but we must understand that the Body of Christ is our greatest protection. Satan cannot again touch the Body of Jesus Christ, and we are safe from all his attacks as we participate in His Body, through the act of communion. But to take communion and have no appreciation for the Body of Christ is to throw away our protection and leave ourselves potential victims to sickness, spiritual weakness and even premature death.

Signs that we don't recognise The Body

There were several issues surrounding the Corinthian church that led to their failure to recognise the Body of Christ.

1. The separation of the Body

"My brothers and sisters, some from Chloe's household have informed me that there are quarrels among you. What I mean is this: one of you says, 'I follow Paul'; another, 'I follow Apollos'; another, 'I follow Cephas'; still another, 'I follow Christ."

(1 Corinthians 1v11-12)

Rather than seeing the Church as the Body of Christ, they saw the Church as a group of separate, individual ministries and ministers. As a consequence some would recognise the ministry of Paul, but not the ministry of Peter. Some would recognise the ministry of Peter, but not Apollos. Some would say "I follow Christ", perhaps indicating that they "only needed Jesus" and didn't need any human minister. Paul attacks this mind-set in very strong terms "Is Christ divided? Was Paul crucified for you? Were you baptised into the name of Paul?" (v13). The answer of course is that Christ's Body, which they were baptised into, cannot be divided and portioned off into separate ministries and compartments. There is one Body and Paul is trying to get them to see this Body rather than ministries separate from the Body.

In a day when people's ministries are celebrated and promoted, particular via the internet and Christian television, we must remember that we are never told to follow an individual minister or ministry. Paul says this is humanistic thinking and not spiritual: "You are still worldly. For since there is jealousy and quarrelling among you, are you not worldly? Are you not acting like mere humans? For when one says, 'I follow Paul,' and another, 'I follow Apollos,' are you not mere human beings?" (1 Corinthians 3v3-4). We are called to love, serve, honour, give to and be a part of the Body of Christ, not just specific ministers or ministries.

It is also vitally important in a local church setting, where there may exist several leaders, preachers or music ministers, that we understand this principle. Our human nature finds it easy to honour and serve the pastor that we connect with the most, the preacher we find the most inspiring or the worship leader whose style we appreciate the most. Sadly, this can then lead to unfair comparison and criticism against the others who we don't prefer as much. Paul says that this is wrong. We are not to pick and choose which ministers we honour and serve. There is one Body. We love and honour and submit and serve everyone in that Body, otherwise we have totally failed to see what the Church is.

Paul tells us that we have been given much more than just Paul, Apollos and Peter. All things are ours! We have access to every gift, every ministry, and every blessing that is in Christ, who is in God (1 Corinthians 3v21-23). Don't limit yourself by separating the body into individual ministers or ministries. Enjoy all.

It is very important that we don't consider our own ministry as being anything other than a ministry that is part of the Body. More danger is done because of this than anything else in local church life. When we have the attitude "I lead the worship team" or "I run the youth ministry", we have immediately made our ministry a separate entity to the Body of Christ. There are no "departments" in the Church – only one Body. The Corinthians were very proud of their individual ministries (4v6) and failed to see the whole Body of Christ. Sadly, church splits have taken place or great arguments have broken out because people thought their department or ministry was more important than someone else's. Read the New Testament – there is no youth ministry, worship ministry or social action ministry anywhere. There is only the ministry of the Body. Of course, we have own gifting and callings, but we use them to serve the Body. Paul says "*we* are God's fellow workers" (3v9). He never saw his ministry as anything other than that which was part of the Body of Christ and one of a number of other ministries that were all equally necessary and valuable.

2. Disease in the body

Another failure in the Corinthians to recognise the Body of Christ was in their willingness to allow blatant immorality to thrive in their midst. Paul, speaking of a man who was in a sexually immoral relationship with his stepmother, is shocked that this kind of behaviour has not been dealt with and he has not been put out of the fellowship (5v2). Paul is very clear here that he is not talking about non-Christians who come into church with an obviously sinful lifestyle. We are called to love and accept unbelievers of all lifestyles, knowing that God's grace can love and transform them (v9-11). Neither are we talking about Christians who are struggling with sin, but are genuinely trying to be reformed. No, Paul is here talking about a Christian who is in blatant, public sin and refuses to repent or change his behaviour.

What is the problem here? Perhaps the Corinthians thought that this man's behaviour was between him and God, and nothing to do with them. Paul disagreed. Using the analogy of yeast and bread, he says that if one part of the body becomes contaminated the whole body becomes contaminated. If my foot gets gangrene, I can't afford to think "well, that's my foot's problem". It will affect my whole body if not dealt with.

When my wife became pregnant we went to antenatal classes and a whole evening was spent talking about the effects of smoking, illegal drugs and alcohol consumption among pregnant women. Of course, this didn't affect us, but it was amazing how women who were big drinkers suddenly stopped all together once they found out that they were pregnant, or men, who had tried to stop smoking for years, stopped instantly they knew their wives were pregnant. They knew that they couldn't allow anything to damage the body of the little one inside of them and were ruthless in cutting out anything poisonous or harmful for their baby. They now saw themselves as custodians of someone else's body.

As part of the body of Christ we are responsible for keeping His body clean and pure and not allowing anything poisonous into it. Because the Corinthians failed to see the body, they allowed immoral behaviour to go unchallenged as they failed to see the sickness they were allowing into the Body. It amazes me how many Pastors welcome Christians from other churches without ever checking with their previous church as to how and why they left. I have known Christians attack and slander their previous church and leadership, leaving a wake of division and rebellion, only to be welcomed with open arms by the Church down the road. Sometimes these same people have been put into positions of ministry just a few weeks later by pastors who were either foolish enough into thinking their behaviour didn't matter or naïve enough to think that the fault was with the previous church or leader.

There have been occasions when I have dealt with Christians turning up at my church from somewhere else with a real hatred and bitterness towards their previous church or pastor. They refuse to forgive and insist on how they were right and everyone else was wrong. They now carry anger and resentment in their heart and refuse to deal with it. If I don't see the Body of Christ, I can think "well, that's between them and God" and do nothing to confront that attitude. Or I can discern that this is a potentially dangerous and poisonous toxin that is coming into my Body that will pollute every part of the Body unless properly dealt with. There then has to be a gentle and loving suggestion that they make peace with their former leader before they think about joining us and at the very least a phone call to their previous leader for a character reference before we even think about allowing them to be involved in any form of ministry. Of course, the leader who sees Church as a meeting thinks that what I have said is out of date or legalistic nonsense, as for them the bigger the crowd and the more gifted the congregation the better. But the leader who sees the church as the Body of Christ will be in wholehearted agreement knowing that the health of a body is far more important than the size!

3. Lawsuits

Another way in which the Corinthians failed to see the Church as the body of Christ was in their keenness to take each other to court (6v1). The thinking behind a lawsuit is fairly logical. I, as an individual, feel that you as another individual have wronged me in some way so therefore I am doing to take you to court. Paul however cannot understand this concept at all. He doesn't see the Church as a group of individuals but as a united body. Therefore to take another Christian to court is like one part of the body fighting against another part of the body. When one part of the body fights against another part, there are no winners, only losers. Even if I as an individual win, the fact that another part of the Body that I am a part of has lost means that I have lost, as my body has been damaged. This is why Paul tells them that it would be better to be wronged than cause any damage to the Body (6v7).

The practical outworking of this is clear: we are not here to insist that I have my way and oppose and attack anyone who would come against us. We are here to make sure that the Body is healthy. Any behaviour, even if I think it is right, that causes damage to the Body, is a sin against Christ (8v12). This is why Paul writes that "I have become all things to all men so that by all possible means I might save some" (9v22). He was even willing to change his lifestyle that he might be a blessing, and not a hindrance to the Body of Christ.

4. Head covering

All of this brings us to another controversial passage in Corinthians – the section on head covering: "But every woman who prays or prophesies with her head uncovered dishonours her head – it is the same as having her head shaved." (1 Corinthians 11v5) Some conveniently ignore this verse in the Bible, saying it has no relevance to us today. It is a very dangerous ground, though, when we dismiss Bible passages as being culturally irrelevant. The problem most of us have is that we think that Paul is telling women that they cannot prophesy without wearing a hat. That is not what Paul is saying at all. Paul is once again getting them to see the Body and each person's part in that body. The head covering was a sign that the woman was under authority (v10). To prophesy without a head covering was to exercise her gift without any regard to her husband, the church leadership or the need to submit to or recognise the body of Christ. Paul is not making a fashion statement. Paul is not bothered whether the women in your church on Sunday wear a hat or not. What Paul is concerned about, is that women recognise the need to honour, submit to, and respect their husbands, their church leaders, and the wider spiritual body that they are a part of.

This applies not just to women, but men too. Paul goes on to say "In the Lord, however, woman is not independent of man, nor is man independent of woman" (1 Corinthians 11v11). In other words, there is no self-dependence in the Body of Christ but rather interdependence. We need each other!

5. Spiritual gifts

The problem the Corinthian believers had regarding spiritual gifts was not that they didn't have them. As we have already seen they had them all! Neither was it, as some mistakenly think, that they had too many spiritual gifts in operation. Paul actually encourages them to eagerly desire spiritual gifts (14v1). The ignorance (12v1) that they had with the gifts was they failed to see their purpose. The purpose of all spiritual gifts is not to draw attention to ourselves, or to promote our ministry, or make us seem more spiritual than others. The purpose of spiritual gifts is "for the common good" (12v7). They are to benefit the Body. Using spiritual gifts but failing to recognise and appreciate the Body of Christ is a misuse of the gifts. This is why, in-between the two teachings on spiritual gifts, Paul first of all tries to get them to see themselves as part of one body (12v12-31) and then teaches them that without a love for the other members of the body, all gifts are useless (1 Corinthians 13).

The purpose of the revelation gifts like prophecy, is always to strengthen, encourage and comfort the Body of Christ (14v3). Any gift that attacks, tears down and condemns the Body of Christ is not a genuine spiritual gift or it is a misuse of a gift.

Paul writes about the difference between the gift of tongues and the gift of prophecy. He says that the gift of tongues is to build yourself up, but the gift of prophecy is to build the Church up. Paul concludes that, whilst speaking in tongues is important, it is better to prophesy, as it is better to build up the

Church than yourself (14v5). Paul tells us that the whole purpose of desiring the gifts of the Spirit is not to draw attention to ourselves but to build up the Body (14v12). Anybody who only desires that they are built-up is a spiritual infant (14v20). Sadly, we see this all the time, with Christians who desire a spiritual experience or a spiritual gift but have no desire to use that gift or experience to build up the Body.

Paul closes his teaching on spiritual gifts by directing any prophet who is using his gift to submit his gift to the rest of the prophets and be willing to restrain his gift at times for the benefit of the Body (14v26-33). When Paul writes that in the Church everything should be done "in a fitting and orderly way" (v40), in no way is he trying to restrict the moving of God's Spirit or instructing us to be programme-led rather than Presence-driven. The fitting and orderly way is this – let the Holy Spirit have free reign, use all the gifts, desire all the gifts, BUT do everything to benefit the Body, serve the Body, love the Body, submit to the rest of the Body and build up the Body.

6. Change of model

The model that Paul wanted to get the Corinthians to follow is found in chapter 14v26: "What then shall we say, brothers and sisters? When you come together, each of you has a hymn, or a word of instruction, a revelation, a tongue or an interpretation. Everything must be done so that the church may be built up."

The New Testament model was that people didn't go to church to be entertained or watch a show. Instead everyone was part of the Body and therefore everyone had something to contribute. How different is this to our platform-driven church services of today. This was the same problem that the

Corinthians had. The spectacular ministry of a few was celebrated, the ordinary ministry of the many was ignored. Paul said, "No, you are all One Body. You are all a part of this thing we call the Church. You all have something to do, something to give, something to bring". If we see Church as a meeting we attend instead of a living organism that we contribute to, then we have failed to see the Church as the Body of Christ.

Some things never change

By the time we get to 2 Corinthians it seems like the Corinthians still failed to see the Body. Paul has to rebuke them, as the man who they had thrown out of fellowship had now repented. But they still refused to forgive him. Paul tells them to bring him back into the Body (2 Corinthians 2v8). He goes on to outline the New Testament ministry of reconciliation which is at the heart of all Christian ministry (2 Corinthians 5v11-21). The aim of this ministry is not just to get sinners to "make a decision for Jesus" but actually to reconcile them and bring them into the Body of Christ. The famous verse "therefore, if anyone is in Christ, he is a new creation; the old has gone, the new has come" (2 Corinthians 5v17) is not actually to do with us seeing ourselves as new creations. The context is all about seeing others as new creations, and forgiving, welcoming, and accepting each other and uniting together as one Body.

Sadly, the Corinthians don't seem to have managed this! Paul ends his second letter by rebuking them because of their quarrels, jealousy, anger, factions, slander, gossip, arrogance and disorder (2 Corinthians 12v20). In other words, everyone was just concerned about themselves and not about the Body.

Conclusion

1 Corinthians 16 ends with a command and an urging. The command is to love one another (v14), the urging is to submit to one another (v16). Both command and urging are designed to encourage us to focus, as individuals, on something bigger than ourselves: the Body of Jesus Christ, whose members we are called to love, honour, appreciate and submit to.

The Corinthians, for all their wonderful church services, failed to see this vital reality. Let's continue to look at Paul's teaching to see how we can avoid their problem.

13

HONOURING THE BODY

"And He is the head of the body, the Church."

(Colossians 1v18)

The revelation of the Church as the Body of Christ runs throughout Paul's letters in the New Testament. Whatever our views and opinions are of Church, we cannot ignore God's view and opinion. When God looks at the Church, He recognises it as the Body of Christ. Jesus is the Head and His Body is comprised of every Church member. It is vital that we see this because it has very important consequences as to how we will treat, value and recognise the Church.

The image of a body is something that we can all relate to because we all have one. If we don't, we are dead! Therein lies the most simple and basic truth that we must grasp if we are to see the Church as God sees it. You cannot separate the head from a body and expect it to live. Likewise, the Church cannot separate itself from the Lordship of Jesus. Without Jesus, we cease to exist. Churches that abandon their love for and recognition of Jesus have their candlestick removed (Revelation 2v5). However, in the same way that body and head cannot be separated, it is equally true that body part and body part cannot be separated. Many Christians have a strange view that they can be in right relationship with the Body as a whole whilst not being in right relationship with certain other members or parts of the Body. Still others have an even stranger idea that they can remain in right relationship with Jesus but not be a part of His Body.

God uses the analogy of a body because it is simple to grasp - and yet how many of us don't grasp it? If any part of my body decides to become disconnected to any other part of my body, the result is pain and a lack of function. If a part of my body becomes totally separate from the rest of my body, although my body may continue to function, the separated body part will die. Take (for example) my arm. Imagine I decided to take an axe and chop off my arm. The first result would be intense pain to the rest of my body. Now, through medical help, the pain would eventually go away but now I would be severely limited in performing certain tasks. And what about the arm itself? It would not feel the pain that the rest of my body felt at the point of separation because it would be dead! No matter how much I love my arm, no matter how useful it may be, my arm only has life when it is connected to my body. No body = no life. Likewise, a Christian only has the life of God flowing into them when they are a part of the Body. A Christian that decides to refrain from relationship with one or more members of the Body of Christ, through un-forgiveness, jealousy, minor doctrinal arguments etc. immediately brings pain to the entire Body. A Christian that decides to walk away from the Body of Christ may not feel any worse off because of it. However, after a while they will spiritually die. It is impossible to remain spiritually alive without a spiritual connection to the Body of Christ. The book of James tells us "the body without the spirit is dead" (2v26). Likewise, it can be said that the spirit (our human spirit) is dead without the Body.

How does all of this affect our relationship with Jesus? Again, if we see the Church as the Body of Christ, it makes things very simple. The head enables the rest of my body to function, but each member of my body is only connected to my head as it is connected to the other parts of my body. So imagine, my big toe loves being connected to my head, but hates all the other toes! It decides to become separate from all the other toes. What then happens to its relationship with my head? Simply put, there is none! My big toe only receives the life that comes from the head for as long as it stays attached to my foot. In the same way, Christians who think that they can remain connected to Jesus and be disconnected from the Body are deluded. The life that comes from the Head flows into us as we remain part of the Body.

In speaking of the birth of Christ, the book of Hebrews says "a body you have prepared for me" (Hebrews 10v5). Although Jesus was the Lamb of God, slain before the foundation of the world, He could not come to earth and begin His ministry of salvation without God preparing a body for Him to dwell in. If God Himself knows the importance of abiding in a body, how much more should you and I? In some ways, abiding in a body would have been a very frustrating and limiting experience for Jesus. Abiding in a body, Jesus would have felt tiredness, hunger and weakness. Abiding in a body, God would experience temptation for the first time. Abiding in a body, God would have been limited to time and geographical boundaries. And yet, without abiding in a body, Jesus could never have taken away the sins of the world, because it was the death and subsequent resurrection of that body that brought salvation to us. Likewise for us, we can often find it very frustrating having to be in relationship with other Christians. Having to submit to and serve a local church and acknowledge leadership and spiritual authority can at times be very limiting. The thought of breaking away and doing our own thing and living a form of Christianity that is purely private rather than public is a genuine temptation at times. Let's face it, being part of a Church exposes you to pain, betrayal, disappointment and hurt more than anything else in life. And yet, quite simply, the Body of Christ is still the method God uses to bring salvation and life to the world. In being a part of His Body, for all the pain and frustration and limitation it can cause, it is the only way to receive God's life and salvation - and the only way we become a conduit of that life and salvation to the world.

Discerning the Body

As we looked at in the previous chapter, Paul's first letter to the Corinthians is all about trying to get them to discern, see and recognise the Body of Christ rather than their own individual needs and wants. I believe that the heartbeat of the letter is chapter 12 verses 12-27. Paul spells out the revelation of the Body very clearly to us; and as much as it was important for the Corinthians to see this in their day, it is equally important for us to grasp it in our day.

"Just as a body, though one, has many parts, but all its many parts from one body, so it is with Christ." Paul here makes plain the simple truth that the Church is the Body of Christ. As the Church cannot function without Christ, there is also a sense in which Christ cannot "function" without His Church. Christ and His Church are joined, united and bonded together. Likewise each member of His Church is joined, united and bonded together with every other member of the Body and in doing so are joined, united and bonded together with Jesus.

"For we were all baptised by one Spirit so as to form one body" (v13). Here we see the true purpose of baptism. I was baptised at my local church when I was twelve years old and had to go through a baptism course beforehand to make sure that I properly understood what baptism was. Sadly, I don't think I did fully understand and the course didn't help! The emphasis was always on baptism as an affirmation of our personal commitment to Christ. Baptism (I was told) was a public confession of a personal faith, symbolic of my sins being washed away and my new resurrected life in Christ. Whilst all of this is true, baptism is much more than this. Baptism is not just a symbolic act, but a very important spiritual reality. Baptism is a recognition that I have died to sin and this world and have been buried with Christ. However, baptism is also me being baptised into something. That something is the Body of Christ, the Church. That is perhaps why salvation was always immediately followed by baptism in the New Testament, because the apostles recognised that the moment someone confessed Jesus as Saviour they needed to be baptised into, and become, part of His Body, the Church. This is why it is ludicrous to say that you no longer want to be part of the Church. To walk away from the Church is to somehow "un-baptise" yourself - as if that were even possible!

"Even so the body is not made up of one part but of many." (v14) Paul here recognises the diversity that there is in the Body. In fact, it is diversity that makes our bodies complete. Being united in the Body of Christ does not mean that we become robots, where we all think, feel, say and do the same things. We all have different personalities, ministries and gifting. Each church differs in style. Being part of the Body of Christ is choosing to belong and unite, in spite of our differences.

"Now if the foot should say, "Because I am not a hand, I do not belong to the body," it would not for that reason stop being part of the body." (v15) Now here is a scary truth … just because a part of my body says that it isn't a part of my body, that doesn't mean that it isn't. Also, just because a part of my body may feel that it isn't part of my body, that doesn't mean it isn't either. Feelings or desire don't come into it. My body is connected whether it likes it or not. Over the years I have heard many Christians say things like "I don't feel a part of this church" or "I'm not sure I really fit in here". The truth is, that in receiving Jesus we have become part of His Body in a very real way. Our saying that we aren't a part of the Body of Christ doesn't mean that we aren't. Even feeling that we aren't a part of the Body of Christ doesn't mean that we aren't.

Many Christians make the mistake of talking about the Church as if it is somehow separate to them. I recently read a blog from a Christian writer about the problems he had with "the church". That is as bizarre as my leg talking about the problems it has with "Andrew Murray". My leg belongs to Andrew Murray; it is a part of me, not separate to me. Any Christian who talks about "The Church" as anything separate to themselves has failed to see the Church as their body. When we talk about the Church, whether good or bad, Christians should always speak of "us" and "we" rather than "the" and "them". The Church is us! We cannot stop being part of the Body unless we stop following Jesus altogether.

"And if the ear should say, "Because I am not an eye, I do not belong to the body," it would not for that reason stop being part of the body. If the whole body were an eye, where would the sense of hearing be? If the whole body were an ear, where would the sense of smell be? But in fact God has placed the parts in the body, every one of them, just as he wanted them to be. If they were all one part, where would the body be?" (v16-19) Here we see three important principles, the first one being that God has placed you in His Body. The Greek word here for "place" means "to set, to put, to be placed by order, command or design". The Bible here is showing us that you are not part of His Body by chance or design. Neither are your gifts and callings given to you haphazardly. No, God deliberately placed you where He wanted you in the Body and deliberately gave you the gifts and callings that you have. To argue about where you are and what you do and to negatively compare yourself with others is a case of the clay arguing with the potter.

The second thing we see in this verse is that each member of the Body has a purpose in being there. For the eye it is to see, for the nose it is to smell, for the ear it is to hear. Likewise, for every member of Christ's body, God has a plan and a purpose. God has a ministry, a work and a role for all.

The third thing we see in these verses is that purpose is only found in the Body and never in isolation. A mouth on its own is pretty useless, but connected to a body it suddenly has a vital role to play in helping the rest of the body communicate and take in food among other things. In the same way, our purpose can only truly be discovered in connectivity to the Body.

"The eye cannot say to the hand, "I don't need you!" And the head cannot say to the feet, "I don't need you!" (v21) Paul is very blunt in his language here. No member of the Body can say that it doesn't need another member of the body. Paul very plainly says this cannot happen. It is totally unbiblical and foolish for any Christian to say that they do not need the Church. It is spiritual suicide to decide that we no longer need to be a part of Christ's body. We simply cannot function without it.

"On the contrary, those parts of the body that seem to be weaker are indispensable, and the parts that we think are less honourable we treat with special honour. And the parts that are unpresentable are treated with special modesty, while our presentable parts need no special treatment. But God has put the body together, giving greater honour to the parts that lacked it." (v22-24)

Here we see the contrast between God and man and are once again amazed by the beauty of God's grace. As humans we tend to value people according to what we deem to be their usefulness. Often we determine this by their gifts and the benefit we get out of them. Others that we see as being less useful we tent to set aside and dis-count. When it comes to honour we tend to honour the gifted, the talented and those that seem to have it all together. But God is the opposite of this! God recognises and values every member of His Body. Those that man says are weak and insignificant, God says are indispensable. God delights to give special grace to those who are in the background, His hidden saints, unknown by man, but special in His sight. God loves to honour the broken and the unlovable. He delights in showing favour to the undeserved. Thank God! God makes sure that every member of His Body is honoured.

God's Promises

If we are truly to honour the Body of Christ then we must understand that God Himself honours the Body of Christ. There are wonderful promises in the scriptures that are connected to the Body. Many of them are found in the letter to the Ephesians.

1. Jesus died for the Body

"For he himself is our peace, who has made the two groups one and has destroyed the barrier, the dividing wall of hostility, by setting aside in his flesh the law with its commands and regulations. His purpose was to create in himself one new humanity out of the two, thus making peace, and in one body to reconcile both of them to God through the cross, by which he put to death their hostility." (Ephesians 2v14-16)

In thinking of the cross, we often emphasise the personal aspect of our redemption. Jesus loved me, Jesus died for me, Jesus saved me. It is true that even if we were the only person on the planet Jesus would still have shed His blood for us. However, this is just one aspect of the cross. The other aspect is that through the cross, we could be united together as the Body of Christ. Jesus didn't just die to save individuals. Jesus died to form a new Body, His Church. He died so that the many could become one in Him.

2. Jesus gives access to His Body

"For through him we both have access to the Father by one Spirit." (
Ephesians 2v18)

One of the most amazing things about Christianity is that it is not a formal religion but a real and living relationship with our Abba. The promise here in Ephesians 2 is that through the Holy Spirit we now have intimate access to the Father. We can know Him, talk to Him, listen to His voice and abide in His presence. Interestingly in the context here, Paul is talking about the Body. The promise is to the Body. God promises His corporate Body complete, unhindered access to His throne of grace.

3. The Body partakes of Jesus

"This mystery is that through the gospel the Gentiles are heirs together with Israel, members together of one body, and sharers together in the promise in Christ Jesus." (Ephesians 3v6)

Notice that this promise is to the corporate Body. All that is Christ's He shares with His Body - His promises, covenants, blessings, favour and goodness. He gives His Body His Spirit, His presence, His Word, His blood, His power and His anointing. Jesus enables His body to partake of His divine nature. This is why Communion is so important. 1 Corinthians tells us that "is not the bread that we break a participation in the body of Christ? Because there is one loaf, we, who are many, are one body, for we all share the one loaf." (1 Corinthians 10v16-17) Paul is not directing our attention here to seeing the bread itself as having mystical properties. He is encouraging us to see the Body, which is what the bread represents. Communion is a process of participating in true fellowship and unity with each other and as such we feed on Christ Himself, enjoying His blessings and His presence.

4. Jesus gives authority to His Body

"And God placed all things under his feet and appointed him to be head over everything for the church, which is his body, the fullness of him who fills everything in every way." (Ephesians 1v22-23)

Jesus is above everything in heaven, in earth and under the earth. Jesus has supreme authority to rule and to reign. He is above death, disease, sin, satan and all the powers of hell. But God doesn't just crown the Head, He crowns the whole Body too. A monarch may wear a crown on their head, but that gives their whole person the right to rule. The Body of Christ shares the authority of the One who is crowned with many crowns and each member of His Body has the right to rule and to reign in life (Romans 5v17)

5. God strengthens His Body

> "So Christ himself gave the apostles, the prophets, the evangelists, the pastors and teachers, to equip his people for works of service, so that the body of Christ may be built up until we all reach unity in the faith and in the knowledge of the Son of God and become mature, attaining to the whole measure of the fullness of Christ ... Instead, speaking the truth in love, we will grow to become in every respect the mature body of him who is the head, that is, Christ." *(Ephesians 4v11-13, 15)*

At the centre of all God's plans and purposes is the Body of Christ. God gives gifts to His Church, He equips His Church, unites His Church, gives knowledge to His Church and matures His Church. The purpose of it all is that the Body would become like the Head, that we would attain to the whole measure of the fullness of Christ. There is no one individual who can be fully like Jesus of course, but as a corporate Body that is what we are growing into. Because of this, we can never be like Jesus without each other. We need each other to become what we were destined to be – like Jesus.

God hates division

Now that we can see how much God values and loves His Body, we can perhaps understand a little more clearly why God hates any trace of division in His Body. The Bible warns us time and again about those who would try and bring division into the Body of Christ. Paul tells us very clearly in Titus 3v10 "Warn a divisive person once, and then warn them a second time. After that, have nothing to do with them."
Bringing division into the Body of Christ can be something that can be very blatant and it can also be something that is very subtle. People who speak against leadership, who refuse to submit to authority, who slander, gossip and judge are all obviously bringing division into the Body of Christ. If we carry jealousy, unforgiveness and bitterness in our hearts, we are again obviously bringing division into the Church which is clearly wrong.

However, being a divisive person doesn't just mean that we are deliberately trying to attack the Body. Going back to 1 Corinthians 12, Paul tells is in verse 25 that division is caused when people have a greater concern over one part of the Body over another. When people are only concerned about their ministry, their vision, their happiness and their needs being met, they are actually bringing division into the Body. Any ministry or church department that is concerned only for itself rather than the needs of the overall Body is a divisive Body member.

Being divisive can be even more subtle than that. Paul goes on to say "If one part suffers, every part suffers with it; if one part is honoured, every part rejoices with it. Now you are the body of Christ, and each one of you is a part of it." (v26-27) Apathy may to us be a passive noun, but according to the Bible it is an active verb. In not doing something, you are actually bringing division to the Body. A failure to care, to suffer, to rejoice, to empathise with others, to distance yourself emotionally from the other members of the Church is to actually be a divisive person, as others will undoubtedly care about your lack of empathy.

In 1 Kings 2 there is the famous account of two prostitutes who come to King Solomon to enquire of his wisdom. One of the women explains that during the night, the other woman accidently smothered her baby. Dismayed by her actions, she switches her dead baby for her friends live one. The second woman claims that this is a lie, that the live baby always belonged to her. There was no proof as to who the baby belonged to, as this was well before DNA testing, and Solomon needed some godly wisdom. Solomon's solution is to ask for a sword. He proposes that he will cut the baby in half and give half to one woman and half to the other. The woman whose baby had died was happy with this arrangement. However, the true mother was horrified by this suggestion. She knew that to bring division and separation to the body was also to bring death. She willingly offers to give up her son to the other woman, allowing him to live. Solomon now knows which woman is telling the truth: the real mother is the one who wanted to preserve the unity of the body even if it meant giving up her rights. The principle here is that division in the body always brings death. The only way to keep the life in the Body is to keep the Body united. The person who truly sees the Church as the Body of Christ and truly honours the Church as Jesus does, is the person who will willingly give up their rights and their desires so that the Church can remain a united body.

In speaking of the Church as the Body, God always emphasises the one-ness aspect: "There is one body and one Spirit, just as you were called to one hope when you were called." (Ephesians 4v4) There is only one Body; this is something that the New Testament clearly teaches. There are no denominations in heaven, only one Body. Any separation between races, genders, classes, ages, nationality or whatever else we use to divide the Body of Christ up, does not advance the cause of the Kingdom but only destroys it. We are told over and over again to make sure we keep the Body as one: "Therefore each of you must put off falsehood and speak truthfully to your neighbour, for we are all members of one body." (Ephesians 4v25); "Let the peace of Christ rule in your hearts, since as members of one body you were called to peace." (Colossians 3v15)

Our need of the Body

"And he took bread, gave thanks and broke it, and gave it to them, saying, "This is my body given for you; do this in remembrance of me." (Luke 22v19)

A friend of mine, Pastor Billy Price, who leads a church in Cincinnati, Ohio, teaches on this passage explaining that Jesus gave His disciples both the bread and the wine during the Last Supper. In doing this Jesus was showing them that they needed both the Body and the Blood and needed to be continually reminded of their need for both. Sadly, many Christians only celebrate the blood of Jesus, and recognise their need for the blood of Jesus. We cannot be saved without the precious blood of Christ, but Jesus never told them that the wine was the only thing necessary or that the blood was the only thing they needed to remember. Equally, they needed the bread, the Body. They needed to partake of the Body, feed on the Body and remember the Body. They couldn't have one without the other. Thank God for the precious blood of Jesus, but let us also acknowledge our need for the Body of Christ too, the Church. Both are equally important in God's plan of salvation. One would be powerless without the other. Church attendance without receiving the forgiveness found in Jesus' blood cannot save us; likewise, receiving God's forgiveness whilst rejecting His Body means we are rejecting God's method of protecting, strengthening and maturing us.

Hate or honour?

There are two contrasting attitudes towards the Body of Christ. The first is found in Ephesians 5v29:

"After all, no one ever hated their own body, but they feed and care for their body, just as Christ does the church"

There are two things to point out in this verse. The first is that Christ feeds and cares for the Church because we are His Body. The second is that as the Body of Christ, how can we possibly hate the Church? Love here is shown as feeding and caring, so hatred can be shown by actively attacking or simply neglecting. When we neglect the Church, for whatever reason, it is akin to neglecting to eat or clean ourselves. Ultimately, the person most damaged will be ourselves.

The correct way to treat the Body of Christ is found in Chapter 26 of Matthew's gospel:

"While Jesus was in Bethany in the home of Simon the Leper, a woman came to him with an alabaster jar of very expensive perfume, which she poured on his head as he was reclining at the table. When the disciples saw this, they were indignant. "Why this waste?" they asked. "This perfume could have been sold at a high price and the money given to the poor."Aware of this, Jesus said to them, "Why are you bothering this woman? She has done a beautiful thing to me. The poor you will always have with you, but you will not always have me. When she poured this perfume on my body, she did it to prepare me for burial. Truly I tell you, wherever this gospel is preached throughout the world, what she has done will also be told, in memory of her." (v6-13)

At great personal expense, this woman poured perfume on the body of Jesus. She showed special love and concern for the body of Christ and made sure it was taken care of and honoured in a way that was considered extravagant to many. I am sure that the disciples of Jesus would have claimed to have loved Him, yet they were not concerned about His body. They even claimed that the anointing of His body was a waste. Yet true lovers of Jesus know that there is no greater expression of love and devotion to the Master than to honour His Body and to show respect to His Body. There is no greater use of our time and resources than to pour ourselves out for the sake of His Body. When we truly devote ourselves to the Body of Christ, others will criticise us. Even followers of Jesus will question our motives and the use of our time and money. "Surely there are better things to be doing in life than giving all your time to the Church?" Jesus defended this woman publicly. Jesus will always defend those who love His body. He said that what she did was "a beautiful thing". There is nothing more beautiful in the eyes of Jesus than our ministry to His Body and our love for His Body. Jesus made sure that this woman was honoured and that she would be remembered forever in His Word. The feeding of the poor was a legitimate need and a legitimate ministry, but this woman refused to be drawn away from serving His Body. All true lovers of Jesus know that all ministry begins with ministry to His Body before anything else. If we desire to draw the favour and attention of Jesus, then let us be willing to sacrifice ourselves for the sake of His Body and to give our lives in poured out devotion to His Church.

Conclusion

In this chapter we have looked at how God honours the Body of Christ, the Church, and how we must do likewise. Next, we will look at how each member of the Body is called to serve one another and how this is key to the growth of the Church.

14

SERVING THE BODY

"… to equip His people for works of service, so that
the body of Christ may be built up … "

(Ephesians 4v12)

The understanding of the thoughts and principles in this chapter is essential for any Christian who wants to be part of a growing and thriving church. In the verse above, Paul writes about the Body of Christ, the Church, being "built up". No doubt Paul was talking here about a church growing not only numerically, but spiritually. Paul says that the way that this happens is when God's people are equipped to serve. This is something he repeats again just a few verses later:

"From him the whole body, joined and held together by every supporting ligament,
grows and builds itself up in love, as each part does its work." (Ephesians 4v16)

Notice two key words here are "grows" and "builds". Surely the desire of every Christian – leaders, especially - is to be part of a church that is both growing numerically and being built into what God wants it to be. I have often been asked in leadership forums, "How do you think we can grow the local church?" Thousands of leaders every year attend "church growth" seminars to find out the latest tricks and techniques in how to grow and build their church. Yet Paul tells us very clearly in the

Bible what grows and builds a church. In verse twelve he tells us that this happens when God's people begin to do "works of service", whilst in verse sixteen he talks about each part of the body doing "its work".

The truth of the Bible is that the local church does not grow and is not built up by church meetings. That is a modern cultural idea, not a New Testament Biblical model. Though essential, great preaching, powerful worship, a relevant programme and moves of the Holy Spirit are in themselves not going to grow and build the Body of Christ. The Body of Christ grows when every member of that Body begins to serve, begins to be active and begins to get involved in service and ministry.

Paul is again using the analogy of a body and talking about the members of the Body (me and you) being like supporting ligaments. Any ligament or muscle that isn't used for a long period of time grows weaker and weaker. Sadly, there are many like this in the Church today. They may attend church every week, but aren't actually committed to any form of service or ministry. As they become less and less active in serving the Body with every passing year, every area of their spiritually begins to weaken. In the natural, how do you begin to grow your body, strengthen and develop those muscles and ligaments? You get to work! You run, you lift weights, you exercise, and you put your body to work. We even call it a "work out". The more your body works, the stronger and healthier it becomes (I am feeling convicted just writing this!) It is exactly the same with the Body of Christ. As each member of the Body gets to work, serving one another, "supporting one another", the local church gets stronger and healthier and begins to grow.

A lazy church is a dead church. An active church is a growing, thriving church. Although every church needs the ministry of gifted men and women preaching and teaching the Word, it is actually the intention of God that His Body "builds itself up", not sit around thinking that it is the Pastor's job to build the church. How do we build up the Church? By serving, by working, by doing.

This concept goes against a lot of modern Ecclesiology, where people treat church as though they are going to the movies or attending a concert – a place to unwind at the end of a week, entertained by the musicians and preacher. Having received and eaten our fill from God's restaurant, we pay the bill, give our compliments to the chef and go home, returning the following week for more of the same. As we look through the Bible, we can see how alien this is to the New Testament church. The truth is, we are all here to serve. Church is not a restaurant where we eat and eat and get fatter and fatter, but a gymnasium where each member of the Body is put to work and in doing so gets stronger and healthier. If Church were a restaurant, God would have us in the kitchen or waiting on tables, not sitting down tucking in! The idea of attending merely to receive and be served is abhorrent to New Testament Christianity.

The modern consumerist approach to church means that people have seen themselves as customers rather than a Body. "I didn't like it this morning", "I wasn't too keen on the music today", "I didn't really enjoy Pastor's message today" are all typical comments from people who have failed to see the Church as the Body of Christ. We are not here to enjoy it: we are here to be a part of it. We are not here to critique it: we are here to serve it. I often heard Christians say, "I didn't get anything out of the meeting today" and I wonder "what did they *put into* the meeting today?!" A selfish Christian believes that the life of their church revolves around them - *their* needs, *their* desires, *their* preferences. Christians who think like that get upset when the Pastor doesn't shake their hand, or offended when no one has visited them when they were sick. A biblical Christian takes their eyes off themselves and places them on others. This is not about me getting from others, it is about me serving others, visiting others, encouraging others, loving others, giving to others.
Seeing the Church as the Body of Christ means I see myself as being placed in the

Church to serve the rest of the Body and that I have a work to do. Paul says in Romans 12v4-8:

"For just as each of us has one body with many members, and these members do not all have the same function, so in Christ we, though many, form one body, and each member belongs to all the others. We have different gifts, according to the grace given to each of us. If your gift is prophesying, then prophesy in accordance with your faith; if it is serving, then serve; if it is teaching, then teach; if it is to encourage, then give encouragement; if it is giving, then give generously; if it is to lead, do it diligently; if it is to show mercy, do it cheerfully."

Paul is not talking about the pastor or the board of elders; he is talking about every member of the Body; he is talking about me and you. He says that every member of the Body has a "function". We all have something to do. The context here is not serving God outside church, in our secular jobs, although of course we do that as well (our whole lives are to be given in service to God), but he is speaking specifically about functioning and serving within the Body of Christ. We have all been given gifts to use and, summing up what Paul is saying here, "get on with it!" Whatever your gift, use it to serve the Body of Christ.

The honour of service

Today's modern church glamorises the pulpit and gifted leaders and ministers can often become overnight celebrities within the Christian world. That means that we often aspire to become "a leader" because they are the ones honoured and blessed by God. Actually the word leader is only mentioned six times in the King James Version of the Bible. The word servant, however, is used over nine hundred times!

Abraham, Moses, Isaac, Jacob, Caleb, Joshua, Hannah, Samuel, David, Solomon, the priests, Nehemiah, Job, many of the prophets, Elijah, Hezekiah, Mary, Paul, the disciples, Timothy – what do they have in common? They were all called servants of God. Sometimes, when I have asked people to describe their ministry, what God has called them to do, their heads have dropped with embarrassment: "I just serve". Let me tell you, if you serve, you are in pretty good company!

Elijah said " … as surely as the Lord lives, whom I serve … " (1 Kings 18v25) whilst Paul said "Last night an angel of the God to whom I belong and whom I serve stood beside me … " (Acts 27v23). These two men are almost boasting, proud of the fact that are simple servants of God. Their glory was not in the task, but in the One that they were doing it for.

James and Jude were both apostles and were actually the half brothers of Jesus - two pretty big titles that they could have boasted about - "Brother of Jesus" looks pretty good on the website! Yet, both of them are happy and content to refer to themselves as servants of Christ in their epistles. The Psalmist said, "I would rather be a doorkeeper in the house of my God than dwell in the tents of the wicked." (Psalm 84v10) It might have been the most menial of tasks, but for the Psalmist, serving God, serving in His house, was an honour to be prized above all others.

No matter how gifted or anointed we are (or claim to be), let us never think that we are too high or too great to serve someone. When speaking of God's children in heaven, the book of Revelation describes us as "servants" who "serve Him". (Revelation 22v3) Even with a resurrected, glorified body, we are still going to be serving. We never get promoted beyond serving. Some Christians think that serving is where we start, then we get promoted to leader, then senior leader and then an apostle etc. No! We start out serving, we continue serving and we spend all eternity serving.
Serving within the church is the greatest honour that there is. Romans 12 talks about the gift of serving. Numbers 18v7 tells us that the Levites were "given the service of the priesthood as a gift". We must never see serving within church as a burden or

inconvenience; we should never look at those on the platform or in public ministry and become jealous or bitter. If God has called us to serve, it is not a task He has burdened us with, but a gift He has bestowed upon us.

Service is the example of Christ

"Jesus said to them, "The kings of the Gentiles lord it over them; and those who exercise authority over them call themselves Benefactors. But you are not to be like that. Instead, the greatest among you should be like the youngest, and the one who rules like the one who serves. For who is greater, the one who is at the table or the one who serves? Is it not the one who is at the table? But I am among you as one who serves." (Luke 22v25-27)

"For even the Son of Man did not come to be served, but to serve, and to give his life as a ransom for many." (Mark 11v45)

If anyone had the right to demand that people serve Him it was Jesus, God's Son, God-Himself - and yet Jesus gave His life to serving others. When Isaiah prophesied about Jesus hundreds of years before His birth he described Him as "the servant of the Lord" and "the suffering servant". Whether it was His parents, His disciples, the crowds He ministered to, Jesus was always serving.

Perhaps the greatest example of Jesus serving is found in John 13. The Bible tells us that it was here that Jesus showed His disciples "the full extent of His love" (v1). How? He would serve them. Love's greatest manifestation is in service. The passage goes on to describe how Jesus would take off His rabbi's cloak, the very cloak that the sick had touched and received healing through, and began to wash His disciples feet. Jesus was secure enough in who He was - "Jesus knew that the Father had put all things under His power" (v3) - that He was prepared to lay aside the thing that outwardly identified Him as a teacher and a miracle worker and expose the heart that was behind it all, the heart of a servant. Never try and spiritualise the washing of the disciples feet by saying He was "washing them with the Word" or "cleansing them with the Holy Spirit", although the passage can be applied that way. No, this was a very real situation, with very real people who had dirty, messy, smelly feet and Jesus served them. The moral of the story? "You should do as I have done." (v15)

This reminds me of the famous passage in Philippians where Paul talks about Jesus "taking the very nature of a servant" (2v7) and exhorting us to have the same attitude (v5). Hebrews tells us that Jesus is a High Priest, not in the order of Levi but in the order of Melchizedek (Hebrews 5v10). When reading about Melchizedek in Genesis 14, you don't find Abram bringing gifts and offerings to him, as was the case with the Levitical priesthood. Instead, you find Melchizedek serving Abram, bringing him bread and wine. This is the example of our Great High Priest, Jesus, the servant of the Lord, who didn't come demanding anything of anyone, but who came and gave His whole life away in service. We must understand that we are never more like Jesus than when we are serving others.

We are saved to serve

"How much more, then, will the blood of Christ, who through the eternal Spirit offered himself unblemished to God, cleanse our consciences from acts that lead to death, so that we may serve the living God!" (Hebrews 9v14)

According to this verse, one of the very reasons why Jesus died on the cross and shed His blood was so that we could serve God. The Bible is very clear; God expects every one of us to serve Him in some way. Romans 12 talks about our "reasonable act of service" in response to God's mercy. Giving our time and energy in serving the Body of Christ should never be considered some great sacrifice or heroic endeavour on our part. On the contrary, it is quite reasonable that this is the fruit of our understanding of all that Jesus has done for us.

I love the words of Jesus in Luke 17:

> *"Suppose one of you has a servant ploughing or looking after the sheep. Will he say to the servant when he comes in from the field, 'Come along now and sit down to eat'? Won't he rather say, 'Prepare my supper, get yourself ready and wait on me while I eat and drink; after that you may eat and drink'? Will he thank the servant because he did what he was told to do? So you also, when you have done everything you were told to do, should say, 'We are unworthy servants; we have only done our duty.'"* (Luke 17v7-10)

What Jesus is saying here is that even after performing menial task after menial task, a servant doesn't expect a standing ovation, celebration or even a "thank you" because of what they have done. They don't expect anything. They serve because they are servants. Many in the Body of Christ feel that after they do something for God or the Church they are now entitled to something. Many become bitter, complaining that "no-one ever thanks me for all I do for the church", "no-one honours me", "no-one appreciates me in that church". Others get angry because they saw their act of service as the first step towards promotion to a more public ministry. Whilst it is good to honour and appreciate those who serve in the church, those of us serving must never expect his. We must never serve for the applause of man, future promotion or even the acknowledgement that we are doing a good job. Serving is both our duty and our privilege, not a bargaining chip or a way to receive praise. Neither should we serve God because our lives are dull and unproductive and we want something to do. If your life is boring – get a hobby! If you understand all God has done for you – get serving!

The greatest command God gave His people in the Old Testament was to "serve the Lord your God with all your heart and with all your soul" (Deuteronomy 10v12). The Hebrew word for serve is the word "abad" and it can also be translated as "to minister", "to work", or "to worship". I remember once a lady in church asking to be removed from a particular service rota that required her to miss the worship part of the meeting, as she felt like she was missing out. She failed to recognise that, by serving the Body, she was worshipping God more than she could by singing songs! One of our greatest acts of worship is to serve the Body of Christ.

Service is a lifestyle

One complaint that I often hear Christians make is that within their local church they are never asked to do anything. "I just don't feel like I am being used" is a phrase frequently uttered by those who are waiting on the pastor to give them something to do, who understand service as "a task" and "a position" rather than a lifestyle and an outflow of love and generosity. It isn't about what you do, it's about who you are. True servants are not those who wait for the pastor to give them a job, but those who give away their entire lives away as laid down lovers of Christ, His Church and the lost. Serving is never about a job we do, it is always about a lifestyle. It is what comes out of our hearts.

" … whoever wants to become great among you must be your servant … " (Matthew 20v26). Notice that is not about "doing" service, it is about "being" a servant. There is a big difference!

Jesus tells us in Luke 12 to "be dressed ready for service" (v35). The King James phrases the word "dressed" as "let your waist be girded". In the custom of the day, Jewish men would wear long flowing robes. When they were about to perform a menial task of service, they would tuck their robes in around their waist. When the task had been completed they would un-tuck their robes and let them hang loose again. This is what Jesus is referring to here, although notice He never tells us to untuck our robes. Instead our robes are to be always girded; we are to always be ready to serve. Our natural posture is that of a servant.

The Amplified version of Colossians 3 sums up the heart of a servant:

"Servants, obey in everything those who are your earthly masters, not only when their eyes are on you as pleasers of men, but in simplicity of purpose [with all your heart] because of your reverence for the Lord and as a sincere expression of your devotion to Him. Whatever may be your task, work at it heartily (from the soul), as [something done] for the Lord and not for men, Knowing [with all certainty] that it is from the Lord [and not from men] that you will receive the inheritance which is your [real] reward. [The One Whom] you are actually serving [is] the Lord Christ (the Messiah)." (v22-24)

The rewards of service

As we have already said, we should never serve God to get anything, but serve in response to who He is and all that He has given us. Saying that, the Bible promises wonderful rewards to those who, without any other motive than love, serve their God and His Body.

The first thing to understand is that God sees every act of service that we do for His Body. I remember being quite amused when reading the list of all David's leaders, officers, mighty men etc in his kingdom to find that listed among all the great and important people were Obil, who was in charge of the camels; and Jehdeiah, who was in charge of the donkeys (1 Chronicles 27v30.) How bizarre that God would make a note, in His Word, of those who looked after the camels and the donkeys! Perhaps God is showing us here that He notices and records the ministry of every one of his servants, no matter how boring or mundane the task appears to be.

The second thing to understand is that God will always honour and reward those who serve Him. Sometimes we may feel that our service goes un-rewarded and perhaps it often does in this life. Nevertheless, we can hold onto the promises of God's Word and "serve wholeheartedly....the Lord will reward everyone for whatever good he does" (Ephesians 6v7-8). Jesus Himself promises us that "My Father will honour the one who serves me" (John 12v26).

Paul made sure that a lady called Phoebe was honoured and commended to the whole church in Rome. Why? Because she had a great public ministry? No, because she was "a servant of the church...a great help to many" (Romans 16v1-2). How much more will God honour and commend those who serve and help His Church?

Finally, God will open doors, not for the best networkers or those who are best at self-promotion but for those who will serve. Jesus said in Luke 12v37, "It will be good for those servants whose master finds them watching when he comes. Truly I tell you, he will dress himself to serve, will have them recline at the table and will come and wait on them." Service opens the door to intimacy and friendship with Jesus.

Service is the key to positioning ourselves to receive the good things God has in store for us. God's best gifts are always on the bottom shelf. We have to stoop down in service in order to get to them. When ordinary people serve, a door to God's extraordinary life of blessing is opened up for them.

The key to service: faithfulness

As someone who was involved in local church leadership for fourteen years, I can tell you that without a doubt the number one quality any good leader looks for is faithfulness. You can never promote short term zeal and enthusiasm, but you can always trust those who have faithfully served long-term in something. Someone who has never been faithful to a local church and has never served in the same ministry position for a good amount of time is someone you can never use. Anyone can be excited about getting involved in ministry when they first get the passion for it; and everyone is excited about their church the first couple of years after they have joined, but can you still be faithful when it's less exciting, more predictable, harder work than you expected or it's failed to lead to the greater things that you were hoping?

Sadly, that is often when people feel "the call of God" to move into something else or lay that ministry down. Of course, we are often not called to the same place or same ministry for a lifetime, but people who don't have a good track record of being faithful to something for a long period of time, in good seasons and in bad, are probably not the kind of people who can be entrusted with greater ministry responsibility.

Remember the words that we all want to hear Jesus say to us when we stand before Him: "Well done, good and faithful servant!" (Matthew 25v21). Jesus won't commend us for the size of our ministry, but on whether we were faithful with the tasks we were entrusted with. It is those who are faithful with little to whom more will be given. (Luke 16v10). Now one thing we know about God is that He cannot lie. He will not say "Well done, good and faithful servant!" just to encourage us. He will only say it to those who actually have been good and faithful!

Christians can be some of the most frustrated people on the planet, because within every true Christian there is a willingness and longing to do something great for God. Though sometimes driven by selfish ambition and ego, most often it is a genuine God-given passion and desire. However, many of us don't know how to go about doing something for God, so we sit around waiting to be asked to preach at a crusade or invited to lead a great ministry. Others constantly harass the pastor for a speaking opportunity or a leadership position. Others try to push open doors and, out of frustration and desperation, attempt to promote themselves and what they can do. Often, our motives are good, we just want to do something for God - to advance His Kingdom and to use our gifts for His glory - but we don't really know how to do it.

The great ministers of the Bible were faithful in serving other people before God called them into their destiny and gave them a ministry of their own. Jacob faithfully served Laban; Joseph faithfully served in both Potiphar's house and in the prison; Moses faithfully looked after sheep in the desert; Ruth faithfully served in the fields of Boaz; Samuel faithfully served Eli; David faithfully served both Jesse and Saul; Elisha faithfully served Elijah; Nehemiah faithfully served as cupbearer to the king; Daniel faithfully served various foreign leaders; the disciples faithfully served Jesus; Stephen and Phillip faithfully served the church as deacons. I could go on and on.

When we feel the call of God on our lives, or we have a dream and a passion to serve Him, the best way to come to a place of fulfilment is to give our lives to serving someone else faithfully until God releases us into our own ministry.

It is a challenge to do this when we have heard God's Word that we have been called into something greater than where we are currently at. When it is prophesied over us that we have been called to the nations, or called to preach or lead, the temptation is to drop everything and get on with it; but God's call done in man's timing can lead to disaster. Zechariah was a man who received a genuine prophecy from God. Whilst he was serving in the temple, the angel Gabriel appeared and told him that he and his wife Sarah were going to have a son. Now, without getting crude, before that prophecy was fulfilled, Zechariah had to go and lie with his wife! Rather than rush off immediately to do so, the Bible tells us that it was only "when his time of service was completed, he returned home" and "after that his wife Elizabeth became pregnant" (Luke 1v23-24). It must have been difficult for Zechariah to continue to serve in the temple, when he knew that, on returning home, the prayers and desires of his heart would be fulfilled; however, as a good and upright man, Zechariah knew that, whilst God had promised, there was a time of service to be completed first. Zechariah had to be faithful before he could be fruitful.

I have learnt in life that if you will give yourself to serving someone else's vision, God will give Himself towards serving your vision. For eight years after God called me to the nations, spreading the message of revival and preaching the gospel, I continued to serve my pastors and my local church. This wasn't disobedience to the heavenly vision, but rather serving the vision of others. Eventually, my time of service was complete and I was released to fulfil the call that was on my life. The church that I served for fourteen years is a small village church in the North of England. I recall one pastor turning his nose up, saying, "You're still based there? Why not move to a bigger church? You'll never fulfil your potential there!" I have never been concerned about fulfilling my potential, only about serving the Body of Christ. If I could give one piece of advice to any young person with the desire for ministry it would be this: Never try and be successful. Be faithful and God will make you successful.

Service starts with what is in front of you

"I tell you, open your eyes and look at the fields! They are ripe for harvest."

(John 4v35)

How do I begin serving? Jesus said that as we open our eyes we see need all around us. One man of God says "the need is the call". Our area of service doesn't usually begin with the call to the mission field or to preach to thousands, it begins with serving whatever is in front of us and the local church that we are a part of. "What's in your hand?" "What is in your house?" were all questions asked to God's servants in the Bible.

How do you find out the will of God for your life or what your ministry is? The will of God is usually revealed in a very general way. "Serve the Body" comes before a more specific way. Get on with meeting the needs around you - pick up litter in the church car park, help move chairs after service, make an encouraging phone call to those who need it, volunteer in some behind-the-scenes ministry, serve your Pastor in whatever he needs doing.

All of this sounds very mundane, but we find miracles in the mundane. Whether it was David taking bread and cheese to his brothers, Moses looking after sheep in the wilderness, or Jesus chatting with a woman at a well, mundane tasks performed with an open and grateful heart transformed into open doors of destiny.

Who knew that Lot's decision to serve two men who were in the city square and show them hospitality would not only result in angelic visitation in his home, but would ultimately save him and his family from destruction?

Who knew that Elisha simply being Elijah's attendant and pouring water on his hands faithfully for years, would lead to his receiving of the prophetic mantle and the double portion anointing? As I look in scripture and at my own life too, I find that simple acts of service and obedience unlocks the doors of the miraculous.

Conclusion

As members of the Church as the Body of Christ we are active ligaments, serving one another and getting on with the task God has assigned to us. God's Church is not grown by great preachers or great worship leaders but by great servants.
Some argue that after a busy week, working Monday to Friday and then having family and household duties on a Saturday, Sunday is their day to rest and relax: "I'm too busy to get involved in church activity", "I'm just too tired", "I don't have

the time". In our busy lives, we can genuinely feel so exhausted that we just want to come to church and receive a "top-up" before another hectic week. The idea that our Saturdays, Sundays or evenings could be given to serving in the Church is just too much for many of us to comprehend.

Let us remember though the promise of Proverbs 11v25: "A generous person will prosper; whoever refreshes others will be refreshed".

In pouring into others - our time, our finances, our energy, our encouragement, our service - we shouldn't become more drained and more weary. On the contrary the Bible promises that the more we serve others the more refreshed we will be.

Before we move on from seeing the Church as the Body of Christ, I want us to look at something that has become more and more common in Christianity today: people serving God outside the context of a local church. The modern day title for this kind of ministry is "Para-ministry".

Let's look at whether Para-ministry is Biblical and what our attitude towards the Church should be, if we are involved in this kind of ministry.

15

PARA-CHURCH

"So after they had fasted and prayed, they placed their hands on them and sent them off. "

(Acts 13v3)

A Para-church is a modern-day term used for a faith-based ministry or organization that usually carries out its mission independent of local church oversight. The prefix Para is Greek for beside or alongside, so a Para-church ministry is one that will often come alongside a local church with its specialist gifting, whilst not necessarily being run or managed by a local church body of elders or pastors. Examples of a Para-church may be the ministry of an itinerant evangelist or prophet; a mission organization; a group that offers debt relief or helps feed the poor; a media group such as Christian television, radio or publishing; a group of Christian musicians and singers or a travelling worship ministry. The ministry that I founded, 'Generation Builders', which travels all over the world preaching the gospel and empowering believers, is one example of a Para-church ministry. My brother and his wife run a ministry called 'One by One', which rescues children from poverty and provides them with food, clothing and education - another example of a Para-church ministry.

The truth is that some ministries are only called to impact their local community, but some ministries by nature of their calling, gifting and size of their vision are called to impact a much wider geographical area. Some ministers and ministries are called to impact a nation or even nations. They cannot therefore be restricted to just ministering in one local church; their calling is bigger than that. That is why Para-church ministries are in operation.

The reason I wanted to write a chapter about Para-church ministry is because it is something that is becoming more and more common. With the invention of the internet and the popularity of social media, it is now very easy to network and make your name known around the world. As a consequence, more and more individuals and groups are setting up their own ministry or organization independently of a local church oversight. To some of the more social ministries, government funding can be a great way of paying the salary of its workers and funding the work that they are doing, so setting up a ministry of this sort without the financial support of a local church is much easier than perhaps it was in the past.

With more and more believers involved in Para-church ministry and more and more of these organizations starting up; I think that it is very important to ask ourselves two questions: Are Para-ministries Biblical? For those involved in Para-church ministries, What should our attitude be towards the local church?

Is Para-church ministry biblical?

As someone who runs a Para-church ministry; I have to honestly look in the scriptures and when I do, I find that the idea of any ministry acting independently of local church oversight to be an unknown concept to the first century Church. I find very little scriptural evidence of anyone "starting their own ministry". Instead, when I look in the scriptures I find that every major ministry that had a wider remit than one geographical locality was birthed in the local church, sent out from the local church and then returned to the local church. This is the Biblical apostolic model.

Perhaps the clearest example is found in Acts 13. The Bible tells us that "Now in the church at Antioch there were prophets and teachers: Barnabas, Simeon called Niger, Lucius of Cyrene, Manaen (who had been brought up with Herod the tetrarch) and Saul." (v1) Notice that all these different ministries were "in the church". The idea of any ministry gift not being in the church was totally unknown to the New Testament church. They were not "in the church" in a vague sense of being loosely joined to some fellowship or network, but they were planted in a local church that they were committed to and were all actively involved in ministry there.

Now among this group of local church ministers, there were two for whom God had a wider remit. The Holy Spirit would speak to Saul (later Paul) and Barnabas and call them to an apostolic ministry which would mean that they would no longer be able to devote themselves exclusively to ministry in their local church in Antioch, but instead would have an itinerant ministry travelling the known world, preaching and teaching and planting churches. How did Saul and Barnabas respond to this call? How did their local church respond? How should we respond if we know the Lord is calling us to a wider ministry than our local church?

It is very important to notice the wording in the next verse: "While **they** were worshipping the Lord and fasting, the Holy Spirit said, "Set apart for me Barnabas and Saul for the work to which I have called **them**." Now there is no doubt that Saul and Barnabas would have been aware of the call of God that was on their lives, but the wording in this verse shows us that the Holy Spirit also spoke to their fellow local church leaders about what He was calling them to do. This is a very important Biblical principle. **Local church leadership will always acknowledge all ministry that is genuine Kingdom ministry** before it is released into wider ministry. The first question that anyone called to any form of ministry should ask themselves is "what do my leaders say?" If someone is genuinely called of God, the Holy Spirit will speak not only to them, but also to their church leadership too. Without the dual call, it is not a genuine call. I know in my own situation that my pastor had told me many times the ministry that he felt God was calling me into, even before I had heard clearly the voice of the Holy Spirit for myself.

We see this principle in operation later on in the ministry of Timothy. Paul writes in 1 Timothy 4, "Do not neglect your gift, which was given you through prophecy when the body of elders laid their hands on you." (v14) Note here that the whole body of elders had publically acknowledged the ministry that Timothy had. Timothy was not going around telling everyone that God had called him to ministry - although he undoubtedly had. Neither was the approval of just one man, Paul, his apostle, enough to make his ministry genuine. What made Timothy's ministry genuine was that the entire group of local church leaders had said that it was. They were willing to lay hands on him and confirm the call that was on his life. This may be unpopular, but biblically it is never enough to have just the Holy Spirit call you. Neither is it enough to just have some distant apostle as your "covering" or "oversight". It doesn't matter if an angel from heaven calls you and the greatest apostle in the world agrees to cover you; unless your local church leadership agrees with the gifting and call that is on your life and is willing to publicly acknowledge it, it is not a genuine call according to the Bible! The answer to the problem that "my pastor just doesn't recognise my calling" is **always** to stay humble, stay submissive, stay serving and take the matter before God in prayer; it is never, ever to just break away and start your own Para-church ministry out of frustration or find another pastor who will support you.

Going back to Acts 13, we see that Saul and Barnabas had heard the call of God, confirmed by other leaders hearing the same thing. What happened next? "So after they had fasted and prayed, they placed their hands on them and sent them off." (v3) Now we know from other scriptures that the ministry Saul and Barnabas were being called to was an apostolic ministry. Apostle simply means "sent one" or "one who is sent". So the question is, who sent them? Verse 2 clearly tells us that the Holy Spirit sent them. Verse 3 clearly tells us that the church that sent them. So which was it? Obviously it was both. All true New Testament ministry that operates outside a local church is sent out by the Holy Spirit first, then the local church that the ministry was birthed in. Without the dual sending out, there is no genuine ministry.

No genuine New Testament ministry is self-appointed. The great danger with any Para-church ministry is that someone can start it out of their own imagination or zeal without a genuine call of God. That is the worst case scenario. An equally dangerous scenario is that people who have genuinely heard the call of God follow it without ever having been sent out by their local church. A friend of mine coined the phrase "some were called, some were sent, others just bought a microphone and went!" Sadly, it is very common in the Church today for people to start their own ministry, travelling all over the world serving Jesus, but never having been sent to do it by any local church. There is no record of any genuine New Testament ministry (with one exception that we will look at later) that just "went" and did ministry. New Testament ministers were always "sent" from their local church.

In Acts 14 we read of how Paul and Barnabas "appointed elders for them in church and, with prayer and fasting, committed them to the Lord" (v23). Even the local church elders were not self-appointed, but were appointed by the apostles, who themselves had been appointed by others. Again, notice the apostolic pattern of church planting. This wasn't a bunch of people randomly planting a church in a locality because they "felt the call". The new church plants were recognised and acknowledged by the local church in Antioch and no doubt came under some kind of apostolic covering. They wouldn't have acted independently of the church that had birthed them.

The true Biblical pattern we see time and again is that, no matter how gifted or anointed someone is, the idea of responding to the call of God or following your destiny without being released into it by the local church is alien to the scriptures. In Acts 15, some false teaching had crept into the church and a counsel was held of all the apostles in Jerusalem. By now, Paul and Barnabas had a proven and fruitful apostolic ministry and would have been well within their rights to attend the counsel and give their opinion, but twice the Bible emphasis how Paul and Barnabas didn't go until they were sent by their local church. "Paul and Barnabas were appointed along with some other believers, to go up to Jerusalem" (v2) "The church sent them on their way" (v3). When they arrived in Jerusalem it was not as "Paul and Barnabas Apostolic Ministries International", but as men who were part of the ministry at the local church in Antioch and were being sent by that church.

So we can see that true New Testament ministry is always birthed in the local church, recognised by the local church and then sent out by the local church. Like today, however, the New Testament church had problems with false ministry. As we have already seen there were some ministries in Acts 15 who had infiltrated the Church with false teaching. In addressing these false ministries, notice what was said about them: "We have heard that some went out from us without our authorization and disturbed you, troubling your minds by what they said." (v24) The accusation labelled at these men was that they had gone out from their local church preaching and teaching without their ministry having been authorized. They were acting independently of the local church (similar to a Para-church ministry), but their ministry was immediately condemned as false, not just because of what they were teaching, but because of how it had started - without any kind of acknowledgement or release from the local church.

This is something that Paul would address again in Colossians 2: "Do not let anyone who delights in false humility and the worship of angels disqualify you. Such a person also goes into great detail about what they have seen; they are puffed up with idle notions by their unspiritual mind. They have lost connection with the head, from whom the whole body, supported and held together by its ligaments and sinews, grows as God causes it to grow." (v18-19) Paul is writing here about people who were greatly gifted and had wonderful testimonies of great spiritual encounters and experiences that they had had. Yet Paul uses the analogy of the body to talk about how they had lost connection with the head and consequently the rest of the ligaments and sinews. Paul wrote very clearly not to associate with any ministry, no matter how spectacular or how great a work that they were doing that failed to see and be connected to the Body of Christ.

For anyone involved in any form of Para-church ministry, we must understand that God never recognises any ministry that we do. There is only one ministry that God sees and accepts and that is the ministry of the Body of Christ. Jesus is the Anointed One and it is only that which is done in and through His Body that God accepts, anoints and blesses. No matter how many gospel crusades we preach at, no matter how many poor people we feed, no matter how many people attend our concerts, if we are acting outside the Body of Christ, it may be good deeds, but it is not ministry.

I think the description of the Menorah, the lamp stand in the tabernacle, is a wonderful description of true ministry. In Exodus we read of the various parts of the lamp stand – the six branches, the three cups on each branch, the buds and branches on each cup. Yet each piece of the lamp stand was made not made independently and then moulded together. No, Exodus 25 tells us "The buds and branches shall be all of one piece with the lamp stand, hammered out of pure gold." (v36) There were different out-shoots branching out, but they were all connected to the same piece of gold. This shows us how God wants His Kingdom to operate. There can be many different ministries, branching off, producing fruit and spreading light, but they are all connected to the ministry of the one Body, the Church; all part of the Church and flowing out of it.

Acts 11 gives us yet another clear picture of how the New Testament Church operated: "News of this reached the church in Jerusalem, and they sent Barnabas to Antioch." (v 22) Again, we see that Barnabas was sent out by the church, to the church. This is true Body ministry.

We have a problem!

As we have seen, the modern definition of a Para-church - "a faith based ministry or organization that carries out its mission usually independent of local church oversight" - is an un-Biblical concept. All ministry in the New Testament came under local church oversight and was sent out by a local church oversight.

This means that we have a big problem as more and more ministries are being set up that are not necessarily local church ministries. For those of us, like myself, who operate a Para-church ministry, how do we respond? Is there any Biblical model for what we do? I think there is. In Acts 8 we find the closest thing to a New Testament Para-church ministry, and that is the ministry of Philip the evangelist. Here is what we read about him, in verses 4-5 and 40:

"Those who had been scattered preached the word wherever they went. Philip went down to a city in Samaria and proclaimed the Messiah there." (v4-5)
Philip, however, appeared at Azotus and travelled about, preaching the gospel in all the towns until he reached Caesarea. (v40)

Unlike the false teachers who had gone out without any covering or acknowledgement from the local church, Philip is a genuine ministry gift to the Church who is always spoken of in complimentary terms in the New Testament. However, unlike the common Biblical pattern of Paul and Barnabas, Philip doesn't seem to have been sent out by any particular local church. Instead, circumstance (the persecution in

Jerusalem) caused him to flee and on his travels he just did what came naturally to him – the preaching of the gospel. The next thing he knew he had his own revival ministry, shaking an entire city in the region of Samaria and before he knew it he had his own itinerant evangelistic ministry, seemingly acting independently of any local church oversight. Philip is the closest thing we can see to a genuine New Testament Para-church ministry. Therefore, we must look closely at the life of Philip and learn some important lessons for anyone involved in any kind of Para-church ministry.

Lessons from Philip

The first time we read of Philip is in Acts 6 when the apostles were wearying from having to feed the widows as part of the church's feeding programme. It was proposed that seven deacons would be appointed who would wait on tables and allow the apostles to give their time exclusively to preaching the word and to prayer.

It says in Acts 6 verses 3 and 5:

> *"Brothers and sisters, choose seven men from among you who are known to be full of the Spirit and wisdom. We will turn this responsibility over to them ... This proposal pleased the whole group. They chose Stephen, a man full of faith and of the Holy Spirit; also Philip, Procorus, Nicanor, Timon, Parmenas, and Nicolas from Antioch, a convert to Judaism."*

Here are several things we notice about Philip:

1. Philip was part of a local church: " ... choose seven men from among you ... " Before Philip started his own itinerant ministry he was a faithful and committed member of a local church. This is incredibly important for anyone wanting to be involved or lead any Para-church ministry. Sometimes people

are involved in these kinds of ministries because it is a paid job or it gives them a sense of fulfilment. The test of whether someone is a true minister or simply a hired hand or someone on an ego trip is always the question "have they seen the church?" Long before Philip had his own ministry he saw the need to be part of a local church and he was faithful to it and committed to it. This is why God recognised him as a genuine ministry gift, even if his ministry wasn't technically "released" as others were. God will always recognise those who recognise His Church.

2. Philip had a good reputation within the local church " … known to be …" Philip didn't publish on his website that he was full of the Holy Spirit and wisdom; he was **known** to be full of the Holy Spirit and wisdom. Over the past few years I have preached in dozens and dozens of churches and on only one occasion has a pastor that has invited me taken the time to contact my local church pastor to ask "What is this guy like? Is he someone that you would recommend? Is he a good guy?" Pastors often assume that because a Para-ministry is fruitful and successful the people running it are people of Christ-like character. Yet ministry scandal after scandal show that this is not the case. Local church, among people we are in relationship with and submitted to, is always the testing ground of character. If you want to know what Philip was like, don't ask the people who were saved at his crusade in Samaria. They were a testimony of his gift. The members and leaders of his local church were the ones who could give testimony to his character. Thankfully they could say this man is "known to be" a good person. Of course, my website is going to tell you what a great ministry I have. But who endorses my character? What do my wife and children say about me? What does my pastor say about me? What do my previous employers say about me? This is vital before we get involved with any Para-church ministry and for those who are involved in Para-church ministry, one of the most important reasons to be involved in a local church

and keep our characters accountable.

3. Philip served in the local church. The job of a deacon was not a glamorous ministry position. It was simply waiting on tables, serving food to widows. It was a behind-the-scenes service ministry. We don't know how long Philip did this, but the scriptures seem to indicate this it was for some time. This is a very important principle. Before Philip launched out into his own evangelistic ministry, he was faithfully serving behind the scenes in his local church for possibly a number of years. Any person who wants to start their own ministry or be involved in a ministry outside their local church who doesn't have a track record of faithfully serving in their local church, is I believe, a scripturally false minister and not a true servant of God. Servants serve others, not just themselves. The difference between Miriam and Aaron and Moses was that Miriam and Aaron wanted people to recognise their ministry, "Hasn't the Lord also spoken through us?" (Numbers 12v2) whilst Moses was "faithful in all God's house" (v7). True men and women of God serve the entire House, not just their own ministry or pet project. How you serve others, support others, and give to others within the church is the genuine test of whether what you do will be backed by God.

4. The local church acknowledged Philip: "They presented these men to the apostles, who prayed and laid their hands on them." (v6) As we have already seen, it seems as though Philip's evangelist ministry was not covered by a particular local church; however that doesn't mean that Philip himself wasn't. Here we clearly see that Philip submitted to his local church leadership and came under their blessing and prayer covering. Para-Church ministries can be very helpful in accomplishing things that one local church just simply can't do on its own. The very nature of a Para-church ministry means that it often needs its own legal structure and organisation as well as its own separate leadership

team. However, all those involved in this kind of ministry must, like Philip, recognise the need to submit to a local church leadership and come under its blessing and prayer covering. The covering that the Para-church ministry provides is never enough. Remember the blessing and anointing flows down from those who are part of the Body of Christ, the Church.

As Philip begins his itinerant ministry we see him becoming more and more successful, as the whole region of Samaria comes under the influence of his evangelistic preaching. What happens next is very important. Verses 14 onwards explain how the apostles in the church in Jerusalem send Peter and John to where Philip is to find out what is happening and take apostolic covering and oversight. Peter and John lead the converts of Philip's ministry into baptism in the Holy Spirit (v17) and take their own teaching and preaching ministry into Philip's revival (v25).

We can learn several lessons here from Philip:

> 1. Philip kept a correct attitude towards the local church. The moment the local church stepped into Philip's revival to inspect it, he didn't get defensive about what he was doing or dismissive of their input. He welcomed the ministry of the local church and invited it in. Philip's independent success had clearly not reduced his love and respect for the local church. People involved in Para-church ministry usually have a much bigger vision than a local church and often feel frustrated when it doesn't share their vision and see the bigger picture. Others might look down on the local church and consider what they are doing to be more important. Over time, our hearts can become bitter and hard towards the local church and its leadership. This indicates that we have failed or ceased to see the Church and, as a result, the blessing of God lifts from our lives. Although we may not notice the difference if our gift continues to be successful, those around us will no doubt recognise that a certain grace

has disappeared from our lives and families. Even though Philip's ministry had by now far outgrown his local church in Jerusalem and was having a regional impact, rather than just local, he still welcomed the input of his pastors, showing that he still had a genuine love and respect for the local church.

2. Philip recognised other ministries. In welcoming Peter and John, Philip recognised that other ministries and ministry gifts were needed and that they could do things that he simply couldn't do. The danger in becoming heavily involved in any Para-church ministry is that our focus becomes so narrow that we will only see the need for that ministry and fail to see the bigger picture of the Body. For example, a ministry that feeds the poor can quickly think that feeding the poor is the most important and necessary thing in the Kingdom and can become angry and frustrated at any ministry that doesn't do that. A prayer movement can think that the only thing that the Church needs to do is pray and can dismiss any church that isn't focused heavily on that. The truth is, we need all the different gifts and ministries that the body provides and each local church may emphasise one over another in any particular season. The key to any Godly Para-church ministry is to recognise and celebrate and recognise the need for all the diverse ministries that God raises up and not just think that our ministry is the answer to all the problems in the world and the Church.

3. Philip recognised his need for the apostles. The success of Philip's ministry meant that he became very well known in the region – fame being an unfortunate side effect of successful ministry. If we are not careful, this can quickly go to our heads and we can think that we no longer need any kind of spiritual authority over us. As an evangelist, Philip quickly recognised the weight that the apostles carried and happily came under their authority. No

matter how big or successful our ministries become we all need to submit to spiritual authority. We all need apostolic covering and we all need pastors and fathers in the faith. We never outgrow our need for leadership, even if we are great leaders ourselves.

Following on from his success in Samaria, the book of Acts chooses not to focus too much on the ministry of Philip and he is mentioned just once more. "Leaving the next day, we reached Caesarea and stayed at the house of Philip the evangelist, one of the Seven. He had four unmarried daughters who prophesied." (Acts 21v8-9) We learn two important lessons from the life of Philip in these verses:

1. Building the house; It seems that, for several years, Philip had stopped travelling exclusively and now lived in Caesarea where he seems to have had some kind of church or congregation. The Bible doesn't tell us that Philip had stopped his itinerant ministry, but it is clear that, in addition, he was also based in a local area from which his ministry operated.

We must remember that, although Paul and Barnabas were sent out from the local church, they also kept coming back to their local church, too (Acts 14v26). Whilst mission work, itinerant ministry and Para-church ministry can be God's call on our lives, there is also a call for every one of us to have a spiritual home, a spiritual house that we are a part of.

Ezra 5 tells us about the people of Jerusalem. Under their oversight, Zerubbabel and Joshua started to rebuild the house of God. Verse 2 tells us that "the prophets of God were with them, helping them." There was no local church in the Old Testament, so the prophets of God were a little like itinerant ministries, acting independently and coming and going as they liked. But in this passage it tells us that they came alongside the local leadership and helped them build the house. All Para-church ministry exists to come alongside the local church and support and help build the House. No ministry should ever demand that the Church supports it or demand the help of the Church. That is a total failure to see the Body. Instead we are there to support the Church and help the Church. Likewise, no Para-ministry should ever enforce itself on the local church and its leaders. Instead, it offers its services and should not become bitter or angry if they are not required. Prophets are able to prophesy, but they are also willing to quietly and humbly help build houses if that's what is required. All ministers should learn from this.

2. Philip trained the next generation "He had four unmarried daughters who prophesied." In local church leadership you automatically think generationally as there are always children and young people coming through. One of the great dangers of Para-ministry is that we only think one-generationally, only doing what God has called us to do without any thought to what will happen when our ministry is over. Some of the great evangelistic ministries of the past hundred years have ended when the evangelist has died, because they failed to raise up a successor. Great Para-church ministries can impact the whole world, yet when the person dies the ministry dies, too. The great thing about Philip is that, not only did he have a great ministry, but he made sure that the next generation were raised up by having daughters who had ministries of their own. We must remember that the ultimate aim of all ministry is not to do the work of the ministry, but rather to equip God's people to do the work of the ministry. This is easier to remember when we are involved in local church leadership, but easy to forget in Para-church ministry where we can quickly become self-obsessed and focused entirely on doing what God has called us to do. Let us learn from Philip and make sure that we are discipling people, training people and raising up sons and daughters (spiritual as well as natural), therefore making sure that the work of God continues without us.

Conclusion

This chapter is incredibly important for the Body of Christ, at a time when more people are starting their own ministry and an increasing number of organisations are being formed that operate separately from the local church. We must always base our understanding on the Bible. In the scriptures we see that there is only one ministry that God recognises - the ministry of the Body, His Church. All true New Testament ministry is birthed in the local church, recognised by the local church, sent out from the local church and returned to the local church.

That doesn't mean that Para-church ministries can't be helpful and useful to the Body of Christ, but rather than follow in the footsteps of those who Paul condemned, we must follow in the footsteps of Philip. We must make sure that those of us working in a Para-church organisation are part of a local church, have a testimony of good character within that church, have served passionately in that church and have been acknowledged by the leadership of that church. As Para-church ministries grow we must always welcome the support of the local church, recognise that we are just one small part of what God is doing and accept our need for pastors and spiritual oversight. Para-church ministries must recognise the need to help build the House of God and raise up spiritual sons and daughters who can continue their legacy.

The past few chapters have focused on seeing the Church as the Body of Christ. Before we close the book by looking at the Church as the Army of God, I want to briefly, over the next two chapters, see two other aspects of the Church: the Bride and the Sheepfold.

16

THE BRIDE OF CHRIST

"For your Maker is your husband – the Lord Almighty is his name – the Holy One of Israel is your Redeemer; he is called the God of all the earth."

(Isaiah 54v5)

In this chapter I want us to look at one of the most beautiful truths of the Church – that she is the Bride of Christ. Many of us will acknowledge this and perhaps even sing about it – many of our praise songs use the language of love; but have we truly seen it? Have we had a true revelation that we are His Bride and He is our Heavenly Bridegroom? The image of Yahweh as the Bridegroom and Israel as His Bride is seen throughout the Old Testament. For New Testament believers, the ultimate fulfilment of this foreshadowing is seen in Christ and the Church. In Ephesians 5 Paul talks about earthly marriage being a prophetic type of an even greater spiritual reality. He calls this a "profound mystery… Christ and the Church".

As the Church we have entered into a marriage relationship with Jesus. There are so many different aspects to this, but perhaps one of the most wonderful is what Paul chooses to highlight in verses 31-32:

"For this reason a man will leave his father and mother and be united to his wife, and the two will become one flesh." This is a profound mystery–but I am talking about Christ and the church."

As the Bride of Christ the Church has become united in the closest, most intimate way possible. A deep spiritual union has taken place; two spirits have joined together, a deep has responded unto deep. This is why we can say confidently that not only am I in Christ, but also Christ is in me.

The phrase "In Christ" is one that Paul uses numerous times in the New Testament. We don't have time to look at everything that comes from being in Christ, but to name a few: in Christ we are God's children; justified; citizens of heaven; blessed in the heavenly realms with every spiritual blessing; chosen before the creation of the world; holy and blameless; redeemed; forgiven; raised up and seated in heavenly places; brought near to God; have peace; have become a dwelling for the Holy Spirit; are called; have eternal life; are free; healed; part of God's Kingdom; sin has no hold on us. We are born again … overcomers … victorious … a new creation. This is all because we are "in Christ". We are in Christ because we are His Bride.

Not only are we in Christ, but He is now in us. We are the light of the world, the salt of the earth. The greater One lives in us. The same Spirit that raised Christ from the dead lives in our spirits. Jesus, the Hope of the World, is now in us. We become carriers of hope and carriers of His presence wherever we go.

As a consequence of this unity "the two will become one flesh". The marriage relationship Christ has with His Church is so real that Christ and His Church have become one. My wife and I are in one sense two separate people, yet in another very real sense we have become one. So it is with Christ and the Church. Christ always identifies Himself with His Bride. Christ and His Church can never be separated – theologically, relationally and practically. How someone treats His Church is the same as how they treat Jesus. When the Father looks at the Church, He sees His beloved Son, as they have become joined together as one.

The love of the Bridegroom

"Christ loved the Church." (Ephesians 5v25)

To see the Church as the Bride of Christ is primarily to see that we are loved! Many books have been written on what the Church should be, as well as what it should be doing. There are numerous online blogs critiquing the Church and its leaders. It seems that anyone with a keyboard and an opinion is qualified to say how they feel about the Church. A bride, though, really only cares about the opinion of one man, her husband. In this case, the Bridegroom has one thing to say to His Bride: "I love you."

The Greek word "love" here is the word "agape". It means to cherish, to prize, to highly esteem. The Church is what Jesus cherishes, prizes and esteems more than anything else. We are the pearl of great price that Christ purchased when He shed His blood for the whole world.

The love that Jesus has for His Church is not a weak, fickle love. Neither is it cold, emotionless or distant. No, the love that Jesus has for His Church is an intense, fiery love, for "our God is a consuming fire" (Hebrews 12v29). Jesus loves His Church with an intense, all consuming, unquenchable, passionate love.

Jesus is constantly inviting His Church into deeper communion with Himself. It is in the banqueting hall that He covers us with the banner of His love (Song of Songs 2v4). The act of communion is both a reminder and a celebration of our identity as His Bride and the intense love He has for us; and also a prophetic declaration of the coming Bridegroom who comes to take His Bride to the place prepared for her.

It is in communion with her Bridegroom that the Holy Spirit takes the Church into the furnace of divine love. It is in that place that she is changed, transformed, impacted and undone.

The Western Church sees Christ as many things – our friend, our Saviour, our provider, our Lord. But we have failed to see Him as our Lover and Husband. How do I know this? Because "our" Jesus has become too safe! Our meetings with Him have become routine and predictable. We have relegated Christianity to principles, doctrines and church services. Our churches now revolve around vision statements, systems and management programmes. But God is a wild-man whose heart burns with an intense and fiery passion for us. God is a lover who longs for us to discover once again the spontaneity and freedom of just enjoying Him.

The Bridegroom that the Bible presents is a running, hugging, kissing God (Luke 15). Zephaniah 3v17 describes Him like this:

"Yahweh your God is there with you, the Warrior Saviour. He will rejoice over you with happy song, He will renew you by His love, He will dance with shouts of joy for you." (NJB)

Study the original Hebrew of this verse. It describes God as doing much more than just singing over you. It literally means that He will spin and dance and shout triumphantly over you! This verse tells us that because of Jesus, God rejoices, celebrates, dances, sings, laughs, claps, spins round and smiles over us. His love roars over us a shout of victory, as powerful as a hurricane and as mighty as the thunder of a waterfall. His love is also gentle and peaceful leading us to a place where we dwell in the living stillness of His presence, safe and secure around Him.

In prophesying of the coming Messiah, Isaiah declared that He would "wrap Himself in zeal like a cloak" (Isaiah 59v17). The object of His zeal, His burning passion, the apple of His eye, is His Church, His Bride, you and I.

The Bride of Song of Songs discovered the passion her husband had for her: "Listen! My beloved! Look! Here he comes, leaping across the mountains, bounding over the hills." (Song of Songs 2v8) Jesus will do anything to get to His Bride. He will move mountains and leap over hills just to be with her. The Church that sees herself as the Bride of Christ knows that He moves at the sound of her voice. She knows that when she lifts her voice in worship, cries out in prayer or even just turns the affection of her heart towards Him, He comes every time.

1. His sacrifice

> *"Christ loved the Church and gave Himself up for her."* (Ephesians 5v25)

A true loving husband is willing to save and to sacrifice to make his bride happy, blessed and fruitful. An unloving husband only thinks of himself and lives to get his needs met. Christ is of course the greatest picture of a loving husband. Everything Jesus does is for the sake of His Bride. Everything He has He shares with His Bride, the one who has stolen His heart (Song of Songs 4v9). What an incredible thing, that all we have to do is turn our eyes towards Jesus and we immediately find His heart.

Although in today's society there is not a marked difference in the role each sex plays, in Bible days the Jewish husband was very much seen as the provider, the one who would meet the needs, care for and look after His bride. This is what Christ has covenanted to do with us! He has made a promise to supply all of our needs, to never leave us or forsake us and to love us with an everlasting love!

Just as the in the book of Ruth, Boaz, the kinsman redeemer covered Ruth as a sign of his love, protection and provision, Jesus, our kinsman redeemer has covered us with His blood. That is our sign, that we are now His and everything is going to be ok!

Jesus made the ultimate sacrifice for His Bride by shedding His blood for her on the cross. This was the price of redemption, the price that He paid so that we could be His. This is why God takes it very seriously and personally when people attack His Church. We are not speaking against individuals we disagree with or an organisation we don't want to be a part of anymore. We are speaking against His Bride, the One He purchased with His own blood.

> " … to make her holy, cleansing her by the washing with water through the word … feeds and cares for it as Christ does the Church … "
>
> (Ephesians 5v26, 29)

These verses show that God recognises that the Church is not perfect. There are still many areas that she is lacking in and areas of dirt and unseemliness within her, but oh! The love of the Bridegroom! Instead of despairing and giving up on the Church because of her lack, He chooses to continually feed her in order to make her one day complete. Instead of pointing out and condemning her because of her dirtiness, He continually washes and cleanses her in order to make her holy.

2. His gifts

The Bride of Christ has been given wonderful wedding garments to wear by Her Husband. She is to keep these on at all times. She could never afford even one of these garments by herself, but thankfully her Husband is a rich man, and generously paid the price so that His Bride could wear the finest of clothing.

The Church's clothing includes strength and dignity (Proverbs 31); righteousness (Psalm 32); praise (Isaiah 61); joy (Psalm 30); power (Luke 24); compassion, kindness, humility, gentleness and patience (Colossians 3). Indeed, His Bride is even instructed to clothe herself with Christ (Galatians 3v27).

The Bride of Christ has been given royal robes to wear and has been granted unrestricted access to and outlandish favour with the King of Kings. She can come boldly into the presence of her King, knowing that the sceptre of grace has been extended and she can speak freely and confidently in His presence.

3. His covenant

"In the same way, after the supper he took the cup, saying, "This cup is the new covenant in my blood, which is poured out for you."

(Luke 22v20)

A covenant is a formal agreement of legal validity, one under a seal, a binding agreement, a contract a solemn promise. God takes His covenants very seriously. In the Old Testament, God entered into covenants with man, which He always kept and always honoured. If God so kept the covenants made with the blood of animals, He will certainly keep the covenant He made with the blood of His Son.

Seeing the Church as the Bride of Christ is seeing that we are more than just forgiven and going to heaven. We are covenant people. Christ has made a blood covenant with His Church to love her, protect her, care for her, give her all that He has and bring her into her eternal destiny. The Bible declares that "All the promises of God are yes and amen in Christ Jesus" (2 Corinthians 1v20). This is more than a feel good memory verse. It is an eternal covenant we have with our Husband. Healing, provision, protection, favour and so many more things – they are our covenant rights. The Church that sees itself as the Bride of Christ is not trying to impress Jesus or trying to beg things that she needs, but has reached a place of deep security and rest knowing that He will never love her any more or less than He does right now and that all things are freely available to her. Therefore, the posture of the Church that sees itself as the Bride is not to beg and plead but to be thankful and receive.

God will never reject, abandon or divorce His Bride. The future of the Church is as bright as the promises of God.

The love of the Bride

A marriage covenant is always a two-way commitment. Although Christ has covenanted to love and care for His Bride, He can only do this when His Bride is in right relationship with Him. According to Paul, when the Church sees itself as the Bride of Christ she will submit to Him as Lord (Ephesians 5v24). Paul says that we are to submit in "everything". In seeing ourselves as the Bride of Christ we must recognise that we are now no longer "free and single". We belong to another and are called to submit to His Lordship and Headship. As individuals we must never make the mistake of thinking that we can live our lives how we want and make our own plans, which we ask God to bless. We are called to find out the plan that He has for our lives and submit to that. Church leaders are never free to lead the church as they want to lead it. "The Bride belongs to the Bridegroom" (John 3v29) and our response to that is always hearing, submitting and obeying.

The principle of marriage that God lays down in Genesis is this: we "leave" our father and mother and "cleave" to our husband or wife. When we enter into relationship with Jesus, there has to be a "leaving". We have to leave behind everything of the old life. No longer do we live for this world, earthly desires, our plans or ourselves. We truly surrender all to Jesus.

Not only is there a "leaving" but there is also a "cleaving". To cleave means "to stick fast". It's an attitude that says "Jesus I am not going to let you go! I will never stop loving you and serving you". Some want to cleave but are not prepared to leave (this is hypocrisy). Some leave, but never cleave (this is religion). If we are truly in relationship with Jesus, we have to leave everything behind, but also cling to, pursue and take hold of Him.

We must understand that God is a jealous God (Exodus 34v14) whose Spirit in us longs jealously for us (James 4v5). God hates any form of compromise or disobedience in His Bride. We must understand God is not jealous with us, He is jealous for us. He is not jealous because He is needy or insecure, He is jealous because He loves us with a passion, but we cannot full receive His love until we fully surrender to Him. Any space that we give to other loves is a space that He cannot possess Himself. In seeing ourselves as His Bride we become fully His; yielded laid down lovers of Jesus.

The Bride's revelation

One famous theologian was asked towards the end of his life: "You have spent decades studying theology, reading books, expounding the scriptures, giving lectures and becoming one of the most learned men of your generation. What is the highest and greatest theological statement you know?"

The old man thought for a moment before responding with a smile: "Jesus loves me this I know, for the Bible tells me so."

A wonderful man of God from my home church once preached a message on the Apostle John and why it was that in his gospel John would always refer to himself as "the disciple whom Jesus loved". The preacher asked the question: "Was it that Jesus loved John more than any of the others?" No! It was simply that John had "got it!" He had the revelation "I am loved by Jesus!" What a revelation that is:

"If God is for us, who can be against us? He who did not spare his own Son, but gave him up for us all – how will he not also, along with him, graciously give us all things? Who will bring any charge against those whom God has chosen? It is God who justifies. Who then is the one who condemns? No one. Christ Jesus who died –more than that, who was raised to life – is at the right hand of God and is also interceding for us. Who shall separate us from the love of Christ? Shall trouble or hardship or persecution or famine or nakedness or danger or sword?

No, in all these things we are more than conquerors through him that loved us. For I am convinced that neither death nor life, neither angels nor demons, neither the present nor the future, nor any powers, neither height nor depth, nor anything else in all creation, will be able to separate us from the love of God that is in Christ Jesus our Lord. (Romans 8v31)

The day we discover we are deeply and unconditionally loved is the day we are truly set free. The greatest day of our lives is when we can boldly declare, "My beloved is mine and I am His." (Song of Songs 2v16)

The Bride's response

Our response to the simplicity and power of His love is obvious – we are to love Him in return.

I sometimes despair in looking at how complicated we have made Church in the Western World rather than the simplicity of just loving Jesus. Many churches are now focused entirely on increasing numbers, buying better buildings, making more money and putting on better meetings. We focus so much on our business strategy that we have forgotten our marriage covenant. We have focused so much on raising leaders that we have forgotten to raise up lovers. In our desire to become purpose-driven we have failed to see that firstly God calls us to be passion-driven.

God is not looking for slick, polished, professional Church – He is looking for lovers. He has called us into a divine romance. He has called us to fall head over heels in love with Jesus. Our attendance means nothing to Him if He doesn't have our hearts.

Have we become like the church in Ephesus that theologically and doctrinally had everything in place, but had lost that burning desire for Jesus? (Revelation 2v1-7). Or have we become like the church at Laodicea that was outwardly prosperous and inwardly satisfied but had become lukewarm and disinterested in the presence of her Saviour, so much so that He was outside and trying to get back in (Revelation 3v14-22). Both of these churches are told to repent, by Jesus Himself.

There was once an African preacher who was outwardly affectionate and warm towards his wife. One day an English preacher and his wife came to visit them. The Englishman was very cold and distant towards his wife. He would never touch her, speak warmly towards her or give any outward signs of his love. Privately he complained to his friend, "I can't understand my wife. I look after her, provide for her, give her a generous allowance and have bought her a wonderful home. Yet she always seems so sad and miserable." The African passionately grabbed hold of his friend. "Man, can't you see the problem? Your wife doesn't want your gifts and possessions. She wants you to touch her, hold her hand, kiss her lips, take her in your arms and embrace her!"

God is not like the cool, cold English gentleman. He is the very opposite of that, but often we, the church, are like that with Him. We think that as long as we turn up, pay our tithes and do our duty, He is happy. We think that if our churches are growing, prosperous and helping people, He is pleased, but Jesus warns us that many will be rebuked, not because of what they did, but because of the one thing they didn't do – they didn't know Him in an intimate, personal and passionate way.

There are three things that a church that has truly seen itself as the Bride of Christ will do:

1. It will worship extravagantly:

- The church that sees itself as the Bride of Christ will worship with passion. This will express itself in its singing, its giving and its service.
- The church that sees itself as the Bride of Christ hates formula, routine and programme. It loves spontaneity, surprise and adventure in its worship. Worship is a joy, a delight, and the reason it exists.
- The church that sees itself as the Bride of Christ hates performance, but worships and serves for an audience of One.
- The church that sees itself as the Bride of Christ is totally free in His presence. It is comfortable dancing, laughing, crying, shouting or being totally silent.
- The church that sees itself as the Bride of Christ will leap before God and will be willing to look undignified in the eyes of the world and the eyes of the religious.
- The church that sees itself as the Bride of Christ understands that dignity and deity rarely dwell together.
- The church that sees itself as the Bride of Christ will willingly sacrifice everything it has to be poured out in worship for His glory. It will consider it the greatest honour to pour out the perfume of worship. (John 12v3)

2. It gives herself wholly to her Master:

- The true Bride of Christ has "made herself ready" (Revelation 19v7). That means she is wearing her wedding garments and is ready to meet Him face to face.
- The church that sees itself as the Bride of Christ values being faithful to Jesus more than the popularity of this world.
- The church that sees itself as the Bride of Christ will not bow to political correctness or the fear of man, but will hold firmly to the teachings of the Bible.
- The church that sees itself as the Bride of Christ has separated itself from this world and has vowed that there will be no compromise or "shades of grey" within her.
- The church that sees itself as the Bride of Christ is always being pulled "upwards" towards the heavenly calling and refuses to yield to the gravitational pull of money or the things of the world.
- The church that sees itself as the Bride of Christ values purity and holiness and never uses grace as a license for sin.
- The church that sees itself as the Bride of Christ is a busy church, working hard until Jesus returns.
- The church that sees itself as the Bride of Christ invests in eternal things.
- The church that sees itself as the Bride of Christ will joyfully face persecution, imprisonment and martyrdom, rather than betray Jesus.

3. It longs for His presence:

"The Spirit and the Bride say come." (Revelation 22v17)

- The only thing that satisfies the church that sees itself as the Bride of Christ is being in the presence of the Bridegroom.

- The church that sees itself as the Bride of Christ speaks about, longs for and looks for the return of Christ.
- The church that sees itself as the Bride of Christ willingly opens up her doors that He may come in and have fellowship with her. (Revelation 3v20)
- The church that sees itself as the Bride of Christ loves to hear Him speak, knowing that His words are anointed with grace (Psalm 45v2) and bring fullness of joy. (John 3v29)
- The church that sees itself as the Bride of Christ longs for the kiss of heaven; knowing that only His kiss, His touch, an encounter with His presence will satisfy it. (Song of Songs 1v2)
- The church that sees itself as the Bride of Christ loves to declare, praise and worship the name of Jesus, believing that His Name is like perfume poured out. (Song of Songs 1v3)

The destiny of the Bride

The reason that Jesus is gracious towards the Church, despite her faults and failures, is because He sees her glorious destiny and has committed to making sure that she fulfils it.

The destiny of the Church is to rule and reign with Him (Psalm 45v9) and to "shine with the glory of God … its brilliance like a very precious jewel, like a jasper, clear as crystal." (Revelation 21v11)

The destiny of the Church is to be presented to Jesus as "a radiant Church, without stain or wrinkle or any other blemish." (Ephesians 5v27)

That is why Christ can prophetically declare, "all beautiful you are my darling; there is no flaw in you" (Song of Songs 4v7). Praise God, this is not only a prophetic statement, but in Christ a present reality.

In order for the Church to fulfil her destiny, Christ has given her a seal, the Holy Spirit. The Holy Spirit is the One who is both a guarantee of the Church's future inheritance (2 Corinthians 1v22) and proof of our betrothal to Jesus (Ephesians 4v30).

- The church that sees itself as the Bride of Christ recognises her total dependence on the Holy Spirit as the One who is leading her to Christ.
- The church that sees itself as the Bride of Christ also understands that because of the Holy Spirit she is protected by the Name and authority of her husband and is responsible for being faithful to Him.

Yes, the Church is full of hypocrites – but He loves it anyway. Yes, the Church fights amongst itself – but He loves it anyway. Yes, the Church fails to correctly represent the heart of God on so many issues – but He loves it anyway. Yes, sometimes the Church is lukewarm and apathetic towards the purposes of God – but He loves it anyway. Yes, the Church is full of imperfect people, led by imperfect leaders – but He loves it anyway.

If we see the Church as the Bride of Christ it will perhaps change our own attitude towards it. If you invite me to your home, chances are that my wife is coming, too. To reject my wife is to reject me. To say you love me but hate my wife is unacceptable to me. Want to make a man angry? Sit there and pick fault with his wife, tell him everything that is wrong with her. No loving husband would allow you to do that for very long. So why would Jesus be pleased if you tell Him everything that is wrong with His bride? He knows the faults of His Church, yet He continues to love her, continues to wash her and continues to prepare her, knowing that in Him she is perfect, pure and spotless.

Conclusion

The subject of the Bride of Christ is an immense subject and in many ways, is the ultimate expression of what the Church is. Sadly, we cannot devote any more time to looking at the Bride in this book. Instead, we will look briefly at another aspect of the Church: the Sheepfold.

17

THE SHEEPFOLD

"I have other sheep that are not of this sheep pen. I must bring them also. They too will listen to my voice, and there shall be one flock and one shepherd."

(John 10v16)

The image of God's people as sheep is one that we are all familiar with. We probably all grew up memorising Psalm 23 or hearing the story of the Good Shepherd. As we grow older, these familiar texts can be a great source of comfort and encouragement to us. In John 10, Jesus teaches around the theme of God's people being sheep and He discusses such things as the love of the Shepherd, the need to go through the gate and the danger of false shepherds and wolves who mean to do the sheep harm. Jesus also teaches on God's people being "His flock". A flock of sheep is, of course, referring to more than one sheep. Jesus is talking about our gathering together. The sheep pen or sheepfold is the place where the sheep are gathered together. It therefore becomes another aspect of the local church, another revelation that we need to grasp. Have we seen the Church as the sheepfold and what does it mean to do so?

The need for the sheepfold

Firstly, seeing the Church as the sheepfold means to recognise our need for one another. This is something we have mentioned several times in this book, but it is perhaps nowhere clearer than in the imagery of the sheepfold. Any sheep that wanders from the sheepfold immediately weakens itself. It becomes vulnerable and easy prey for wolves or other predators. Within the confinement of a sheep pen there is safety in numbers, the protection of a fence, and the watchful and careful oversight of a shepherd. There is also the knowledge that when the sheep is hungry and thirsty, the shepherd will open up the gate and personally lead it to food and water. Although there are no guarantees that wolves and thieves won't penetrate the sheepfold, there is little doubt that a sheep is much safer there than wandering the hills in isolation. In fact, Jesus revealed that one of the tactics of Satan is to scatter and separate the sheep. (John 10v12)

Hopefully the parallel here is obvious. Whilst being under the leadership of a pastor and submitting to and attending a local church may seem limiting, restrictive and boring to some, the local church and the covering of a pastor is actually our greatest form of protection. Although we fully believe in the authority and power given to us as believers, we must never lose the vulnerability we have in knowing that we are all just sheep. Outside the safety of the local church, we are a target for deception, worldly temptation and satanic attacks.

The famous parable of the Good Shepherd found in Luke 15 is one that we all love and are familiar with. Please read that story again and notice at what point the shepherd had a party and declared that the lost sheep was now found. It was not when he had seen it, found it or put it on his shoulders. It was only when the sheep had been returned home to the sheepfold that the work of rescue and salvation was complete and the celebration could begin. Jesus is here showing us that it is not enough just to be found by the Shepherd. It is equally important to allow the Shepherd to lead us to our spiritual home, the place where we gather with other sheep. The very desire and mission of Jesus, according to John 10, was to bring His lost sheep into the sheepfold and for us to be united as one flock.

The need for a shepherd

"When he saw the crowds, he had compassion on them, because they were harassed and helpless, like sheep without a shepherd." (Matthew 9v36)

The context of this passage is that Jesus is in the midst of a hectic period of itinerant ministry, travelling from village to village and town to town ministering to the crowds of people. It was as Jesus was confronted with the needs of the ordinary people of the regions of the places he visited that His heart broke for them. Seeing their desperate needs – physical, emotional and spiritual – the Bible tells us His compassion for them was great. He describes their condition as "harassed and helpless". It is here that the Bible tells us what the real answer to their needs was. What the people were lacking was not meetings to attend, Bible studies to increase their knowledge or miracles to satisfy their immediate needs. No, what the people were lacking and what they desperately needed were shepherds.

This is something that is repeated in Mark 6v34: "When Jesus landed and saw a large crowd, he had compassion on them, because they were like sheep without a shepherd. So he began teaching them many things."

Jesus' diagnosis towards the people of his time was: these people need shepherds.

Let me ask you a question. Do you have a shepherd? Do we see a need for a shepherd? The word pastor and the word shepherd are of course the same word in the Greek "poimēn". 1 Peter exhorts pastors to be "shepherds of God's flock that is under your care", so it is clear that when the New Testament refers to shepherds, it is speaking of pastors.

Although Christ is ultimately the Good Shepherd (Psalm 23) and the Great Shepherd

(1 Peter 5v4), there is no doubt that God also gives His sheep Under-Shepherds, human pastors who help feed us, guide us, teach us, lead us and protect us. So let me ask you again, who is your shepherd? Do you see the need for one? Do you view your pastor as just some person who stands in the pulpit and gives a talk for 30/40 minutes each week or do you see that without that person and the ministry he provides (not only in the pulpit, but out of it) you are lost, harassed and helpless? (Jesus' words, not mine!)

Being a pastor is one of the hardest jobs and ministries there is. It should never be entered lightly as it brings with it huge responsibility, challenges and sacrifices. Most pastors are overworked, underpaid and underappreciated. Pastors are responsible not only for the legal and practical organisation of a congregation, but are responsible for their spiritual needs too. The pastor is seen as the one who has to come up with "the vision" for the church and somehow has to combine being a C.E.O. of a legal business with being an anointed "man of God". Although some mistakenly think that he only works Sundays, the reality is that pastoring a church takes over his entire life. There are no evenings free or days off from the burden and the concern that he will feel over his congregation. Imagine the pain you feel when a loved one gets sick or dies … or a marriage falls apart … or a family member walks away from God or is struggling spiritually. Imagine the frustration you feel when a close friend is apathetic and lukewarm in their commitment to God or the local church. The pastor has all of those emotions running through him on a regular basis. He carries the burden and the weight of every person's needs and problems.

The pastor is expected to always be there, at the office, the hospital bed or the graveside; and to always be in his pulpit, bringing a fresh word under a fresh anointing to the people.

Pastors bear the brunt of most people's criticism towards the church. If the vision isn't relevant enough – it's the pastor's fault. If the preaching isn't powerful enough – it's the pastor's fault. If the church isn't growing – it's the pastor's fault. If there isn't enough love in the church – it's the pastor's fault. If the community isn't being reached – it's the pastor's fault. If the youth group are a pain – it's the pastor's fault. If the worship team aren't anointed enough – it's the pastor's fault. We unfairly place all of our hopes and expectations on one man who we expect to be the most spiritual, most holy, most compassionate, most anointed person in the whole world. No wonder many pastors leave the ministry worn out, burnt out and fed up!

God always has a special place in His heart for pastors. He identifies with every local church pastor by describing Himself as a shepherd (one of them) on numerous occasions in the Bible. When choosing a king to lead Israel, one after his own heart, He found a shepherd, David. When Christ was born, God chose to send an angelic host to bring the message of joy, not to the religious scribe in the temple or Herod in the palace, but to humble shepherds who were looking after their flocks at night.

In seeing the church as the sheepfold, I believe God wants us to acquire a fresh insight into the love He has for pastors. As such, I believe that we are in turn to love, honour and appreciate our pastors more than we have in the past. God gives pastors according to Ephesians 4. Pastors are a gift that God has given to His Church; therefore, we should receive them with gratitude. We must see our need for pastors and embrace them and allow them to teach us, lead us and yes, even discipline us.

We must thank God for our pastors and pray for them every day. Satan always attacks the pastor and his family first within a church because he knows that if he can "strike the shepherd, the sheep of the flock will be scattered". (Matthew 26v31) Pastors need us to cover them in prayer daily. Attacking a pastor (even because we want what is best for the church) only helps the work of Satan. Instead of our criticism or opinion, pastors need us to stand with them, pray for them and encourage them.

Pastors need our gratitude and thanks. As an itinerant minister, the moment I have concluded my meeting I can leave and never see those people again. Pastors can't do that. They have to be there in every season of life: ready to love, counsel and comfort the broken, the needy and those struggling with problems. People may come up to me as a visiting evangelist and thank me for my ministry, but the poor pastor is often overlooked, as we have become too familiar with him. We take for granted that he will be there every week (after all, that's what he's paid for).

Why not surprise your pastor this week? Why not thank him for his ministry? Why not bless him and his family with some unexpected gift or card? Why not go up to him and instead of telling him that the light bulb in the bathroom has gone out or that there is some litter in the car park, encourage him from the bottom of your heart? The next time someone comes up to you after service complaining that it was too long, not lively enough, that "we are not doing more to outreach", instead of agreeing, respond by saying, "It may be true, but we can't expect our pastor to do it all. He needs our help and our commitment. Let's thank God for this person He has given us and pray that He will raise up more people to help them with the work." Instead of it being a one-off, why don't you let it become a lifestyle? I can guarantee that not only will you surprise your pastor, but you will also gain a smile from heaven.

Being sheep

If we are to see the Church as the sheepfold, we need to see ourselves as the sheep. The applications of this are numerous, requiring, as we do, the protection of the sheepfold and the care of shepherds. Being a sheep means that we also need to allow ourselves to be pastored by submitting to the shepherds God has given us. Submission is a subject in itself, so I will address it in a future chapter. Here, I want to look at just one aspect of what it means to be a sheep.

"He was oppressed and afflicted, yet he did not open his mouth; he was led like a lamb to the slaughter, and as a sheep before its shearers is silent, so he did not open his mouth." (Isaiah 53v7)

Many years ago, as a young man in the church, I was taken on one side by the pastor and asked if I would lead and preach one Sunday morning whilst he was on holiday. What an honour and a privilege this was! I immediately accepted and began to pray and study for a sermon that I thought would be a blessing to people.

The big day arrived and with a few butterflies in my stomach I took hold of the microphone and opened up the service. Two hours later I admit I felt a mixture of relief and pride that everything had seemed to go well. There had been no major disaster. I had even received a few "amens" and nods of approval from the congregation. It had been a success!

As I alighted from the stage, two well-known members of the church approached me wearing their Sunday best. "Can we have a word in private?" they asked. A new sense of pride filled my heart. What more could they want but to tell me how good my ministry was and to offer some words of encouragement? Then another thought popped into my head: perhaps they needed pastoral care and in the absence of the senior minister had come to me for my advice! "How wonderful," I thought. "Another opportunity to speak into someone's life!"

It soon become apparent that their intentions were quite the opposite of what I had in mind. Point by point they began to criticise my ministry! It was unbiblical. It wasn't what people wanted. I had offended them. People would not return if they thought they were going to be subject to this kind of preaching. Then they hit the killer blow: "When the pastor hears about this, he is not going to be happy with you either!"

As I listened to this angry rant, several emotions rose up within me. Firstly, I was genuinely upset. I had tried my best to minister God's Word, but had clearly done it wrong. I struggled to hold back the tears at the thought of letting God and the church down. Then I started to feel panic and fear. What if our pastor heard about it and agreed with them? What if he never let me preach again? What if my ministry was over before it had begun? After those emotions had passed, I began to feel anger. Everything that these men were accusing me of was wrong! I had preached a Biblical, Christ-centred message in a manner that would have pleased my pastor, had he been there. My red hair isn't always a good thing and I could feel the anger rising up within me as I prepared myself for an outburst. This feeling was soon followed by feelings of pride and self-justification. Who on earth were these people to speak to me like that? I looked at them both, two of the most miserable, religious people I knew. "Who do you think you are?" I thought! I am a man of God, called and anointed by God! I know the Bible more than you, I pray more than you. How dare you criticise me!

As I prepared to launch my counter-attack, the Holy Spirit reminded me of the words "as a sheep before its shearers is silent, so he did not open his mouth". I immediately closed my mouth and sat there in total silence as they continued their complaint. When it was quite clear that they had finished, I smiled and stood up and shook their hands. "Thank you so much for bringing this to my attention. I am only a very young preacher and I am learning every day. I am sorry that you didn't like how I preached this morning, but please be patient with me as I continue to grow in ministry. I need the prayers of older gentlemen like yourself, as I really need God to keep teaching and helping me".

That was many years ago. As I think back on that day I am convinced more than ever that I ministered in the will of God that morning and that those two men were wrong in everything they accused me of. They wanted to take advantage of an inexperienced minister by using that moment to try and take control over what happened in the church. However, I am also convinced that if I had reacted in anger or self-justification, it would have hurt my brothers in Christ and caused damage to the Church of Jesus and my own future ministry. I would also have acted in the spirit of this world that always seeks to justify its actions, rather than the Spirit of Jesus, who, when accused (though falsely accused), "made no reply, not even to a single charge". (Matthew 27v14)

Since then I have had many people criticise my ministry and accuse me of various things. Some of these people were right in what they have said and I have had to repent, but many times I have been accused of things that I have never done or criticised for things that I knew God wanted me to do. The flesh always rises up and says "defend yourself, argue back, who do they think they are?", but I have learnt to remain silent, even when falsely accused. People may say, "you are a push over, you are letting people walk all over you", but I disagree. I call it letting God take charge of the situation. When you refuse to defend yourself, God steps in and defends you. He is the One who justifies, He is the One who will honour and He is the One who reveals the truth.

We live in an age when, if you are wronged, you have every right to compensation. If you are falsely accused, you have every right to take someone to court. This attitude can creep into the church where we always have to give our opinion, we always have to be right and if anyone disagrees with us, we have to prove to them that we know best. If we are falsely accused or badly treated, then we have every right to be offended and upset and to tell everyone what they did to me.

In the midst of all this, we have the Bible that tells us to be like sheep. Sheep will submit to the shearer without complaint. Even when led away to be slaughtered, sheep will not protest or argue that "this isn't fair". They silently let it all happen.

What kind of a deal is it being a sheep? Well, a pretty good one actually. Jesus, the Lamb of God, who was falsely accused, found guilty and nailed to a cross, all the while refusing to defend Himself or speak back to His accusers, ultimately became "the shepherd" (Revelation 7v17). The very one who submitted to ill treatment and injustice became the One crowned with honour and glory and power. God always honours those who become like sheep.

Jesus said, "do not be afraid little flock, for your Father has been pleased to give you the Kingdom" (Luke 12v32). God gives the Kingdom, not to those who battle against their enemies, but to those who suffer and submit silently like sheep. The Kingdom of God, God's realm, a place containing joy, peace, righteousness, authority, glory, power, provision and so much more is the sheepfold that we have access to - but only sheep can enter there and sheep have learnt to follow the way of Jesus, a way of quietness, humility and meekness. It can mean being misunderstood, falsely accused and even mistreated, but if we handle it in the right way, in love, honour and grace, allowing God to defend us, it will lead to future promotion, victory and favour.

The Great Shepherd

When we have become like sheep, having recognised our need for pastoral care and entered the sheepfold of a local church, we gain access to the presence of the Great Shepherd – Jesus Himself. The blessings that brings are enormous:

1. Jesus, the Good Shepherd, provides everything His Church needs. (Psalm 23v1)
2. Jesus, the Good Shepherd, brings His Church to a place of rest, a place where it can flourish. (Psalm 23v2)
3. Jesus, the Good Shepherd, is always leading His Church. (Psalm 23v2)
4. Jesus, the Good Shepherd, brings restoration to His Church, restoring our souls, health, spiritual fervour or anything we are lacking. (Psalm 23v3)

5. Jesus, the Good Shepherd, guides His Church, by His Word, His Spirit and His ministers. (Psalm 23v3)
6. Jesus, the Good Shepherd, is always present in the midst of His Church, even through times of great distress or hardship. (Psalm 23v4)
7. Jesus, the Good Shepherd, comforts His Church with the Comforter, the Holy Spirit. (Psalm 23v4)
8. Jesus, the Good Shepherd, is not afraid to correct or discipline His Church, always trying to lead it in the way of righteousness. (Psalm 23v4)
9. Jesus, the Good Shepherd, provides a table of communion that His Church can eat from, a refuge and safe place in a world that hates it. (Psalm 23v5)
10. Jesus, the Good Shepherd, anoints His Church with the Holy Spirit. (Psalm 23v5)
11. Jesus, the Good Shepherd is coming back for His Church, to take it to her eternal dwelling place. (Psalm 23v6)
12. Jesus, the Good Shepherd, knows each member of His Church by name. (John 10v3)
13. Jesus, the Good Shepherd, is always speaking to His Church. (John 10v4)
14. Jesus, the Good Shepherd, protects His Church from all who would harm it. (John 10v12)
15. Jesus, the Good Shepherd, brings healing to His Church. (Revelation 7v17)

In Hebrews 13, Jesus is called "that great Shepherd of the Sheep". Jesus loves His Church passionately. He died, shed His blood, and laid down His life for His Church, for His sheep (John 10v11). Now resurrected as the overseer of His flock (1 Peter 5v2), He is always watching over His Church, knows each individual by name and knows the true spiritual condition of all of His lambs.

Conclusion

Let us thank God today for Jesus, our Good Shepherd. Let us recognise that we were like sheep, lost and hopeless, until He took the initiative and came and found us. Let us see that His desire is to lead us to a local church, where we can gather with other sheep and come under the covering of pastors. Let us thank God for our pastors and allow ourselves to be shepherded by becoming like sheep.

In the book of Zechariah, God says this of His people: "… the Lord Almighty will care for His flock, the house of Judah, and make them like a proud horse in battle." (Zechariah 10v3) How amazing that God describes the same group of people as both sheep and warhorses. Now sheep and war horses are two totally different creatures. Sheep are meek, mild, gentle and submissive. They yield to the voice of the shepherd. A warhorse, on the other hand, is a fierce, strong, powerful, mighty and majestic creature.

In our relationship with God and with each other within the church we must become sheep. However, we must also remember that we are on a mission, taking the good news of Jesus in the power of the Holy Spirit into the world. Some of the places we go into are dark, dry and hostile. We need the power and authority of a mighty horse in battle! God says that if we learn to become sheep, He will give us what we need to go out into this world as warhorses, on a divine commission from heaven. This leads us to the final aspect of the Church: the army of God.

18

MARCHING ORDERS

"Put on the full armour of God, so that you can take your stand against the devil's schemes."

(Ephesians 6v11)

The final aspect of the Church that we are going to look at is that of The Army of God. Battles, armies and warfare feature throughout the Old Testament. The battles that God's people fought against their enemies become, for the New Testament believer, a prophetic picture of their type of battle: " … not against flesh and blood, but against the rulers, against the authorities, against the powers of this dark world and against the spiritual forces of evil in the heavenly realms." (v12)

Paul uses the language of the army in several of his epistles, calling God's servants soldiers in 1 Corinthians 9v7, Philippians 2v25, 2 Timothy 2v3-4 and Philemon v2. When we join the Church of Jesus Christ we are enlisting into heaven's army, which brings with it incredible privilege and challenge. The wonderful thing about being in heaven's army is that our victory is already assured. "The Lion of the tribe of Judah has triumphed!" (Revelation 5v5) and He promises that the gates of hades will not overcome His Church.

Every soldier on active service is sent out on mission and it is the missional aspect of the Church that we will look at in the next chapter. In this chapter, however, I want us to look at something that is drilled into every soldier from the moment they enlist: the importance of submitting to those in authority.

As we discovered in the previous chapter, a basic structure of authority exists within the sheepfold. The shepherd leads and the sheep follow him. Whenever the shepherd is mentioned in scripture, he is always leading, guiding or instructing his sheep. A Middle Eastern shepherd would never go behind the sheep and drive them along. Instead he would walk ahead of the sheep and invite them to follow him wherever he was going. They would do this by hearing and obeying the sound of his voice. Sheep automatically learn to follow the shepherd and those that wander off and go their own way will soon find themselves in danger. In seeing Jesus as our Good Shepherd we quickly grasp the importance of hearing from Him and following His instructions. The basic call of discipleship is one of "come, follow me". (Matthew 4v19) However, as we saw in the previous chapter, Christ also gives His Church human shepherds: pastors, leaders, elders etc. In the same way that we follow and submit to Christ, we are instructed to listen to our human shepherds and follow and submit to them.

Every army works on a structure of authority and submission. According to the British Army official website, "The rank system forms the backbone of the Army's structure and it defines a soldier or officer's role and degree of responsibility. Soldiers and Officers have different rank systems. Broadly speaking, officers have more leadership duties. However, many Officers start off as soldiers, before gaining their commission."

Within the British army, Generals hold the most senior rank and under them come Lieutenant Generals, Colonels, Captains and Lieutenants right down to Sergeants and Privates. Each rank of the army has authority over the rank below (a private has authority over civilians in certain situations). However, each rank also has to submit to the ranks above it. Even the most senior of army officials has to submit to the government. Understanding the vital need to follow orders and submit to authority is of importance to any army. Any soldier, even those with high rank, if they fail to submit to their senior officers will face severe disciplinary procedures - for example, being facing a court martial or, in some countries, even facing execution.

One of the very first things that anybody joining the army will learn is how to obey instructions. Recruits will often have to take part in seemingly meaningless drills and march up and down, stopping and starting and turning all at different paces and rhythms at the orders of a commanding officer. In a practical sense, these seemingly endless drills might be of little help in a battle situation, but what they are doing is teaching the young cadets to follow instructions from those in authority. These drills are performed endlessly so that hearing a command and obeying it becomes ingrained in a soldier's psyche. Of course, what the commanding officer is concerned about is not whether a unit can march in time, but that in a battle situation, when chaos and fear are present, the soldiers will obey an order immediately and without question. This is the only way that their safety, the safety of the rest of the unit and the success of the mission can be guaranteed.

Why do soldiers have to be taught this? It is precisely because submission to authority is something that every person hates. Ever since Adam and Eve failed to submit to God and rebelled against His commands, rebellion has been an intrinsic part of human makeup. No one has to teach a child to rebel against its parents. Rather they have to be taught to obey. Even as you are reading this chapter on submission, your carnal nature will be hating every word that you read and disagreeing with it all, and yet as we see from scripture, submission to authority is such a major part of what we are called to do as Christians.

Jesus said that the house with a strong foundation was a picture of the person who "hears these words of mine and puts them into practice". (Matthew 7v26) Hearing the words are not enough. There also has to be a submission to the words. The very foundation of the House of God is obedience. If there is no obedience in the house, then no matter how attractive it is, it will come crashing down. Whatever we are building will rise or fall depending on our ability to obey instruction. This leads us to the question – who are we to obey?

Submission – yes - but to who?

The obvious answer to this question is "to God". The book of James tells us "Submit yourselves, then, to God. Resist the devil, and he will flee from you." (James 5v7) This verse gives a little clue then, that power and authority are found in submission.

Submission to God is something that should be obvious to all Christians. Once we receive God's free gift of grace, we are called to obey Him and to submit to His Word. However, the Bible never gives us the option of "I'll just do what God tells me" or "I'll only obey Jesus". If only this were true! No, the Bible tells us - over and over again - that God expects us to submit to human authorities, too.

Romans 13v5 tells us, "Therefore, it is necessary to submit to the authorities, not only because of possible punishment but also as a matter of conscience." Whilst 1 Peter 2v13 says, "Submit yourselves for the Lord's sake to every human authority: whether to the emperor, as the supreme authority, or to governors, who are sent by him to punish those who do wrong and to commend those who do right."

This is speaking about how, in society in general, the Christian is expected to submit to every authority that is in place (with the exception of governments that command its citizens to disobey God, such as Babylon in the book of Daniel). Notice that the Bible says things like "for the Lord's sake" and "who are sent by Him". The

Bible teaches that God chooses to link Himself to all those who are in any form of leadership or authority, even secular authorities. Our submission to them is very closely linked to our submission to God.

Submission to authority is to invade every area of our lives, at work and at home: "Slaves, in reverent fear of God submit yourselves to your masters, not only to those who are good and considerate, but also to those who are harsh." (1 Peter 2v18) Children are commanded to obey and submit to their parents all the way through scripture (Hebrews 12v9), while wives are instructed to submit to their husbands. (Ephesians 5v22, Colossians 3v18 and 1 Peter 3v1)

In seeing the Church, it is obvious from reading the New Testament that it was never intended to be run as a democracy where everybody had a say and an opinion and a right to do what they wanted. God has clearly set up an authority structure within the Church and seeing the Church as The Army means recognising those that God has placed in a position of leadership and submitting to them.

In speaking of those who were in leadership of a particular local church, Paul wrote, "I urge you to submit to such people and to everyone who joins in the work and labours at it." (1 Corinthians 16v16). This teaching is backed up by Peter in 1 Peter 5v5 and by the writer of Hebrews who in chapter 13v17 says, "Have confidence in your leaders and submit to their authority, because they keep watch over you as those who must give an account. Do this so that their work will be a joy, not a burden, for that would be of no benefit to you."

It is clear then, that we are not only to submit to God, but also to those human authorities who He has placed above us. In his book, Spiritual Authority, Watchman Nee uses the analogy of Adam and Eve. Nee explains how Adam (whom he uses as a type of Christ) had to submit to God, but how Eve (whom he uses as a type of the

Church) not only had to submit to God, but also to her husband Adam. Nee explains that this shows that we, as the Church, submit not only to God, but to His delegated authorities, too. A careful reading of the Genesis account would indicate that the command to not eat of the tree of knowledge of good and evil was given to Adam only. If this is so, then Eve's disobedience was not a rebellion against God directly, but a rebellion against her husband. However, in God's eyes, rebellion against His delegated authority is the same as rebellion against Him. Nee says, "submission to God is not possible unless we submit to those He has placed over us".

According to the dictionary the word "submission" means "the act of allowing someone or something to have power over you". Oh, how we hate the word "submission". Our flesh hates and despises this word and yet it is something that God instructs us to do over and over again. We prove our love to the invisible God by loving those we can see and prove our submission to the invisible God by submitting to those leaders we can see.

Paul tells us: "Let everyone be subject to the governing authorities, for there is no authority except that which God has established. The authorities that exist have been established by God. Consequently, whoever rebels against the authority is rebelling against what God has instituted, and those who do so will bring judgment on themselves." (Romans 13v1-2)

These are strong words from Paul, but he makes it very clear that every authority has been put there by God, that every authority is God's servant (v4) and that every authority is to be obeyed. Within the life of a local church the implications of this are pretty clear. Every pastor and elder has been appointed by God (even the ones we don't like or think are useless!) and as such we are to honour and submit to them.

The way of submission

In a very practical sense then, how are we to submit to those who are in positions of authority within a local church? I would suggest three things for us to consider:

1. Honour

Paul writes in 1 Thessalonians, "Now we ask you, brothers and sisters, to acknowledge those who work hard among you, who care for you in the Lord and who admonish you. Hold them in the highest regard in love because of their work." (5v12-13).

Here Paul places an emphasis on inner attitude, rather than outward obedience. Submission is always a heart attitude before it is a physical act. Paul first tells us to "acknowledge" those who are in authority. This speaks of recognising that our leaders are God's gifts, God's delegated authority and those who God has placed in a position of leadership within the church. It also means to recognise and be grateful for them and for all that they do.

Next Paul tells us to "hold them in the highest regard" which means to respect and honour them. Other translations of this verse use phrases like "esteem them very highly", "hold them in very high and affectionate esteem", and "overwhelm them with appreciation".

Finally Paul tells us to love them. This means that we are not submitting because we have to but because we genuinely love and appreciate our leaders. In some cases this can be easier done than in others, but it is quite possible to genuinely and deeply love all those in leadership over us through the work of the Holy Spirit.

2. Recognise the importance of covering

Teaching on spiritual covering can, like any teaching, be misunderstood, manipulated and abused. People can debate all they like about how practically we submit to those in authority and which areas of our lives we are to submit. I personally have chosen as best as I can to make sure that whenever I make an important decision in my life, I seek out those in spiritual authority over me for their wisdom and guidance. Whether that was when I began dating my wife and I asked for the blessing of my senior pastor; proposed in marriage when I asked for the permission of her parents; moved to another church, when I asked for the release of my old church or ministry decisions where I need the advice of my trustees … I have come to learn how important it is to come under spiritual authority. In each of these cases I am not coming in with a "this is what I am doing now, bless me" attitude, but with a humility and openness that says "what do you think I should do in this situation?" "Will you release me to do this?" "Do I have your genuine support and blessing to do this?" I am open to correction, rebuke and reluctance to bless each time and am willing to submit my will and desires to someone else.

You might say, "This sounds a bit extreme, God has given you a free will, whatever He tells you to do, go ahead and do it". The Bible though is full of examples of those who went ahead and did what they wanted without any recognition of spiritual authority and the disaster that this led to.

Leviticus 10 tells us the story of Nadab and Abihu who were put to death for offering unauthorised fire before the Lord. As priests of God, Nadab and Abihu had been given permission by God to offer incense in His presence, but only under the supervision of their father, Aaron, the high priest. Because they had the call, the access and the ability to do this, they mistakenly thought it was alright to just go ahead and do it without recognising their senior leader and seeking his blessing and approval before they started this ministry. But God will never bypass the authority structure that He has put in place and their genuine fire became false fire because of this lack of submission.

In Acts 19, Luke tells of the sons of a man called Sceva who decide to cast a demon out of a man in the name of Jesus, only to find that they had no authority over the demon, who proceeds to beat them up. The account seems to imply that the sons of Sceva were not part of any local church and therefore under no kind of spiritual authority. They were doing what they considered a spiritual ministry, but with no kind of submission to God's delegated authorities in their lives. Therefore, they had no power over Satan and no ability to perform any miracle.

The accounts of both Nadab and Abihu and the sons of Sceva teach us the importance of having accountability and covering in our lives, especially in our service for God. Even the angels of God don't worship without having a covering (Isaiah 6). If we fail to recognise those who God has placed in leadership in the church; if we dismiss their teachings, warnings and advice; if we think that we know better; if we think we can just go ahead without seeking out the support and blessing of recognised leaders in God's church, then not only will what we do fail to have any backing from heaven, but we have no power over the enemy and become an easy target for his attacks.

Instead, let us follow the example of Nehemiah, a godly man who, when he was burdened by the state of Jerusalem, went firstly to God in prayer before asking the king for his permission and release to do what God had put on his heart to do. Because Nehemiah submitted to the authority of the king and came under his covering, the king gave him letters of approval as well as the protection of his army as Nehemiah set out on his journey. When opposition came, Nehemiah could show his enemies the letters of approval as proof that he was a man under authority and that the task that he was doing he had first submitted to his leaders.

3. Sensitive to rebellion

A person who is under authority will not tolerate any form of rebellion in others and will refuse to participate in any. Titus 3 tells us "warn a divisive person once, and then warn him a second time. After that, have nothing to do with him." The Bible makes it very clear that if anyone in the church speaks against anyone in authority or makes any move to attack them or displace them, then those of us who recognise that God's leaders are God's delegated authorities are to disassociate with those who fail to see that.

David refused to honour the man who had killed his enemy Saul. Instead he killed him, saying "why were you not afraid to touch the Lord's anointed?" (2 Samuel 1v14)

A number of years ago, a group of people from my old church wanted to approach the leadership to question them about a number of decisions that they didn't agree with. Upon listening to their questions and complaints it seemed that they had reasonable points in various issues. Yet behind it all was a heart of rebellion that was unwilling to submit to those in authority. I sought out the advice of my spiritual father, who warned me "you must submit to the leaders of the church and honour them. If you join in with this group your ministry will be over". I immediately went to the ringleader of the group and told him that I wanted no part in what he was doing. I then went to the pastor of the church and told him that although I, too, was concerned about certain things concerning the church, I was going to submit to his decisions, support and honour him and serve him. I look back on that situation as being a real test from God, one which by His grace I passed and one which led to me being released into a ministry of my own.

The source of rebellion

Rebelling against authority is one of the most serious offences in the eyes of God. In the Bible, God forgave murder and adultery but struck down dead those who rebelled against their authority. There is no doubt that when people complain against leaders, publicly speak about them in a negative way, try to usurp authority, blatantly disobey what they have been told to do or take the lead in any kind of church split or breakaway group, they come under God's judgement. A kind of spiritual death takes place.

Examples of God's judgement coming on the rebellious include Miriam and Aaron in Numbers 12 and Korah and his followers in Numbers 16.

On each of these occasions someone spoke against one of God's leaders. God took it as a personal attack on him and also stood on the side of His delegated authority.

Many times when people attack someone in leadership, they will try and justify themselves, like Saul did when he disobeyed Samuel in 1 Samuel 13, or Gehazi when he disobeyed Elisha in 2 Kings 5. They will try and claim that they have every right to give their opinion and will often point out faults and failures that are genuine. God never claims that His leaders are without fault. Even the greatest of leaders will make mistakes, but their weakness should never be an excuse for us to attack or rebel. We submit, not because of the perfection of the leader but because of the command of God.

Rebellion can often be quite subtle. Absalom didn't start out by attacking his father, David, the king. Instead he seemingly quite innocently said, "If only I were appointed judge in the land….", but behind this innocent comment was the spirit of rebellion. Likewise, people who may innocently say things like "If only I was on the leadership of the church!", "If only I was in the worship band!", "I could take so much pressure off the current leaders!", "I could be such a help!", "I have so many better ideas!" are often covering their rebellion and thirst for control behind a mask of helpfulness.

The reason God hates rebellion so much is because that was the sin of Lucifer. Rather than submitting to God, Satan rose up and said, "I will ascend to the heavens; I will raise my throne above the stars of God" (Isaiah 14v13). Satan not only rebelled against God, but he led others into rebellion as well, with a third of the angels listening to him rather than God. God hates any form of rebellion and calls it witchcraft (1 Samuel 15v23). Whenever we refuse to submit to leadership, speak against them or criticise them we are following the way of Satan, no matter how we try and justify it or cover it up.

When submission is needed

"I can't submit to my pastor because…." then usually follows a list of disagreements in style, vision, theology or dislike of decisions that have been made. The decision is then made to leave that church and find a pastor who they agree with because then they can submit. Of course, this fails to see the very point of submission. If I agree with everything a person says or does, then I don't need to submit! Submission is only necessary when there is a disagreement. The fact that we don't agree with something that our leaders do is not an excuse to leave the church, it is a test of our submission. Submission can only be tested when there is conflict. The heart that says, "I might not like this but I am going to support and serve anyway" is a heart that has learned true submission.

The only exceptions to this rule should be when a leader is preaching clear heresy, is in open, unrepentant sin or is misusing their authority to control, manipulate or bully. In these cases we should leave the church and come away from their influence. Even then, there should be no public accusation made but simply a willingness to allow God to deal with them: "Even the archangel Michael, when he was disputing with the devil about the body of Moses, did not himself dare to condemn him for slander but said, 'The Lord rebuke you!'" (Jude v9)

The way of Jesus

If the way of Satan is rebellion, the way of Jesus is submission. The Bible tells us that, in everything, Jesus submitted to His Father. Even when this was hard to do, in the Garden of Gethsemane, Jesus submitted His own will to that of His authority: " … not my will, but Yours by done." (Luke 22v42)

However, Jesus wasn't just obedient to God, He was also submissive to God's delegated authorities too. Luke tells us that He was obedient to His parents (Luke 2v51), whilst His eagerness to be baptised by John the Baptist was in some way indicative of his desire to come under the ministry of someone else before He began His own ministry. He was even willing to come under soldiers who came to arrest Him, refusing to defend Himself or speak out against those who were accusing Him.

Submission to authority is a beautiful thing because, as we do so, we take on the character of Christ and follow in His footsteps and example.

A church or a cult?

Some may say that a church that teaches its members to submit to its leaders is a cult rather than a group of free children of God. Indeed, many have tragically manipulated the Biblical principles found in this chapter to try and exert control over those that were under them.

The Bible gives a wonderfully balanced view on submission. Nowhere are leaders told to exert authority over the church. If any leader demands that you submit to and obey him, he is a controlling leader who should be avoided. The emphasis in the Bible is not on the leader exerting authority over you, but on you voluntarily submitting to them. Biblical submission is never enforced or insisted upon, but is always something that you freely and willingly choose to do.

The Greek word submit in Romans 13 is used in the reflexive (middle voice), which implies that it is the person under authority who initiates the act of submission upon themselves for their own benefit.

It is important to note that in recognising our leaders as God's delegated authority, we are in no way suggesting that they are better than us, more loved, more valuable or more important. All children of God have His Spirit and can hear His voice. In fact, we could possibly know God more intimately than any of our leaders. Recognising authority relates to recognising people's functions in the church. It is nothing to do with our identity in Christ.

Remember that in order to have a holistic approach to life we must see every aspect of God's Church. In seeing the Church as the Body of Christ, for example, we see that everyone is equally valuable and that we are all one in Him. In seeing the Church as the army we see that there is a definite authority structure that God has put in place and then we must *submit* to those He has placed in authority over us. If we see only the first then we mistakenly think the Church is a democracy and we all have a right to dictate what happens; if we only see the latter, we mistakenly think that God values leaders over others. This is clearly not the case.

Therefore ...

"… God exalted him to the highest place and gave him the name that is above every name." (Philippians 2v9)

God gave Jesus total authority and glory because he lived a life of total submission. Independence is never the pathway to glory in God's kingdom. The road of submission and obedience is the way to the abundant life that God desires for us.

God's desire is that His disciples would have both power and authority (Luke 9v1). Power means the ability to do something, authority speaks of the right to exercise power. If I own a gun I have the power to shoot someone, but unless I am a member of the police or armed forces I have no authority to do that. Many Christians today think that all we need is the power of God, but this is not true. We can have great power, but we also need the authority to exercise it. Acquiring power is easy – it comes from an in-filling of the Holy Spirit (Acts 1v8) - but no encounter with God can give you authority. Authority only comes one way – submission. Unless we come under authority we will never be given authority. The more we submit the more authority we will possess.

The Roman centurion in Matthew 8 was of course familiar with how an army works. Notice his statement "I am a man under authority with soldiers under me." (Matthew 8v9). This soldier was both under authority and at the same time had authority. The two were linked together. If he had removed himself from the authority of his superiors, he would have been discharged from the army and would have lost any authority he possessed over anyone else.

As soldiers in Christ's army, God want us to have authority over sickness, Satan and the circumstances of life. He wants our prayer life and worship life and ministries to possess His authority so that they are powerful and effective. But it is only our willingness to come under authority that releases authority into our lives.

Remember Psalm 133? The oil flows downwards upon the beard of Aaron. God always anoints his leaders and in coming under godly leadership in honour and submission we position ourselves to receive the downpour of heaven's oil. If we move out of alignment with our leaders, choosing to act in isolation, independence or rebellion, we move out of the flow of God's Holy Spirit. When we come "under the beard" we find life and blessing forevermore. (v3)

The submitted life is a blessed life. In submitting, not only do we receive authority of our own and position ourselves to be soaked in God's Spirit, but there is something about a life of submission that seems to attract God's favour. God's command to Hagar to go and submit to her mistress (Genesis 16v9) was immediately followed by a promise to bless: "I will so increase your descendants that they will be too numerous to count." Famously the command to honour our parents is the only one that brings with it a promise: "… so that it may go well with you and that you may enjoy long life on the earth." (Ephesians 6v3) When understood in this context we see that submission to authority is not a chain that restricts us, but a covering that protects us, the means by which God releases His blessing and favour upon us.

K.P. Yohannan in his book Touching Godliness says the following: "Anyone who desires to have God's best must unconditionally surrender our lives to Him, which includes submission to our delegated authorities. This choice, however will not come without suffering in the flesh. There is one thing I am certain of: anyone who deeply hungers to know the living God and to touch godliness will relentlessly pursue submission to God and to His authority."

Conclusion

As soldiers in the army of God we have each been given orders to follow. Sometimes these orders come directly from heaven, but often they come to us through heaven's delegated authority. Sometimes we may question these orders or think that we know a better way, but it is our obedience to these instructions that bring us safety and protection and enable us to complete our mission and fulfil our assignment. Let us all be yielded vessels to God's government today.

In the next chapter we look at the purpose of every army – to advance and take territory in the name of their government.

19

AN ARMY ON THE MOVE

" No one serving as a soldier gets entangled in civilian affairs, but rather tries to please his commanding officer."

(2 Timothy 2v4)

In continuing to look at the Church as the army of God we will now look at the mission of the Church. Paul, again using the imagery of the army in the above verse, is basically instructing Timothy not to get distracted. The priority of any soldier serving in any army is to keep focused on the mission and fulfil the orders of their commander officer. Anything that takes the soldier away from the mission at hand is an unnecessary distraction.

Similarly, the Church of Jesus, as the army of God, is also on a mission: to "go and make disciples of all nations" (Matthew 28v19) … to go, to move, to be led where our Commanding Officer leads us. The church that sees itself as the army of God is a missional, pioneering church that is always going, always moving, always taking new territory for its King. The members of the church that sees itself as the army of God, have a deep passion for world evangelism, a deep passion for souls and see their primary calling as evangelists and missionaries on planet Earth.

God is a moving God

Everywhere you look in the scriptures, you see a God who is moving, who is active and who is doing. The very first mention of the Holy Spirit in the Bible, is as One who was "hovering over the waters" (Genesis 1v2). The Holy Spirit was moving, hovering, waiting for the Word to come, so He could be released into action.

One of the very first things God does after creation is to go for a walk in the garden (Genesis 3v8).

When Jesus came, we see that movement and mission were two key components of His life and ministry. Acts 10v38, tells us that "Jesus went around doing good and healing all who were under the power of the devil". Jesus moved, He went places, and He did things. In His very first recorded sermon, Jesus stood up and declared that the Spirit of the Lord was upon Him (Luke 4). This is followed by a key word "Because". The Holy Spirit hadn't come upon Jesus just to make Him feel good, or to make Him appear more spiritual to others. There was a "because", a purpose to the anointing. In this case it was to "proclaim good news to the poor … to proclaim freedom for the captives … recover the sight of the blind … set at liberty the captives … proclaim the year of the Lord's favour".

There is always a "because" to the anointing of the Holy Spirit. The Holy Spirit never anoints us just to make us feel good! He never moves upon a church so that it will become famous or attract disillusioned members of other churches. The Holy Spirit comes upon us to empower us to be missionaries: in our communities and to the nations of the world.

Acts 1v8: "But you will receive power when the Holy Spirit comes on you; and you will be my witnesses in Jerusalem, and in all Judea and Samaria, and to the ends of the earth" is meant to be normal Christianity. There is no hint in this verse that Jesus is only speaking to full-time Christian workers or people who have "too much time on their hands". He is speaking to every Christian, in every nation, in every age of Church history, from the first century until His return. We are called to go.

Every Christian is called to reach their local community with the gospel. Many Christians somehow put evangelism down to the local church pastor. "What is the pastor doing to make the church grow?" "If only the pastor would put on more evangelistic events…" Jesus never said that evangelism was the responsibility of church leadership. It is the responsibility of all those who belong to God.

The early Church took its responsibility seriously and that is why daily, people were saved (Acts 2v47). There is no mention of special gospel campaigns or the hiring in of a guest speaker. Just simple, ordinary believers who "continued to testify to the resurrection of the Lord Jesus, and much grace was upon them *all*." (Acts 4v33)

Looking at the book of Acts we can see that mission was never a programme put on by leaders but a lifestyle lived out by believers. Christianity was always a movement before it was a meeting. It was always about personal evangelism before public events.

Not only do Christians blame the lack of souls being saved on pastors, but often we dare to put the blame on God! I have often been in prayer meetings where Christians have prayed for God "to bring in the harvest" or speak about how they are waiting on God to bring a revival and then their community will get saved.

If world evangelism was purely down to God, the world would have been saved long before now. The heart and desire of God has not changed – He loves the world and wants everyone to be saved. He paid the ultimate price for people to be saved through the death of His Son and has given the responsibility of sharing this good news to His Church.

Nowhere in the New Testament do you find any instance of the Church praying for God to save people. Instead you find them praying for God to give them boldness in their evangelistic efforts and then you see them going out on mission, sharing the good news in the power of the Holy Spirit.

To ask God to "bring in the harvest" is a totally unbiblical prayer. Jesus Himself told us that "the harvest is plentiful". What is needed is more workers. This is what we are to pray for (Matthew 9v37-38).

The church that sees itself as the army of God understands that it is responsible for the eternal souls of the men, women and children of their community; and will be willing to do whatever it takes to compel people into God's Kingdom (Luke 14v23). Not only is every believer responsible for evangelism in their community, but they are also commanded to take the gospel to the nations through overseas mission. Some Christians say that mission "is not their ministry" or "they need to pray about it" but the same command to preach the gospel in Jerusalem (our local area) is the same command to go "to the ends of the earth". There is no need to pray to find out if overseas mission is God's will for you. God has made His will plain. It is to go. Of course we should pray about where we should go, when we should go and how long we should go for; but we must make sure that at regular points in our walk with God we go overseas on mission. Unless we are physically unable to do so, we are living in clear disobedience to the command of Jesus if we do not.

A moving people

If God is a moving God, then it stands to reason that His Church is a moving Church. Jesus tells us that "The wind blows wherever it pleases. You hear its sound, but you cannot tell where it comes from or where it is going. So it is with everyone born of the Spirit" (John 3v8). So one of the very signs that we are filled with the Holy Spirit is not in how powerful our altar calls are, but in the fact that we are moving. A Spirit filled and Spirit empowered church is a moving church.

Paul said that "those who are led by the Spirit of God are the children of God" (Romans 8v14). One of the very things that identify us as God's children is that the Holy Spirit is leading us somewhere.

In Matthew 11v12, Jesus described the Kingdom of God as a moving, advancing, increasing Kingdom. It is important to understand that Jesus has given the keys to the Kingdom to His Church (Matthew 16v19) and if the Kingdom is to move, advance and increase, as God intends it to do, it will do so because the Church moves, the church advances, the Church impacts the nations with the message of the gospel.

Just as in the Old Testament, the priests carried the Ark of the Covenant as the nation moved, today the Church is to be a carrier of God's presence to the lost, broken and hurting. But unless the Church carries the ark and moves, it isn't going anywhere. Some Christians complain that "God isn't moving in our area", but the only reason why God doesn't move is because the Church doesn't move. The Church is the move of God, the revival that is on Earth today. We must see ourselves as this and get moving!

Mark 16 tells us of the early church that "the disciples went out and preached everywhere, and the Lord worked with them" (v20). Please notice the order: they went and then God worked. Many times we hope that God will work and then we may have the confidence to go. But that is never the divine order. The divine order is always: you go, you speak, you move, you act and heaven will back you up! But unless you go, God will not work.

God is drawn to movement

Whether it was the wise men following the star, David running towards Goliath, the woman with the issue of blood pressing through the crowd, Peter walking on water, the children of Israel walking around the walls of Jericho or Paul on his missionary journeys, it seems as though God is always drawn to movement.

As one man of God says, "God is a God who works with workers and moves with movers, but He doesn't sit with sitters".

In the Bible, God curses the sluggard (the lazy one who doesn't want to do anything) and rebukes the one who sleeps during harvest time, calling him a disgraceful son (Proverbs 10v5). Jesus had harsh words to say about the workers who failed to produce fruit (Matthew 21), the man who buried his talent (Matthew 25) or the fig tree that was barren (Matthew 21). A church that is not moving will eventually stagnate and will become so inward-focused that it eventually destroys itself. A church that is missional in approach should have a constant stream of love, grace and power flowing into it, as it releases love, grace and power to those in need.

We find in the Bible that things begin to happen in response to our movement.

1. Blessing follows movement:

> *"The Lord had said to Abram, "Go from your country, your people and your father's household to the land I will show you. I will make you into a great nation, and I will bless you; I will make your name great, and you will be a blessing."* (Genesis 12v1-2)

The desire and heart of God was to bless Abram. But I want us to notice that the plan of God to bless Abram was dependent upon Abram's willingness to move. God could only bless Abram as he moved.

Moving for Abram involved cost. It involved him leaving his comfort zone, leaving a familiar place and going into the unknown. As Abram moved, however, he was moving into blessing. God could not bless him where he was. The command to go was intended to reposition Abram into the fullness of God's blessing.

I firmly believe with all my heart that God wants to bless us. I have also found that receiving the blessing of God usually involves movement on my part. It means me hearing the voice of God, and moving in response to it.

A Christianity that is content to just sit in a pew and wait for the second coming is safe and comfortable. There are no risks to it. But it also a life devoid of the fullness of God's blessing. A believer that sees the church as the army of God lives a life of risk, adventure and sacrifice. There are material sacrifices as it can cost money to go. There are emotional sacrifices at leaving behind family and friends. There are spiritual sacrifices at laying down my agenda and following the call of God. But as we step out in faith and follow the call of God, we find that God is moving us into blessing and abundance.

The times when I have felt closest to God have been when I have gone in response to His call, for that is when I need Him the most. The times my faith has been strengthened the most is when I have taken a step of faith, totally trusting that He would come through for me. The times I have seen God's provision the most is when I have stepped out with nothing but a word, and He has met my need.

The highlights of my Christianity have been times when God has used me to impact lives, families, churches and areas. This has always been when I have been willing to move, been willing to go.

Not only did God want to bless Abram, He also wanted Abram to be a source of blessing to the nations. But Abram could not do this unless he moved. The Church contains the greatest message, the greatest hope, and the answer to every need, problem and situation on planet earth; but unless we are willing to move and go, that blessing will never impact the nations like God intended it to do.

2. Miracles happen in movement:

As I look in the Bible, I see time and time again that miracles often happened in response to people's obedience. Many times we want a manifestation of God's power, when God is looking for a movement from His people.

I have a passion for the miraculous. I read books on healing, pray for the gift of healing on a regular basis and will often ask for prayer from men and women of God who are used in healing. Praise God, God has used me over the years to see many healings and miracles take place. I notice one thing though. God never used me to heal someone when I was reading a book on healing. I never saw a miracle when I was asking for miracles. I never saw God use me while I was on the carpet soaking in God's presence. Although all of these things are good, I have found that the only times I have ever seen a release of the miraculous has been when I have moved towards need and gone and prayed for someone. Stepping out in faith and doing it is the one obvious, but most neglected, key to being used in healing and miracles.

In 2012, I was on mission in the nation of Argentina. Ministering in the city of Cordoba we had been in some large church meetings where God had done some incredible things. On a day off (a rare occurrence on mission), our team guide, Paul Bendele, asked if we would mind visiting his friends in the nearby town of Chancanni. Although I had been looking forward to a rest, I reluctantly agreed. What Paul neglected to tell us was that Chancanni was several hours' drive away, over horrendous terrain, a journey that led me to thinking we were about to die on several occasions! I don't travel well at the best of times, and so when we eventually arrived I was feeling sick, shaken and thoroughly fed up.

As I looked around at my surroundings I was even more unhappy. Chancanni seemed totally deserted and looking at our humble accommodation for the night, it seemed clear that we were not going to be living a life of luxury during our stay. Paul informed me that Chancanni was a tiny community of about 500 people, with a small church of around a dozen believers. Because of the remoteness of the community from the rest of the province, it found itself in great need. Alcohol addiction, spousal abuse and even incest among family members was common. To hear about the condition of this place depressed me even more and made me long for the comforts of home.

Paul informed us that we would be holding a meeting in the town square that night. Now, my interested was aroused. Perhaps I would get the chance to preach to a big crowd of several hundred people. Paul told us that there may be only 10 or so people there (his prediction proved accurate). Now I was really mad! Why had we come all this way, to minister to so few?

I will never forget, sitting in the back of the car in a sulk, asking God "Why on earth have you brought me here?" At that moment I looked up and saw a young lady in her early twenties. As I saw her, the Holy Spirit spoke to me and said, "I have brought you here for her".

I discovered that she was the daughter of one of the local church leaders. Having strayed from God many years before she had become pregnant outside wedlock. Now engaged to be married, neither she nor her fiancé were interested in serving God and her parents had been desperately praying to Him for their daughter's restoration.

I immediately knew why God had sent me to this place. After repenting of my bad attitude I promised Him that I would preach the gospel with all my heart, if only he would give me this one soul.

I preached the gospel that night to this small group as though I was preaching to thousands. What a joy that the first person to respond to the salvation call was this girl. The second was her fiancé. They were both weeping at the altar, getting their life right with God.

As we were preparing to leave the meeting, someone grabbed me - would I pray for a lady that needed healing? This woman was in her mid-40s and what I didn't know at the time was that she had been deaf and mute from birth. I quickly turned and prayed in the name of Jesus. Both of these woman's ears popped open, her tongue loosed and she heard and spoke for the first time in her life.

Chancanni had been in a three year drought without a drop of rain. Everything was dry and barren. As soon as we stepped into our vehicle to leave, the heavens opened and rained poured down all night long.

As I lay in bed that night I was so grateful for the incredible miracles that I had seen that day. God reminded me of my vow to preach the gospel with all my might if only that girl would be saved. The Holy Spirit spoke to me right there and said these words: "If you will always be willing to go anywhere to reach one person with the gospel; signs and wonders will always follow your ministry."

I became conscious of the times we pray for God's power when God is looking for our movement, whether that be to our next door neighbour or the most distant mission field. When we are willing to go and reach the lost with the gospel, we will find that God's power will follow us. The power is only released in the going.

3. Transformation happens in movement:

> *"Come, follow me" Jesus said, "and I will make you fishers of men."*
> *(Matthew 4v19)*

The call to discipleship was a call to move, to go and to follow. It was in the going that a transformation would take place. As they went, Jesus would make them into the thing that they were not, into the thing that He desired them to be.

We frequently excuse ourselves from serving God when issues in our lives get in the way - the areas in our life we need God to change. "Change me and then I will be ready!" we say; or we use our circumstances as an excuse as to why we cannot go: "Change this situation and then I can go!" I have found that often transformation happens when we go, not before it. It is in the going, the doing and the obedience that the Holy Spirit comes upon us and not only changes our circumstances, but changes us too.

As we go in response to the call of God, we find that in the process, Jesus makes something out of us, and we step into something that we never thought possible.

Passion for souls

"During the night Paul had a vision of a man of Macedonia standing and begging him, "Come over to Macedonia and help us." After Paul had seen the vision, we got ready at once to leave for Macedonia, concluding that God had called us to preach the gospel to them." (Acts 16v9-10)

Paul and his missionary group were travelling from place to place when suddenly Paul had a vision of a man crying out for help. This vision so gripped Paul that he immediately stopped what he was doing and responded to this call. This world, audibly or not, is crying out to the Church to come and help it. In a world that is messed up, broken, hurting and in desperate need, the cry still comes to the church "come and help us". The church that sees itself as the army of God has seen this vision, has heard this cry and will lay down its agenda to go and preach the gospel to those in need, whoever or wherever they are.

I must admit to being a very reluctant evangelist. I grew up in church with no real passion for souls or heart for the lost. But in January 2007, I had an encounter with the Holy Spirit that would change my life and ministry forever.

When you have a true encounter with the Holy Spirit, a spiritual heart transplant takes place and He gives you the heart of Jesus. The heart of Jesus burns for souls. It was this passion for souls that compelled Him to die the most horrific death on a cross. It was God's love for the world that caused Him to send Jesus (John 3v16). There can be no salvation unless someone goes.

The heart of Jesus breaks over a lost and dying world. It was His passion for reaching the lost that He described as His food (John 4v34). The very thing that sustained Jesus was mission. Jesus was intensely focused and committed to bringing God's salvation to the lost: "As long as it is *day*, we must do the *works* of him who sent me. Night is coming, when no one can work." (John 9v4)

It was this very heart that was in the apostle Paul when he said, " … I am compelled to preach. Woe to me if I do not preach the gospel!" (1 Corinthians 9v16)

It was the timidity of the flesh that caused the first disciples to gather together with the doors locked for fear of the Jews (John 20), but it was an encounter with the resurrected Christ and the fire of His Spirit that caused Peter and John, just a short time later, to boldly enter the temple, the very centre of Jewish religion (Acts 3v1).

The church that fails to see itself as the army of God is happy to just meet together and lock the doors out of fear, trying to keep the darkness at bay. The church on fire for the Holy Spirit doesn't try and keep out the darkness. Instead, it moves towards the darkness, goes in for a head-on collision with the powers of hell, knowing that it possesses a message and a power that is far greater than anything that the devil has and is able to bring hope and transformation to the most hopeless of situations.

It was as Peter and John went to the temple that they were faced with a need - a man at the gate of the temple, who was crippled. Many times we are so focused on the needs that are within the church, we ignore the fact that outside its doors are the cripples, the beggars, those desperately needing an encounter with God. We don't have to go too far outside our church doors to be faced with need.

I wonder how many people had passed the beggar that day. I wonder how many times the Church passes by the spiritual beggars in our communities? Peter and

John had a fire burning in their hearts. No doubt they could still hear the words of the Master ringing in their ears: "You shall be my witnesses." Peter and John were men on a mission. Nothing would distract them from fulfilling the commission of their commanding officer to "Heal the sick, raise the dead, cleanse those who have leprosy, drive out demons. Freely you have received; freely give." (Matthew 10v8)

And so we draw near the end of looking at the various aspects of what the Church is. It is appropriate that we should conclude with seeing the church as the army of God. If we fail to see this, we will become happy and content, secure in our personal salvation but blind to the needs of a lost and dying world. Or we can allow God to open our eyes afresh to see today, that as His Church, we have a mission that must be completed. This mission is for all of us and we must obey. The souls of the lost are dependent on our obedience.

Keeping the main thing, the main thing

I will conclude with the following story for us to ponder over:

On a dangerous sea coast where shipwrecks often occur, there was once a crude little life-saving station. The building was just a hut and there was only one boat, but the few devoted members kept a constant watch over the sea and with no thought for themselves went out day and night, tirelessly searching for the lost. Some of those who were saved, and various locals, wanted to become associated with the station and give of their time, money and effort for the support of its work. New boats were bought and new crews trained. The little lifesaving station grew.

Some members of the lifesaving station were unhappy that the building was so crude and poorly equipped. They felt that a more comfortable place should be provided as the first refuge of those saved from the sea. They replaced the emergency cots with beds and put better furniture in the enlarged building. Now the lifesaving station became a popular gathering place for its members and they decorated it beautifully and furnished it exquisitely, because they used it as sort of a club. Fewer members were now interested in going to sea on lifesaving missions, so they hired lifeboat crews to do this work. The lifesaving motif still prevailed in this club's decorations, and there was a miniature lifeboat in the room where the club initiations were held.

One night a large ship was wrecked off the coast and the hired crews brought in boatloads of cold, wet, and half-drowned people. They were dirty and sick. Some of them had black skin and some had yellow skin. The beautiful new club was in chaos. So the property committee immediately had a shower house built outside the club where victims of shipwreck could be cleaned up before coming inside.

At the next meeting, there was a split in the club membership. Most of the members wanted to stop the club's lifesaving activities, since they were unpleasant and a hindrance to the normal social life of the club. Those who insisted upon lifesaving as the club's primary purpose, who pointed out that they were still called a lifesaving station, were voted down and told that if they wanted to save the lives of all the people who were shipwrecked in those waters, they could begin their own lifesaving station down the coast. They did.

As the years went by, the new station experienced the same changes that had occurred in the old. It evolved into a club and yet another lifesaving station was founded. History continued to repeat itself and if you visit that sea coast today you will find a number of exclusive clubs along the shore. Shipwrecks are frequent in those waters, but most of the people drown.

Conclusion

Before we finish looking at the Church as the Army of God, I want to look at one other way in which we can advance the territory of God's Kingdom - and that is through prayer. Prayer and spiritual warfare are vast subjects, of course, and we cannot cover everything in one chapter, but allow me to share with you one principle of prayer that relates to the Church of Jesus.

20

THE KEY OF DAVID

"I am the Living One; I was dead, and now look, I am alive for ever and ever! And I hold the keys of death and Hades."

(Revelation 1v8)

As we conclude our look at the Church as the army of God we can rejoice, knowing that although we are in a battle, we serve One who has already overcome! Jesus has already defeated sin, hell and the grave and triumphantly holds the keys of victory in His hands!

In Revelation Chapter 5, the apostle John has a vision of a scroll that is sealed with seven seals. As heaven asks who is worthy to break open the seals, John is devastated to learn that there is no one in heaven, earth or under the earth worthy enough to break open the seals. Suddenly, a triumphant cry comes from one of the elders "'Do not weep! See, the Lion of the tribe of Judah, the Root of David, has triumphed. He is able to open the scroll and its seven seals." (Revelation 5v5) The elder was of course referring to Jesus Christ, the One who is worthy and able to break open the seals.

Many churches today are desperate for a breakthrough that often seems impossible. However, there is no need to weep and despair. Jesus Christ is still worthy and able to bring breakthrough into the most hopeless of situations.

A few years ago I was ministering in a prison in Kenya. It was a slightly daunting place with guards who had machine guns and prisoners wearing black and white striped uniforms. I shared a few words before my pastor preached the gospel and several of the men gave their lives to Jesus. At the end of the message, the Kenyan pastor who had arranged the visit announced that we were to go and lay hands on the men who had responded. A little reluctantly I moved among these criminals and started to pray for each one. When I got to one man, I paused. The Holy Spirit had given me a word for him. "Sir", I said, "God has brought you to this prison because He wanted to meet with you here. But very soon you will be released from this prison and when you are on the outside you will serve God". As I gave the word a few people around me began to laugh.

Afterwards they told me what was so funny. The man was in prison for murder. He was under a life sentence. "In our country life means life. This man will never be released. He will die in this prison."

A few weeks later I received an email from the pastor in Kenya. It seemed that there had been a problem in that prison with overcrowding. The government had never before done this in history, but they had produced a list of prisoners who were in that jail for minor offences and had pardoned them to make room for more serious felons. For some reason that no one could explain, that man's name was on the list! His sentence cancelled, he walked through the doors a free man, upon which he contacted the pastor to tell him the news and dedicate his life to serve God.

Friend, we truly serve a God of breakthrough! A God who makes a way where there seems to be no way! A God who still holds the keys of victory to every battle that the Church faces and a God who holds the keys to any and every situation!

The keys of the Kingdom

As encouraging as this is to know, it is also important to understand that Jesus is not the only one who has the keys. In Matthew 16v19, whilst Jesus speaks directly to Peter He is also speaking prophetically to all who would become members of the Church that was built on the rock. Jesus promises us, "I will give you the keys of the kingdom of heaven; whatever you bind on earth will be bound in heaven, and whatever you loose on earth will be loosed in heaven."

Not only does Jesus have the keys – He has given the keys to His Church! When I married my wife, she moved into the apartment that I owned. The first thing that I did after we got married was to give her a copy of the keys. What kind of husband would I be if I said I was the only one who could have keys? As the Bride of Christ, Jesus has given us a copy of the keys to His Kingdom! He has said of His Church, "We (me and the Father) will come to them and make our home with them" (John 14v23). As He makes His home in us, He gives us a copy of the keys to His Kingdom.

The Kingdom of God is God's realm. It contains His presence and His "stuff". The Kingdom is a place of joy, abundance, peace, grace, forgiveness, mercy, healing, strength, righteousness, wisdom and so much more. Whoever has the keys has the access and the right to obtain all that God is and all that God has.

Prayer and the Church

Jesus has said that His Church should be a place of prayer: "It is written," he said to them, "'My house will be called a house of prayer." (Matthew 21v13)

As the army of God, we must use the weapon of prayer in order to see God's Kingdom advance. It is only through prayer that we will see the victory. You cannot win a spiritual battle with carnal weapons.

When we pray, however, we must see that the Church has already been given the keys to the Kingdom. Perhaps, you have found yourself in the unfortunate position of being locked outside, having lost your keys! You hammer on the door, trying to get someone's attention, hoping someone will answer. How foolish would it be to do that if you already had the keys! You could open up the door and walk straight in.

Many churches treat prayer like they are beggars, shivering in the cold, hammering away, trying to get God's attention. When we realise that Jesus has already given us the keys and we have access to an open door it changes the way we approach prayer.

When I started working at Bethel Church in Barnsley in 2001, one of the first things they gave me was a copy of the keys. That meant I had access to the church any time day or night. If I wanted to, I could enter the church at 3.00 am. If the police stopped me I could show them that I had the keys and they knew I had a legal right of entry. When I left that church in 2014, I had to hand my keys back. Now I am restricted to accessing that building only when it is open to the public. It doesn't matter that I was there 13 years. It doesn't matter that I know the pastor. I don't have the keys, so if I enter without permission I am a thief.

The church will never pray correctly and never be victorious, praying like it doesn't deserve to pray, but when we understand that we have the keys to God's Kingdom and can access His throne room any time, day or night, we have discovered a powerful truth!

The master key

A number of years ago I was ministering in the nation of Zambia. On the last day we were flying home and needed to leave the hotel very early in the morning. I contacted reception the night before and asked them to give me an early morning wake up call. The next day I woke up suddenly, and looking at my watch, realised they had forgotten to call me! I had only a few minutes to get downstairs. Quickly dressing I grabbed my bags and went to the door handle. Disaster struck however as I pulled it, only for the handle to fall off in my hand with the door still locked! I began to shout, but it would do no good - even if my friends heard me, they only had keys for their doors.

Eventually I got someone's attention and a porter came with something very special. He had a master key to the hotel. It was the key that opened up every door and he quickly used that key to let me out.

Notice that Jesus spoke about the "keys" to the Kingdom, plural. There are many keys in the Kingdom, but hidden in the Word of God, is a master key. This is a key that opens up any and every door and it is a key that God longs for His Church to discover.

This key is called the key of David. Jesus spoke about this key in Revelation 3v7: "These are the words of him who is holy and true, who holds the key of David. What he opens no one can shut, and what he shuts no one can open."

Whatever He opens remains open, so not only is the Key of David a master key that opens every door, but it brings permanent breakthrough. Many times in church life we see the same old problems reoccurring, but the key of David enables things to open and shift and remain that way. Not only does the key of David open things, it also shuts the door. How we need our churches to shut the door to sickness, negativity, unbelief, immortality, luke-warmness and so many other things. The church that has the key of David is able to do this.

What is the key of David?

I believe that in naming this master key after King David, the Holy Spirit is pointing us to the life of David. There are two distinguishing marks of the life of David. Firstly, he was a worshipper. Secondly, he was pursuant of God's presence.

Church, as the army of God, this is where our victory lies! In being a church that puts on the garments of praise and boldly and passionately lifts up the name of Jesus we are given the keys of victory. And when like David we say "My heart says of you, seek His face; your face Lord I will seek" (Psalm 63v1) we find the master key that gives us access to keys to Kingdom breakthrough.

Several weeks ago I lost the spare key to my car and couldn't find it anywhere. That car is being sold today and the new owner insisted on having the spare key. Faced with the prospect of knocking loads of money from the agreed price I was in a panic and looked all over the house, but couldn't find it anywhere. I went to bed that evening and prayed saying, "Lord, you know where that key is, you need to tell me". As soon as I woke up, the Lord told me where it was, in a very obscure place, but I found it straight away. The lesson? I worried and stressed and couldn't find that key, but as soon as I prayed, the key was there. Easy.

God said:

"Many of my people are faced with closed doors, they are hammering on the door trying to get it to open and are begging for the keys. Others once knew what it was to live with the open door but now all doors have closed and there is a panic that the keys seem to have been lost.

There are keys that open up doors to finance, ministry opportunities, family being saved, marriages' being restored. There are keys to abundance, joy, peace and deliverance. For church leaders there are keys to new buildings, keys to your city and community. For evangelists there are keys to nations, regions and miracles. As long as you stress, panic, strategise and try to find the key to your breakthrough in your own strength, the way will remain hidden. But in my presence, keys are found. The key to your breakthrough, the key to your open door.

For the Lord says, "I am the One who holds the key of David, what I open no one can shut and what I shut no one can open". The name David means "Beloved". As you walk in the reality of being the Beloved of God, as you embrace your identity as His Bride, as you rest, enjoy and abide in His presence and live in the simplicity of being a lover of Jesus, it is in that place that keys are found. Christ still gives the keys of the kingdom to His Church, not the Church that walks in the flesh, but the Church that walks in the Spirit.

I see in the Spirit keys, lost keys, abandoned keys, keys long forgotten, but keys ready to be found and put into locks that will open with ease to those who have the keys. There is a door of blessing, a door of breakthrough, a door of destiny and Christ has the keys. The Lord urges His people to go back to His presence, back to the place of prayer and fasting, back to the intimacy of worship, become His beloved and find and pick up the keys He intends for you to have."

Heaven on earth

In Psalm 62, David says "I have seen you in the sanctuary and beheld your power and your glory." Have you ever stopped to think that, under the Old Covenant, David wasn't actually allowed access into the glory of God? Only the High Priest could access God's glory and he only once a year.

Yet because David was a worshipper and a pursuer of God's presence, he found the keys to a dispensation that would only come later, after the death of Jesus.

Although we are now in the Church age, there is another dispensation coming - the dispensation of the Kingdom. In that age, there will be no more death, sickness, pain or injustice. In that age we will see Him face to face and be like Him.

Some churches are content to live in defeat and bondage on earth, waiting for that future dispensation that is coming. However, if we as the church will discover true "Spirit and Truth" worship and start to really hunger and thirst after God's presence, maybe we will find the keys to enable us to access what is coming in the future, right now. Maybe that is what it means in Hebrews 6 when it talks of those "who have tasted the goodness of the Word of God and the powers of the coming age".

When we have the key of David we can taste heaven now, we can taste resurrection power, healing, glory and justice now. This is what God longs to show His Church.

The keys of destiny

The city of Jerusalem was David's destiny and inheritance. The only problem was that between David and his inheritance was an enemy. The enemy mocked David saying "'You will not get in here; even the blind and the lame can ward you off.' They thought, "David cannot get in here" (2 Samuel 5v6).

Like David, we too have an inheritance. Psalm 2 says "Ask me and I will make the nations your inheritance" (v8). Our inheritance is that we will see His Kingdom come in our nations and His glory change our communities. But we too have an enemy that mocks us: "Great Britain [substitute your nation] belongs to me," says the enemy. "The Church is finished, a dwindling minority. Immorality has won, darkness has won. The Church has failed."

Yet the Bible declares, "Nevertheless, David captured the fortress of Zion – which is the City of David." (2 Samuel 5v7)

I want to prophesy a "nevertheless" over your church, community and nation today! It doesn't matter how small or needy your church is … NEVERTHELESS! It doesn't matter what strongholds are over your community … NEVERTHELESS! It doesn't matter how backslidden your nation appears … NEVERTHELESS!

You see, underneath the city was a hidden shaft of water. It was a secret place that not even the enemy noticed. David and his men got on their hands and knees and climbed up that water shaft right into the enemy camp. They might have been a bit soggy, but they had found the key to the city!

The key to taking cities is still the same today. There is a secret place - the secret place of prayer. The enemy cannot see us in the secret place because in that place we "dwell in the shelter of the Most High and rest under the shadow of the Almighty" (Psalm 91). But God sees us in that secret place. He promises:

"But when you pray, go into your room, close the door and pray to your Father, who is unseen. Then your Father, who sees what is done in secret, will reward you." (Matthew 6v6)

In the secret place there is a hidden flow of water. It is called the river of the Holy Spirit. God is calling His Church to fight from their knees. Like David and his men, let us get on our hands and knees in a posture of prayer and worship and enter the river of His presence. As we become immersed in that river and allow the river to carry us to the lost and broken, we find ourselves in the midst of the enemy's camp, not as captives but as victors. We have found the keys to the city God has promised us.

Conclusion

In speaking to the religious leaders of his day Jesus said, "Woe to you experts in the law, because you have taken away the key to knowledge. You yourselves have not entered, and you have hindered those who were entering." (Luke 11v52)

Religion always robs people of the keys to the Kingdom. A church that doesn't have an active prayer life doesn't have the keys of victory that it needs. As the army of God we must discover once again the old secret of the secret place. We must again go back to that secret place of prayer and that river of the Holy Spirit. A Church that responds to the Spirit's call to pray will find the keys to their city and whatever other breakthrough they need. Let us all resolve to be the Spirit filled, praying church that Jesus requires us to be.

That concludes our look at each of the various aspects of the Church. In these final two chapters I want to look at how God desires to flow through His Church, but firstly I will address all those in leadership and ministry and see how we should respond to the Church.

21

PAUL AND THE SUPER APOSTLES

"For such people are false apostles, deceitful workers, masquerading as apostles of Christ. And no wonder, for Satan himself masquerades as an angel of light. It is not surprising, then, if his servants also masquerade as servants of righteousness. Their end will be what their actions deserve."

(2 Corinthians 11v13-15)

For those of us who live 2000 years after the New Testament was written, the place of the Apostle Paul in Church history is in no doubt. Paul is loved and admired as a pioneer, Church father, master theologian and example to all who would follow as one of the greatest leaders and men of God the Church has ever seen. It perhaps seems strange to us then, that in his life time Paul was not universally loved and admired. Indeed there were those who would call into question Paul's apostolic credentials. Some within the Church looked at other leaders who called themselves apostles and actually thought that they were more worthy to wear this title than Paul was. It is in the background of this that Paul writes to the Corinthian church, on one hand questioning the claims of others that were known as apostles and at the same time defending his own right to use that title and exercise the authority that it brought.

In verse 6 of 2 Corinthians 11, Paul ironically calls these other unnamed leaders as "super apostles" whilst he exposes them plainly in verse 13 as "false apostles".

The recipients of this letter were no doubt aware of who Paul was referring to as he questioned the motives of these other leaders within the church. It seems that the "super apostles" were men who enjoyed the glory and popularity of public ministry. They were highly skilled and trained and used their academic qualifications as proof of the legitimacy of their ministry and as an excuse to belittle those who were less qualified. The "super apostles" loved to tell everyone of their ministry accomplishments; they loved to exert their authority over the Church and used every opportunity they could to take money from the people that they were leading. They were heavy shepherds, bullies, people whose authority could not be questioned, money makers, who used the title of "apostle" and the cover of ministry as an excuse to rule God's Church however they wanted.

The "super apostles" were the ministry superstars of their day. They had the big name, the big ministry and loved to use the title "apostle" as a way to appear superior over other leaders and also to exert their authority over people.

The scary thing about the "super apostles" is that outwardly their ministries were considered a huge success. As their name, power and influence grew, they were considered as the leaders that God was using. Meanwhile, that old guy Paul was languishing away in prison, a failure, a relic from a bygone area.

Ultimately, of course, history and God are the true revealers of whose ministry was blessed by Him and whose was rejected. One day every minister will stand before Jesus and "If anyone builds on this foundation using gold, silver, costly stones, wood, hay or straw, their work will be shown for what it is, because the Day will bring it to light. It will be revealed with fire, and the fire will test the quality of each person's work." (1 Corinthians 3v12-13)

It is a true challenge to every leader within the Church to remember that it is to Jesus that we will give an account of our ministries. Could it be that, like in the early Church, there are some with big names and titles and growing churches that will actually have their work burned away in the fire of God's judgement? Could it be that there are those who worked hard and faithfully with little public fanfare who, it will be revealed, were building something of eternal significance? All of us in ministry should learn from the differing examples of Paul and the "super apostles".

Leaders: What do you see?

The biggest failure of the "super apostles" was their failure to truly see and recognise the Church. They saw themselves. They saw their ministries. They saw the numbers. They saw how much money was in the offering. They saw how many names were on the database. They saw "their" vision. They saw their goals and targets. But they failed to see the Church.

As leaders we must remember that we have been given to the Church. The Church has not been given to us.

In speaking to the Ephesian elders Paul warned of false leaders who would "draw away disciples after themselves" (Acts 20v30). In contrast he urged them to "keep watch over yourselves and all the flock of which the Holy Spirit has made you overseers. Be shepherds of the church of God, which he bought with his own blood." (Acts 20:28)

The false apostles see the Church as an opportunity to draw people after themselves. They use the Church as an opportunity to promote themselves and their name, make money and exert power and influence. They see the Church as a tool to fulfil their ambition, their vision and their ministry goals.

The true apostle on the other hand only sees the Church. They love the Church, care for the Church and would lay down their life for the Church.

God takes very seriously how we as leaders see and treat the Church. One of His strongest rebukes was to the leaders of the nation in the time of Ezekiel. In chapter 34 he spoke in incredibly strong terms about the "false shepherds" who were only in a position of ministry to feed themselves. God said that He was against them, would hold them accountable and would remove them from their place (v10).

God was looking instead for shepherd leaders who would strengthen the weak, heal the sick, bind up the injured, bring back strays, search for the lost, clothe the flock and lead with justice and tenderness. This is the job of apostolic leadership. This is the kind of leadership God blesses. Am I this kind of leader?

When Peter was reinstated by Jesus, the command of Jesus was pretty clear to this young leader: "feed my lambs", "take care of my sheep", "feed my sheep" (John 21).

Maybe Jesus doesn't care how many books we sell, how many followers we have on Twitter or how big our network is. Maybe all He asks us to do is see His Church and see the people He has given us to love and look after and make sure that we are doing it well.

Peter would learn this lesson. Writing as an older leader he says:

"Be shepherds of God's flock that is under your care, watching over them—not because you must, but because you are willing, as God wants you to be; not

pursuing dishonest gain, but eager to serve; not lording it over those entrusted to you, but being examples to the flock. And when the Chief Shepherd appears, you will receive the crown of glory that will never fade away." (1 Peter 5v2-4)

Jesus Himself spoke of the hired hand in John 10. The hired hand is the leader who is there for the salary and the opportunity. They have no real concern for the people they are leading and will run away at the first sign of trouble (or the first sign of a better opportunity). They are committed to self but not committed to the sheep. In contrast the true leader, the good shepherd, the one who follows the model of Jesus, is so committed to the people they are serving that they would lay down their lives for them (John 10:11). Indeed it could be said that true ministry is laying down our lives daily for those to whom we are ministering.

Paul: The true apostle

"Some time later Paul said to Barnabas, 'Let us go back and visit the believers in all the towns where we preached the word of the Lord and see how they are doing.'"

(Acts 15v36)

We don't have time to do a comprehensive study on the life of Paul but even just a brief skim through the scriptures will show us the passion and burden that this man had for the Church. His only concern was the Church and seeing how it was doing. He had a single focus, seeing the Church grow and flourish. Today's leaders should read these words soberly, especially anyone who claims to be in apostolic leadership:

"I have laboured and toiled and have often gone without sleep; I have known hunger and thirst and have often gone without food; I have been cold and naked. Besides everything else, I face daily the pressure of my concern for all the churches.

Who is weak, and I do not feel weak? Who is led into sin, and I do not inwardly burn?" (2 Corinthians 11v27-29)

This was a man who gave his life for the Church. He regularly spoke of weeping over the Church (Acts 20v31; Philippians 3v18), these tears coming out of the depth of love that he had for the Church (2 Corinthians 2v4).

I am always challenged by the account in Judges 17 and 18 of a young Levite who became priest of the household of a man named Micah. This man took a position of ministry because he was offered a good salary and it seemed like a good opportunity. When he was challenged by a group of travellers from the tribe of Dan, he was asked three questions: Who brought you here? What are you doing in this place? Why are you here? (Judges 18v3)

The first question addressed the origin of his call, the second question addressed his purpose and the third addressed his motives. The only response this young leader could give was that a man named Micah "has hired me and I am his priest" (v4). In other words, someone gave me a title and they are paying me to fulfil a function in the house. God help us if this is what we have reduced ministry to. Do we know that God has called us? Are we here to lay down our lives for His Church? Are we here to glorify Him? Let us go before God with those same three questions over our ministries. Who brought us here? What are we doing here? Why are we here?

True Biblical apostles:

1. Did not gather people to themselves or their network, but were rather sent to people – apostle means one who is sent not one who gathers (Acts 16v9)
2. Did not demand authority over churches, but rather gave their authority away to local church leaders (Acts 14v23)

3. Were not distant, mysterious figures who were never seen or heard from, but rather fathers who were in deep close relationship with those they considered spiritual children (1 Timothy 1v2)

4. Didn't demand money from the Church, but rather gave money to the Church (2 Corinthians 8v9)

5. More than being great administrators, apostles were men of prayer who moved in signs and wonders (2 Corinthians 12v12)

6. Were not seen as Christian celebrities, but rather the scum of the earth (1 Corinthians 6v13)

7. Didn't see the church as an organisation that they were the CEO of, but rather the bride of Christ that they had been entrusted with (2 Corinthians11v28)

Seeing Jesus

The title of this book is "Seeing the Church" and this chapter is about the great need for leaders today who see the Church rather than just seeing themselves and their ministries. However, if we want to be leaders who build eternal fruit there is another great challenge for us. In seeing the Church, we must never forget to stop seeing Jesus.

Seeing the Church is my assignment, but seeing Jesus is my vision! In seeing the Church we must never forget that it is His Church and not ours.

Paul writes in Colossians 1v28, "we proclaim Him (Jesus), admonishing and teaching everyone with all wisdom, so that we may present everyone perfect in Christ".

We must be so careful when we speak of the Church and we say things like "my church", "my vision", "my team". We can be very well meaning and sincere when we use these terms but we create a dangerous precedent. Paul says that the Church is

"His Body" and "I have become its servant" (Colossians 1v24-25). Let us never move away from that.

In the age of social media it is easy to talk about all the wonderful things "our church" is doing. We can easily talk about how we are growing, how successful we are and how much we are accomplishing. Although it is good to give testimony of God's goodness, there is a danger that we are doing what Israel did when they "held a celebration of honour of what their hands had made" (Acts 7v41). It can be such a subtle thing, but there is so fine a line between glorifying God and boasting of what we are accomplishing. The tragic result of their honouring how good their worship service was is that "God turned away" (v42). Could it be that the presence of God is no longer moving in some of our worship services because they are simply another opportunity for us to delight in what we are building and what we are doing in His Name?

"We preach Christ crucified: a stumbling block to Jews and foolishness to Gentiles, but to those whom God has called, both Jews and Greeks, Christ the power of God and the wisdom of God." (1 Corinthians 1v24)

Leader: who are you preaching? Do we talk more of the church than we do about Jesus? Do we talk more about our vision and strategy than we do about Jesus? Do we spend more time sharing our accomplishments than we do boasting in Jesus?

Conclusion

This chapter is such a challenge to anyone in leadership and ministry and it comes down to the question, what exactly is it that I am building?

"Therefore judge nothing before the appointed time; wait until the Lord comes. He will bring to light what is hidden in darkness and will expose the motives of the

heart. At that time each will receive their praise from God." (1 Corinthians 4v5)

I don't want my life and ministry to be vain. I want to receive praise from God. Therefore I must honestly ask myself: am I building for myself or am I building for others? Am I promoting myself or am I promoting Jesus? Am I seeing my ministry or am I seeing the Church?

Most leaders are sincerely living for Christ and His Church. And sometimes our ministries can look to man small and unsuccessful. We can look at the so called "super apostles" and get discouraged. Yet I am reminded of another Bible hero: David. David was looked down upon by his brothers and father, not even invited to the feast when the prophet called. Yet David had two great passions: He loved God and he took care of the sheep he'd been entrusted with. No one saw David as he worshipped to Yahweh in the fields alone. No one saw David as he risked his life, fighting off lion and bear to protect his sheep. But God saw. "He chose David His servant and took Him from the sheep pens" (Psalm 78v70); "I have found my servant David, with my sacred oil I have anointed Him" (Psalm 89v20).

Leader, you may be discouraged by the size and impact of your ministry. You may feel a failure. Others may look at you and look down at you. But if you will keep your eyes on Jesus and on His Church, then know that God sees you, God will promote you, God will honour you and increase you. He will call you from the place of being hidden in secret. He will make sure the anointing oil finds your head. No one knows the name of these "super apostles" of the day. But we sure know the name of Paul. We know the name of David. Men who loved God and laid down their lives for God's people. Let us be the same.

22

THE TREASURE IS IN THE HOUSE

The wife of a man from the company of the prophets cried out to Elisha, "Your servant my husband is dead, and you know that he revered the Lord. But now his creditor is coming to take my two boys as his slaves."

Elisha replied to her, "How can I help you? Tell me, what do you have in your house?"

"Your servant has nothing there at all," she said, "except a small jar of olive oil."

Elisha said, "Go around and ask all your neighbours for empty jars. Don't ask for just a few. Then go inside and shut the door behind you and your sons. Pour oil into all the jars, and as each is filled, put it to one side."

She left him and shut the door behind her and her sons. They brought the jars to her and she kept pouring. When all the jars were full, she said to her son, "Bring me another one."

But he replied, "There is not a jar left." Then the oil stopped flowing.

She went and told the man of God, and he said, "Go, sell the oil and pay your debts. You and your sons can live on what is left."

(2 Kings 4v1-7)

In this chapter we read of a woman who was in great need. She lived in a time of famine. Her husband was dead. She had no means of support. She was in debt. It is safe to say that this woman was not having a good day!

The need

And yet there was one need that was all consuming. There was a need that far outweighed all the others: "the creditor is coming to take my two boys as his slaves". This mother was about to lose her children. Any parent knows that if we were ever faced with the prospect of losing our children, all other needs would pale into insignificance. The next generation would end up in slavery unless God did a miracle. Her future, her family's future, her future hopes and dreams were all tied up in God breaking in and setting free the next generation from its chains.

Our local churches have lots of needs. We have bills to pay and buildings to maintain. We have programmes to run and services to plan. We have rotas to arrange and pastoral issues to take care of. The list is endless. And yet there is one supreme need that matters above everything else: the next generation. The future of each local church is determined by the spiritual prosperity of our children. Yet for many churches this is a battle that we are losing. As we look at the generation that we are living in, it could be considered the most un-churched generation in modern history. We need a miracle for our children to be set free from their chains and brought into liberty.

In this hour of great crises, the woman approaches the prophet Elisha, God's anointed representative. She comes in a posture of petition begging him to do something. The response of Elisha is interesting. Rather than immediately giving her the answer she was searching for, he turns around and asks her a question instead: How can I help you? What do you have in your house?

The question

Many times the church positions itself in prayer before God, asking Him to do something in its generation. It cries out for God to move and for Him to deliver our children. Whilst prayer and intercession are vital components in what God wants to do (she would have never have received her miracle if she hadn't first come and asked) it is not the answer in itself. It is only one side of the coin. The other side is our response to the question "what do you have in your house?" Many times we are begging God to reach a generation when God is asking us, "What do you want me to do? I have given my Son. I have given my Word. I have given my Spirit. I have done everything. Now what is it that you have in your house?"

What is in your house? What is in your local church? What is in you? What are the gifts, ministries and anointings that God has placed and deposited within you?

The answer is always in the house. The answer to reaching a generation is always within the house. God's miracles are not always done for us, but done in and through us. When a couple cried out for God to send a deliverer to Israel, God's response was that the woman would get pregnant with a warrior called Samson (Judges 13). Her deliverance would come from within her own body. God always puts within His Body, within His House, within His Church, everything it needs to do its job of reaching a generation. The treasure is always in the house.

The answer to Elisha's question "what do you have in your house?" is not exactly a declaration of faith and hope: "I have nothing". Looking around at her lack and poverty she came to the conclusion that she had nothing that God could use.

Many times in our local churches we can feel like we are lacking something – "if only we had a bigger building", "if only we had more money", "if only we had more leaders", "if only we had more musicians", "if only we had more young people", "if only people were more committed"…

The list of our wants and needs could go on and on. The Church always feels like it's lacking something and we can become obsessed with what we don't have. But God can't use what we don't have. He can only use what we do have.

So what do we have? You see this woman suddenly remembered that she did have something after all! Whilst she was overwhelmed by her lack, it would be revealed that within the house would be the very thing that God would use not only to sustain her in famine but also to release a generation from slavery!

The answer

The answer was in the house! The miracle was in the house! The treasure is always in the house.

"Except a little oil"… It wasn't much, but it was enough. Our churches may lack many things but one thing the true Church of Jesus will always have is oil. Jesus always makes sure that there is oil in His Church.

The oil in Scripture of course speaks of the anointing of the Holy Spirit. That anointing God has placed within His Church. It was this same oil that anointed David to kill Goliath. It was this same oil that anointed the prophets, priests and kings of old. It was this same oil that came upon Jesus at His baptism. It was this same oil that came upon the disciples in Acts 2. It was this same oil that has been poured upon all the heroes of faith throughout Church history.

Friends, we may not have much, but we have the oil! The very Spirit of God is within us. The same power that raised Christ from the dead has been deposited within us!

It was need that would reveal what was there all the time. The oil would have remained gathering dust on a shelf without the hour of crises that this woman found herself in. Many times the Church misses out on the wonder of the gospel and the reality of the Holy Spirit within us simply because we don't put ourselves in a position where we need Him.

We don't actually need the anointing of God for a regular church service. The anointing of God was given to help us reach a generation (Acts 1v8) and to destroy the works of the evil one (Acts 10v38). Unless we are doing these things we don't need the oil. So we think we don't have it. But if we deliberately put ourselves in a situation where we need the oil, we will find deep within us the solution to the needs around us. We will actually surprise ourselves by what God does through us because we are drawing on the resources that we never knew existed.

It is remarkable that that which was considered ordinary, that which was considered insignificant and worthless, was the very thing that God would use!

You never know what you've got until you begin to use it. In many of our churches there are vessels of oil that are gathering dust on a shelf somewhere. Ministries, anointings, giftings that are untapped potential. Meanwhile we are complaining, saying that we have nothing! The treasure is right there within the house. We have to use it!

As leaders our job is to search every shelf, every nook and cranny searching for jars of oil! Maybe some of us are those jars of oil and we have been sat on the shelf gathering dust. It's time to come off the shelf. Within you is the very solution the church has been crying out for!

The vessel

*"Then he said, 'Go, borrow vessels from everywhere, from all your neighbours –
empty vessels; do not gather just a few.'"* (2 Kings 4v3 - NKJV)

Get me a vessel! This is the cry of heaven! Whilst we are looking for a miracle, God
is looking for a vessel. You see, without God, man cannot. But without man, God will
not. God only works through His vessels, His people.

I am sure that all these vessels were different shapes and sizes. Some had maybe
been used for noble purposes, some for ignoble. Maybe some of the vessels were
old, maybe some were dirty, and maybe some were cracked. It didn't matter. What
mattered was that it contained oil.

Throughout history God has used all kinds of vessels. Some of them weren't very
refined. Some were maybe a little chipped around the edges. Even the New Testament
reveals God using a man delivered from demonic possession to impact a region and
a messed up woman at a well to impact a village. Even the apostles themselves were
considered "unschooled, ordinary men" (Acts 4v13) but "they had been with Jesus".
They had encountered the Anointed One and now that Anointing Oil, the person of
the Holy Spirit, dwelt within them! They had a treasure within the earthen vessel. It
was that oil that would qualify them. It was the oil that God would use!

The oil only stopped when there were no more vessels. As long as there are vessels
that are willing to be used God will always move.

"Pour oil into all the jars and as each is filled, put it to one side" (2 Kings 4v4). As
the vessels were filled they were set apart. The Bible word for this is "sanctification".
The purpose of our infilling is not to make us feel good or to give us a wonderful

experience. God fills us so that He can set us apart and use us.

God doesn't give His Spirit to His Church just so it can have better meetings. He gives the Holy Spirit to the Church so that His Church can be set apart to be used by Him.

In order to do that, the oil that is within us must be poured out.

The Miracle

"They brought the jars to her and she kept pouring" (2 Kings 4v5). The miracle took place as she began to pour out the little that she had. We love to contain and receive and that is why we miss out on the supernatural deliverance of heaven. God is longing for us to take what we have and release it. It was the act of outpouring that brought the intervention of heaven.

When the Charismatic Church uses the word "outpouring" we often think of a special season of visitation from the Holy Spirit. But notice that in this story, Elisha never even set foot in the house. The woman didn't need him to. She had what she needed all the time! She just needed to release it.

What the Church needs is not an external visitation but an internal outpouring! We don't need a new infilling but an awakening to understand Who already fills us! The outpouring came from within the house.

All over planet earth, God has houses that contain oil. What are these houses doing? Praying for more oil! God is crying out, "You have the oil! Use it!"

God is waiting for an outpouring of you! He is waiting for an outpouring of your church into the towns, villages, cities and regions that He has placed you in. He is waiting for an outpouring of your life in service and devotion to Him.

"Then Mary took about half a litre of pure nard, an expensive perfume; she poured it on Jesus' feet and wiped His feet with her hair. And the house was filled with the fragrance of the perfume." *(John 12v3)*

One of the greatest acts of worship in the Bible was an act of outpouring. When Mary took the treasure in her vessel and poured it out, the result was that the aroma of that which was released changed the atmosphere of the room. When the Church takes the treasure that it has and pours it out, regions and nations are changed. There is a change in the aroma of our communities. There has been a shift in the atmosphere because of our acts of outpouring.

In 2 Kings, as the woman poured out the oil, God so worked that not only did she have all her needs met but her sons were set free. Someone else's miracle is on the other side of our obedience.

"But even if I am being poured out like a drink offering on the sacrifice and service coming from your faith, I am glad and rejoice with all of you." (Philippians 2v17)

The apostle Paul determined that his life would be a life of outpouring. All the revelations, anointings, encounters that God has deposited within him, he determined to pour out on behalf of others.

Jesus Himself, in the ultimate act of outpouring, poured out His blood, His breath, His very life for the sake of the world.

What if we determined as the Church that we existed for one reason and that was to be God's outpouring on this earth. What if we took our time, our finance, our gifts and talents, the anointing of God within us, our very lives – and we poured it all out for the sake of the world.

I think God could do something with a people like that! I think He could move powerfully in a generation that had a Church that lived to give itself away.

Conclusion

"The kingdom of heaven is like treasure hidden in a field. When a man found it, he hid it again, and then in his joy went and sold all he had and bought that field."

(Matthew 13v44)

The treasure of the Kingdom is the Church. Where we look at our churches and see lack and need, God looks and sees treasure. He has deposited treasure within His Church. He put within us the very power, presence and anointing of Himself. All the gifts, talents, ideas, resources, ministries and anointings that the Church needs to reach a generation are already within us.

Christ values His Church so much and so recognises the treasure that it is that He went and paid the ultimate price so that we could belong to Him. Christ then puts His Church back into the field (the world) like buried treasure. It's time for us to come out of hiding!

"But we have this treasure in jars of clay to show that this all-surpassing power is from God and not from us." (2 Corinthians 4v7)

Each one of us contains the treasure of God. Each church contains the fullness of Christ and His glory. We look at the weakness of the vessel but it's the treasure inside that contains the miracle. It's the treasure inside that this world needs. Let's begin to take the vessels off the shelf and pour out what God has placed within us. It's time to be the outpouring that this generation is looking for!

A SUMMARY

"His intent was that now, through the church, the manifold wisdom of God should be made known to the rulers and authorities in the heavenly realms, according to His eternal purpose that He accomplished in Christ Jesus our Lord"

(Ephesians 3v10-11)

God's plan and eternal purpose is that through the Church His manifold wisdom, who He is, would be revealed. Not only is the Church "His" Church but it is His plan. In order for us to understand the plan and purpose of God for our individual lives we must see the Church. The unfolding of our individual purpose only comes about as we perceive, understand and have a revelation of the Church as God sees it.

There is only One God, but there are many aspects to who He is. Likewise, there is only One Church but many different aspects to what the Church is. God wants us to see the full expression of what His Church is so that we can live in balance and be released into the fullness of all that God desires us to be as we take our place in His glorious Church.

The Church is **The Assembly.** This speaks of us literally and physically meeting together. Church is more than a meeting, but nevertheless meeting together is a vital part of what the Church does. We cannot afford to neglect meeting together. The entire Bible empathises the importance that God places on His people meeting together. We need that fellowship with others. We were never created to live in isolation. It is in the meeting together that healing can flow, that faith can be strengthened and that we can be equipped and empowered. Jesus Himself promises to be in our midst when we meet together.

The Church is **The House of God.** Each one of us is a living stone and as we join together we become the House of God. It is a spiritual house that is filled with the very presence and glory of God Himself. The House of God is a place filled with good things. It is a place of abundance and feasting, a House of grace, an "awesome place" in which Jesus is seen. Jesus has promised to reign over His House and cause a river of refreshing and delight to flow through it. How vital that like Jesus we have a passion and zeal for the House of God and remain planted in the place that He has positioned us until He clearly releases us to move elsewhere.

The Church is **The Family of God.** We were all created to flourish within the framework of family. That is why God created the Church. The Church is not a business or organisation. It is a family unit where we are called to love and care for each other deeply as brothers and sisters. Each local church is called to be a "city of refuge" providing grace, protection and safety for all in need. Each local church is called to live out the Beatitudes of Christ and to show the world what a culture of honour really is. Within the family of God, He has placed mothers and fathers and we are called to be good sons and daughters in the family as well as raising up spiritual children of our own.

The Church is **The Body of Christ.** Like the church in Corinth, no matter how good our meetings are, failure to discern and recognise the Church as the Body can lead to disaster. We are one Body, not a separate group of denominations and cliques. I am not just an individual who looks out for himself and misuses my gifts to bring glory to myself. I am part of a Body, here to meet the needs of others and build up others. I am part of something bigger than just myself. God loves the Body of Christ and hates it when it is divided or diseased. Likewise, I too must love, honour and be united within the Body. I have a part to play within the Church and am called to serve the Body of Christ.

The Church is **The Bride of Christ.** Jesus is passionately in love with His Bride. He died for Her and is returning for Her. The Bride's response is to be passionately in love with the Bridegroom. We are called to worship extravagantly, long for His presence and give ourselves wholly to Him.

The Church is **The Sheepfold.** We need the sheepfold and we need the Shepherd, both our local church pastor (s) and of course Jesus, the Great Shepherd over the flock. Likewise we need to be sheep which means being humble, submissive and teachable.

The Church is **The Army of God.** We are called to submit to God and His delegated authorities, understanding that in the Kingdom the way of submission is the way to promotion and honour. As the Army of God, the Church is called to move, spreading the gospel and advancing the Kingdom. We must also understand the authority and power that we have been given and that we can activate through prayer and worship.

CONCLUSION

"How truly wonderful and delightful, to see brothers and sisters living together in sweet unity! It's as precious as the sacred scented oil flowing from the head of the high priest, Aaron, dripping down upon his beard and running all the way down to the hem of his priestly robes. This heavenly harmony can be compared to the dew dripping down from the skies upon Mount Hermon, refreshing the mountain slopes of Israel. For from this realm of sweet harmony God will release his eternal blessing, the promise of life forever!"

(Psalm 133: The Passion Translation)

The will and desire of God for your life is to bless you! He wants to bless your relationships, your finances, your health and your ministry. God desires that above all else "that thou mayest prosper and be in health, even as thy soul prospereth" (3 John v2 - KJV). God wants you to live in the fullness of His blessing, understanding that "The blessing of the Lord makes one rich, and He adds no sorrow with it" (Proverbs 10v22 - NKJV).

God wants you to know His life. This life is the very life of Jesus abiding within you. This life is the life of The Spirit, God's resurrection life. It is a life of abundance, a life of joy and peace, a life of overflow. It is a life of intimacy with the Father. It is a life of purpose and fulfilment, a fruitful life. A life lived in victory, strength and holiness. A life enjoying God and being devoted to Him.

God wants His anointing oil to be poured out upon your life. This anointing destroys the yoke of the enemy in your life. It is an anointing to win souls and move in the gifts of the Spirit. The anointing of God enables you to operate in God's authority and to know the very power that Jesus knew when He was on earth. The anointing of God makes effective your prayer life, your ministry and all you do for God on earth.

The key to the blessing, life and anointing of God operating in our lives is our relationship with the Church. For it is through the Church that God's blessing flows. It is through the Church that God's life dwells. It is through the Church that God's anointing is poured out.

To separate ourselves from the Church or to not see the Church correctly or to carry a bitter or apathetic attitude in our hearts to the Church is to cut ourselves off from the very blessing, life and anointing that God so desperately wants to give us.

But when we truly see and understand what the Church is; when we see the Church as God sees it; when we perceive and understand that the Church is the very plan and purpose of God for my life then everything changes. When we see that we are His Assembly, His Building, His House, His Family, His Body, His Bride, His Sheepfold and His Army, when we see this and understand this, get ready for God to move in our lives!

When we get a passion for the Church and take our place in the Church then we are positioning ourselves for an outpouring of the very blessing, life and anointing of God in our lives!
The key to our success, fruitfulness and effectiveness comes down to this truth: have I seen the Church as God sees it?

Let us pray: *Father, thank You for Your Church. Thank You that You never take Your eyes off of Your Church for a moment. Everything You do is so that Your Church can flourish. Father, thank You that You love Your Church and have promised to build Your Church. Thank You that even the gates of hell cannot prevail against Your Church. Father, help me to see the Church like You do. Help me never to forsake meeting with my brothers and sisters in Christ. Help me to truly know what it is to belong to a family. Give me a loving, generous, forgiving and faithful heart to my spiritual family. Father, give me a passion to serve Your Church and show me areas of service that I can get involved in. Father, give me the same passion and zeal for the Church that Jesus had when He laid down His life for Her. Father, keep me humble, submissive and teachable with all my brothers and sisters, especially to Your delegated authorities. Father, give me a passion for souls and a boldness in evangelism and an authority in prayer that I can help Your Church advance Your Kingdom. Father, open my eyes to see the Church as You see it and help me to see my role within Your Church. Amen.*

"Christ loved the church and gave himself up for her to make her holy, cleansing her by the washing with water through the word, and to present her to himself as a radiant church, without stain or wrinkle or any other blemish, but holy and blameless." (Ephesians 5v25-27)

The Scriptures teach that Christ is coming for a radiant, holy and blameless Church. Some people therefore teach that Christ cannot come back yet because the Church isn't any of these things. But they fail to see the Church as Jesus does. In the eyes of Jesus His Church is radiant. In the eyes of Jesus His Church is without stain or wrinkle. In the eyes of Jesus His Church is holy and blameless. In the eyes of Jesus His Church is beautiful, glorious, powerful, pure and wonderful. Jesus declares over His Church "You are altogether beautiful, my darling: there is no flaw in you" (Song of Songs 4v7). This is the Church that Jesus sees. Do we?

AFTERWORD:
A PRAYER FOR THE BROKEN

My child I am praying for you. I am not only your Saviour but I am also your Great High Priest. I bring your name before my Father constantly. There is not a moment that goes by when you are not on my heart. I know you greater than you know yourself. I see past the surface and see deep within where no one else can see and where you are sometimes too afraid to look yourself. I carry your burdens. I understand your pain.

I pray for all my children but there is a special place in my heart for the broken. There is a special place in my heart for the hurting. I am praying for the ones that were gossiped about. I am praying for the ones who were betrayed by their brothers and sisters. I am praying for the ones who were ignored and rejected. I am praying for the ones whose passion was misunderstood and whose gifts were not recognised. I am praying for the ones who were judged and looked down upon. I am praying for the ones who were used and left feeling burnt out and worn out. I am praying for the ones who were let down by those they should have been able to trust. I am praying for the ones who were the victims of heavy shepherding. I am praying for the ones who were abused by those in leadership. I am praying for the ones who were falsely accused. I am praying for the ones who fell into sin and who had rocks thrown at them instead of the hand of grace. I am praying for the victims of church splits. I am praying for the ones whose leadership committed moral failure. I am praying for the ones who always felt like they were on the outside looking in. I am praying for the ones who spoke against the church and now feel like there is no way back.

My child, I understand. I know what it is to be rejected by my people. I know what it is to be falsely accused. I know what it is to be betrayed. I know what it is to be abandoned by the very ones who I cared for. I know what it is to be beaten, wounded and hurt by my brothers and sisters. I know exactly what you are going through because I suffered it myself.

My child, I understand your pain. I understand your hurt. I understand your anger. I understand that for some the pain is so raw. I understand that for some the pain has turned to bitterness. I understand that for some, the feelings have gone completely and now the heart you had for my Church has become a heart of stone.

My child, I love you. I don't judge you or condemn you. I love you passionately and desperately want to heal you. I know it was never me you had a problem with, it was my Church that hurt you.

But child, this hurt is only hurting you. The pain you carry is eating away at you. The bitterness and anger is only destroying you. You cannot receive the love I so long to show you while your heart is hard towards my Church.

You see, I love my Church. I died for my Church. I am not only praying for you but I am also praying for the ones who hurt you. For they too are hurting, they too are human, they are too are sinners. But they too are loved. And they too are forgiven. I know you say "why should I forgive them". I know you are afraid to trust again. I know you feel that if you were to once again become part of my Church you may be hurt again. And maybe you would. But child, you need my Church and my Church needs you. I miss you in my House. I miss the joy of seeing you worship with your brothers and sisters. I miss the laughter as you fellowship together. I miss seeing you serving within My House, for this is why you were created.

My child, I have created a place of blessing, a place of healing, and a place where you can thrive and flourish. Please do not let the actions of some rob you of the joy that can be yours.

The words "Father, forgive them, for they know not what they do" are harder to say for those who have something to forgive. But my grace and the power of my Spirit can help you say those words and mean them. It is the start of your healing, the start of your restoration.

My child, give me your heart. Give me your pain. Give me your anger. Give me your rejection. Give me your fear. No matter how hurting your heart is I will receive it. No matter how hard your heart is I can heal it. Healing is in my presence. Restoration is in my presence. My child, you have carried this long enough. Let go. Release it to me. Don't hold on to it one second longer. You can do it. I am waiting for you. Waiting for the moment of return to become a moment of celebration.

My child, you are so loved

Your Great High Priest and Faithful Friend

About the Author

Andrew is the founder and director of Generation Builders and travels the world extensively as an evangelist, teacher and revivalist.

Born into a Christian family Andrew has been in full time Christian ministry since the age of eighteen. In September 2001 he began working full time at Royston Bethel Community Church in Barnsley, South Yorkshire. He remained on staff at the church for thirteen years serving initially as an intern and then later as a schools and youth worker.

During this time Andrew, achieved a certificate in Biblical studies from Mattersey Hall Bible College and later became a fully accredited minister with the Assemblies of God UK and Ireland.

In 2006, Andrew was appointed youth pastor and then later assistant pastor at Bethel Church, serving firstly under Pastor John Morgan and later Pastor Dave Jones.

In January 2007 Andrew had a powerful encounter with the Holy Spirit which led to a wonderful move of God in the youth group at the church, with many young people coming and experiencing God's presence. This was the start of Andrew launching "Generation Builders" and beginning to travel to the nations.

For two years, Andrew oversaw the Bethel Internship and Ministry Academy a full time internship programme, where young people were discipled, trained and released into ministry and also taught God's Word for several hours each week.
In 2014 Andrew handed over his pastoral duties in the church and was released by the leadership to run Generation Builders full time. Since that time he has travelled

the world seeing moves of God's Spirit marked by salvations, healings and thousands of people impacted by the preaching and teaching of God's Word.

Andrew is currently a member of Revive Church, a multi-site church based in East Yorkshire led by Jarrod Cooper. Andrew ministers regularly at the church and also is the director of the Revive Academy Full Time College.

Andrew is married to Laura and they have two children Judah and Asher.

Contact Information

For more information about "Generation Builders" ministries please visit our website www.generationbuildes.org

If you have been blessed by this book or are interested in having Andrew Murray speak at your church or event then please email admin@generationbuilders.org

For more information about our full time college including how to apply then please visit www.reviveacademy.com/college

For more information about Peanut Designs please visit www.pnutd.co.uk

For written correspondence please contact:

FAO Generation Builders
Revive Church
Bridlington Avenue
Kingston Upon Hull
East Yorks
HU2 0DU
United Kingdom

Made in the USA
Middletown, DE
03 May 2019